Reforming the Bismarckian Welfare Systems

T0355659

Broadening Perspectives on Social Policy
Series editor: Catherine Jones Finer

The object of this series, in this age of re-thinking on social welfare, is to bring fresh points of view and to attract fresh audiences to the mainstream of social policy debate.

The choice of themes is designed to feature issues of major interest and concern, such as are already stretching the boundaries of social policy.

This is the eleventh collection of papers in the series.

Previous volumes in the series include:

Reforming the Bismarckian Welfare Systems

Edited by

Bruno Palier and Claude Martin

Chapters © 2008 by the Authors
Book compilation © Blackwell Publishing Ltd

First published as Volume 41, Number 6 of *Social Policy and Administration*

BLACKWELL PUBLISHING
350 Main Street, Malden, MA 02148-5020, USA
9600 Garsington Road, Oxford OX4 2DQ, UK
550 Swanston Street, Carlton, Victoria 3053, Australia

First published 2008 by Blackwell Publishing Ltd

1   2008

Library of Congress Cataloging-in-Publication Data

Reforming the Bismarckian welfare systems/edited by Bruno Palier and
Claude Martin.
p. cm.
Includes bibliographical references and index.
ISBN 978-1-4051-8348-2 (pbk. : alk. paper)   1. Public welfare—Europe. 2. Welfare
state.   3. Europe—Social policy.   I. Palier, Bruno.   II. Martin, Claude, 1955–

HV238.R45 2008
361.6′8094—dc22
2008003438

A catalogue record for this title is available from the British Library.

Set in 10.5pt Baskerville
by Graphicraft Ltd, Hong Kong

The publisher's policy is to use permanent paper from mills that operate a sustainable
forestry policy, and which has been manufactured from pulp processed using acid-free
and elementary chlorine-free practices. Furthermore, the publisher ensures that the text
paper and cover board used have met acceptable environmental accreditation
standards.

For further information on
Blackwell Publishing, visit our website at
www.blackwellpublishing.com

CONTENTS

CONTENTS

NOTES ON CONTRIBUTORS

Giuliano Bonoli is Professor of Social Policy at the Swiss Graduate School of Public Administration (IDHEAP), Lausanne, Switzerland.

Daniel Clegg is Lecturer in Social Policy at Edinburgh University.

Barbara Da Roit is a post-doctoral student in the Department of Sociology and Social Research at the University of Milano–Bicocca, Italy.

Patrick Hassenteufel is Professor in Political Sciences at the Université Saint Quentin en Yvelines, France.

Ute Klammer is an economist and Professor of Political Sciences, in particular Social Policy, at the University of Duisburg-Essen, Germany.

Trudie Knijn is Professor of Social Science at the University of Utrecht, the Netherlands.

Blanche Le Bihan is Researcher in Political Science at LAPSS, French School of Public Health, Rennes, France.

Marie-Thérèse Letablier is a sociologist, Director of Research at CNRS and head of the Department of Employment, Labour Markets and Social Policies at the Centre d'Etudes de l'Emploi, Noisy-le-Grand, France.

Claude Martin is Director of Research at CNRS, Centre de Recherches sur l'Action Politique en Europe, Science Po Rennes, University of Rennes 1, and Director of the LAPSS, French School of Public Health Rennes, France.

Jane Millar is Professor of Social Policy and Director of the Centre for the Analysis of Social Policy at the University of Bath.

Nathalie Morel is a Researcher at the Laboratoire Georges Friedmann (Université Paris 1 Sorbonne) and Post-doctoral Fellow at the Centre d'Études Européennes in Sciences-po Paris.

August Österle is Associate Professor in the Department of Social Policy at the Vienna University of Economics and Business Administration, Austria.

Bruno Palier is CNRS Researcher at Sciences-po, Cevipof (Centre de Recherches Politiques de Sciences-po), Paris.

1

From 'a Frozen Landscape' to Structural Reforms: The Sequential Transformation of Bismarckian Welfare Systems

Bruno Palier and Claude Martin

While, during the 1980s, attention was centred first on analysing welfare state crisis, and then on understanding the differences between welfare states, the key preoccupation now is the analysis and understanding of welfare reforms (Martin 1997). In pursuit of this objective, recent comparisons have either analysed all types of welfare regimes (Esping-Andersen 1996; Ferrera and Rhodes 2000; Scharpf and Schmidt 2000; Ebbinghaus and Manow 2001; Leibfried 2000; Pierson 2001; Sykes *et al.* 2001; Huber and Stephens 2001; Swank 2002; Wilensky 2002), or focused specifically on the liberal or else on the Nordic regimes (Pierson 1994; Orloff *et al.* 1999; Kautto *et al.* 2001; *Revue Française des Affaires Sociales* 2003). But to date no systematic comparative research has been conducted on recent developments in the 'conservative corporatist' or Bismarckian welfare regimes based mainly on social insurance mechanisms.[1]

Despite the absence of systematic comparison within the Bismarckian family of welfare systems, the general literature on welfare state change paints a picture of the development of these systems, based on their contrasts with the other regimes. From this standpoint, the general literature usually concludes that – despite the fact that they are facing the biggest challenges and are the most in need of transformation – the Bismarckian welfare systems have proved almost wholly incapable of implementing important reforms.

This collection presents a systematic comparison of the development of social insurance programmes over the last three decades – and demonstrates, on the contrary, that Bismarckian welfare systems have changed a lot. The papers show that, after a period when increasing social expenditure and social contribution to finance a 'labour shedding' strategy was the main answer to economic crisis, they have recently developed policies aimed at restructuring their welfare systems, in line with the dominant social policy agenda set at the international level.

In order to understand these changes, we will start by discussing what the main characteristics of Bismarckian welfare systems are. Second, we will synthesize the main changes that have occurred in these systems, and say why it is appropriate to speak of the 'realignment' of Bismarckian welfare policies to the dominant social policy agenda. Third, we will emphasize the specificity of the trajectory followed to join this common agenda, being highly determined by the typical Bismarckian welfare institutions. We will conclude, finally, that the consequences of these changes are increasing the insider/outsider cleavage.

What Is a Bismarckian Welfare System?

In what follows, we focus on the Bismarckian world of social protection, based mainly on social insurance, or the 'conservative corporatist' type of welfare capitalism. There has been continuous debate about the Esping-Andersen typology.[2] However, instead of trying to read Esping-Andersen's typology as a description of the 'real worlds' of welfare capitalism, it is useful here to conceptualize it as isolating ideal-types, differentiated both in terms of policy goals (logic or conception) and policy instruments ('ways of doing', institutions).

A number of broad normative/ideational elements are (more or less) common to Bismarckian welfare systems. The main aim and emphasis is to provide job and income security for male workers: security seems indeed the basic word (where poverty alleviation could be that of 'liberal' public welfare programmes, and equality the central aim of the Nordic ones). Security appears in the name of the main social insurance schemes: *Soziale Versicherung, sécurité sociale, seguridad social, sicurezza sociale*, etc. Beside this central point, one should also mention the importance of professional belonging in defining individuals' social identities, and the importance of collective protection and collectively negotiated rights. As far as social justice is concerned, these schemes are less concerned about poverty or inequalities than about ensuring the proportionality of benefits with regard to former wages (the so-called equivalence principle, which is a specific conception of equity). There is also a shared historical basis to the Bismarckian welfare systems, linked as these are with industrialization, whose expansion was largely constructed in the (postwar) heyday of Fordist, industrial capitalism – unlike many liberal (Anglo) welfare states that were established earlier (pre-industrial) and social democratic welfare states that only took off later (post-industrial) (Bonoli 2007).

In the Bismarckian systems, the level of social protection offered depends on the employment situation, market performance and merit. As a result of the relatively generous level of the social benefits provided, it also guarantees insured individuals a certain level of independence in relation to the market in the event of a contingency. In this case, dependence on the market is indirect, in so far as the level of social benefits provided by these systems is itself related to prior employment (and family situation). Universality of coverage is therefore dependent on the capacity of society to ensure full employment. As we know from gender studies, these systems were also characterized by a strong orientation towards the support of traditional family roles. This model is frequently associated with a family structure based on the male breadwinner, which implies that women are left with prime responsibility for caring (Lewis 1992). Under this model, the participation of women in the labour market is fairly low (France being an exception).

As far as policy instruments or 'ways of doing' are concerned, Bismarckian welfare systems have (more or less) a number of commonalities in respect of four key institutional variables:

1. Modes of access to social protection are based on work/contribution; these systems were primarily aimed at insuring salaried workers who were paying contributions.
2. Social benefits are merely in cash, transfer-based, proportional, earnings-related, expressed in terms of replacement rates.
3. Financing mechanisms are based principally on social contribution (payroll taxes).
4. Administrative structures are para-public, involving social partners in the management of the social insurance funds (*Kassen, caisses, cassa*, etc.).

This type of welfare system is found mostly in continental Europe. Indeed, most countries of the European continent, having followed the Bismarckian route of welfare state development, can be considered as 'social insurance states' and share these common 'welfare institutions': access to benefits is linked to work position (instead of citizenship or need); most of the benefits are in cash and contributory (instead of flat-rate benefits or social services in kind); much of their social outlays are financed via earnings-related social contributions (instead of general taxation); and they have established a more or less 'corporatist' management of their schemes via funds that are more or less independent from the state. The comparative welfare state literature has shown that Germany, Austria, France, the Netherlands, Luxembourg, Italy, Spain, Belgium, Hungary and the Czech Republic have all developed welfare systems close to this ideal-type (Germany usually being the reference case). Our basic hypothesis is that this similarity of welfare conception and institutions partly explains the similarities in the problem profile and in the trajectories of reform. However, this has not prevented the policies being implemented from changing a lot, from the 1970s to the 2000s.

Bismarckian Welfare Systems Have Gone through Important Changes to Align with the New and Common Welfare Reform Agenda

Recent literature on comparative welfare state development has not focused specifically on the Bismarckian welfare regimes, but has drawn a comparative picture of their development by contrasting them with other types of regime. When he analysed 'national adaptation in global economies' and compared the various capacities of different welfare regimes to face the new economic challenges, Esping-Andersen emphasized the rigidity of the continental welfare state arrangements, speaking of a 'frozen continental landscape' resulting from the 'frozen Fordism' found in Germany, France or Italy (Esping-Andersen 1996). He concluded that 'the cards are very much stacked in favour of the welfare state "statu quo" in these countries' (1996: 267). Scharpf and Schmidt (2000) have shown that if all welfare states present vulnerabilities to the new open economic context, the welfare systems based on social insurance face the biggest difficulties of all welfare states, while Pierson (2001) argues that reforms have been rarest and most problematic in conservative corporatist regimes.

As depicted by the current literature, most of the continental welfare states were supposed to remain the same, not only because their reaction to the crisis (the 'labour shedding strategy' – Esping-Andersen 1996) reinforced their characteristics but also because they seemed unable to implement any structural reforms. While other welfare regimes have been able to overcome their difficulties through the introduction of reforms inspired by their own tradition, Bismarckian welfare systems not only appear unable to find a way out of the crisis in their own traditions, but actually seem to be locked into their difficulties by the very weight of that tradition. However, if one focuses exclusively on Bismarckian welfare systems, and if one includes the most recent reforms (implemented since 2000), one can see that tremendous changes have occurred in the policies implemented.

And yet they changed!

In this collection, we concentrate on the social policy reforms closest to the 'Bismarckian' model: old-age insurance in Germany, France and Italy (Giuliano Bonoli and Bruno Palier), health insurance in Germany, France and the Netherlands (Patrick Hassenteufel and Bruno Palier), unemployment insurance in Germany, France, Belgium and the Netherlands (Daniel Clegg), child- and elder-care policy reforms in the same countries (Nathalie Morel),[3] long-term care policies in Italy, Austria and France (Barbara Da Roit, Blanche Le Bihan and August Österle), activation policies towards lone parents in France, the Netherlands and the UK (Trudie Knijn, Claude Martin and Jane Millar) and the role of firms and social partners in family policies in Germany and France (Ute Klammer and Marie-Thérèse Letablier).

Our common, basic hypothesis is that the similarity of welfare conception and institutions partly explains the similarities in the problem profile and in the trajectories of reform. Our comparisons demonstrate that in continental Europe, welfare reforms have followed a similar path, starting with the well-known 'labour shedding strategy' (in line with the basic conception and institutions of Bismarckian welfare), succeeded in the 1990s by attempts at retrenchment and the spread of 'institutional' reforms; all these enabling – by the beginning of this century – the multiplication of structural reforms (in line with the new global social policy agenda).

France, Italy and Germany (together with Austria and Spain) have all gone through several waves of pension reform both in the 1990s and in the early 2000s, as shown in Bonoli and Palier's contribution to this collection. Comparing the politics of these reforms in various countries shows some similar trends: reforms were usually postponed until European integration and/or economic recession forced governments to act. Before the first wave of reforms, the main 'action' was to increase payroll taxes to finance pensions. In the 1990s, reforms were usually negotiated on the basis of a quid pro quo, whereby benefits were progressively to decrease in exchange for the planned introduction of non-contributory pensions financed from general tax revenues instead of through the insurance schemes. In the second wave of reforms (during the 2000s), more innovation seems to have been introduced, with new goals such as the development of voluntary private pension funds and the emphasis on increasing employment rates among the elderly – and cutting back on early retirement. In the late 2000s, with some hindsight, it is clear that even in Bismarckian countries pension systems are more amenable to reform than had been expected. Reform processes have been difficult, and several governments have lost political capital (and sometimes, admittedly, elections) because of pensions. Nevertheless, the trend suggests that one-time 'pure' social insurance pension systems are, slowly, being turned into multi-pillar ones.

In health insurance, changes are also visible, since competition between insurers has gained in importance in Germany and the Netherlands, and the state is reinforcing its controlling capacities in France and Germany. Up to now, continental health insurance systems have remained Bismarckian (they are still mainly financed by social contributions, managed by health insurance funds, delivering public and private health care, and freedom is still a higher priority than in the national health systems), but a new 'regulatory health-care state' is emerging in Germany, France and the Netherlands (see article by Hassenteufel and Palier). Beyond the remaining role of health insurance funds, they combine a logic of universalization through state intervention and a market logic based on regulated competition. They associate more state control (directly or through agencies) with more competition and market mechanisms. Those changes are embedded in the existing institutions via a type of 'conversion' (Thelen and Streeck 2005). In short, structural changes occur without revolution in the system.

Unemployment insurance systems have also changed, shifting away from the (insufficiently productive) 'labour shedding strategy' towards the development of activation policies. Daniel Clegg speaks of qualified cost containment and reactionary recalibration and shows that activation has developed mainly at the margin, focusing on the 'outsiders' of the labour market (see also the contribution of Knijn, Martin and Millar on income support towards lone parents). In fact, many of these policy changes have helped to preserve the integrity of insurance-based, contribution-financed and managerially autonomous unemployment protection arrangements, though only for a shrinking number of 'insiders', thus heading off pressures for more fundamental institutional change. Activation at the margins has allowed insurance arrangements to renounce, *de facto*, their responsibility for 'bad risks' without undermining the normative primacy of the employment basis of rights to guaranteed income replacement, on which the survival of Bismarckian social insurances depends. Unemployment policies in continental Europe have changed, not in spite of attempts to preserve the institutional status quo, but rather because of them. This process of dualization in unemployment compensation and employment policies has occurred incrementally, with the support of the 'insiders'' own representatives defending their position – at the expense of a growing number of 'outsiders', for whom most of the losses are reserved.

Nathalie Morel likewise traces a U-turn in child- and elder-care policies. During the late 1970s and 1980s Germany, the Netherlands, but also France and Belgium had tried to keep women at home or bring them back there, whereas, since the late 1990s, attempts have been made to facilitate the (re-)entry of (certain) women into the labour market, by the development of formal caring facilities and specific leaves. She shows, however, that care policy reforms have also provided a back door for the introduction of labour-cheapening measures and for increasing employment flexibility in otherwise very rigid labour markets. Here, a focus on promoting 'free choice' has justified the introduction of measures that have simultaneously reinforced social stratification in terms of access to the labour market – meaning that some women now have much more 'free choice' than others – and weakened certain labour-market rigidities.

The analysis of long-term care reforms in Italy, France and Austria also leads to the idea of there being a common trajectory in the continental welfare systems (with specific attention to the share of responsibility between the public and private spheres), centred on the choice of a cash-for-care system. Nevertheless, the pace, methods and, above all, the impact of these choices are different for informal care and for the labour force in this sector, depending on the level of regulation of the scheme and its connection to the issue of labour market regulation and also to the grey market in each country, as Da Roit, Le Bihan and Österle demonstrate in their contribution.

However, looking at social policies towards lone parents and, in particular, lone mothers, the comparison between two continental (France and the Netherlands) and one liberal (UK) welfare system demonstrates in this case the relatively weak specificity of the first two welfare systems in these respects, when compared to the third one. A common trend towards activation policies and towards an 'adult worker' model is evident in all three national configurations. Knijn, Martin and Millar analyse the three social policy trajectories and assess the capacity of their instruments to achieve this common objective. Nevertheless, many important policy variations remain, depending on the degree of workfare orientation (punitive workfare, control and an explicit will to reduce the number of minimum income recipients) as against activation orientation. The political variable plays an important role in this context. Nevertheless, these different welfare systems seem effectively to have realigned themselves to a new common orientation.

The comparison between German and French family policies is also very instructive for understanding common trends. Despite the huge differences between these two welfare systems in terms of intervention in private life, female employment levels, and also childcare policies, a common orientation is gaining ground on the necessity to diversify the offer of services by giving enterprises a new role. Klammer and Letablier offer a detailed analysis of this common trend between two very different traditions of family policy – and underline the differences still existing over the pace of adaptation (rapid in the German case and slow in the French).

In summary, most of the contributions argue that structural, institutional and paradigmatic changes are indeed taking place, over and above mere adaptive reforms. These changes have to be understood as being framed by Bismarckian welfare perceptions and institutions. Their direction is, however, towards the same objectives as those which have been defined for other welfare systems.

Realigning Bismarckian welfare systems

If a large part of the literature on welfare state reforms centred around a hypothesis of convergence – to defend either the progressive development of a 'European social model' or the idea of a 'downward harmonization' – this seems largely inappropriate in respect of the current reforms. By comparing the variations in social expenditure in Europe and OECD countries, Francis G. Castles, wondering whether European welfare states are converging, answered that 'they are in some respects and not in others' (Castles 2004: 91). It seems, indeed, inadequate to defend this idea of a convergence or even a simple downsizing of the welfare states: the bulk of the welfare programmes we are studying remain 'Bismarckian' in their objectives and in their instruments, and, as we will see, they follow a specific trajectory. Nevertheless, considering the policies implemented, we can see big changes in the policy agenda. During the 2000s, governments have adopted new policy objectives, rather distant from the type of 'frozen Fordism' that Gøsta Esping-Andersen once described.

In the new context of the 1970s, the first reaction (typical of Bismarckian welfare regimes) was to remove people (especially women and the elderly) from the labour market by developing specific benefits for them, and to increase social contributions to finance these measures as well as the recurring deficits. The reaction now, however, is to try to encourage (re-)entry into the labour market and to stabilize or even diminish public social spending. Joining the others who did it before them, the governments of Bismarckian welfare systems have now adopted the common or 'orthodox' social policy agenda, as framed during the 1980s and 1990s by the main international agencies.

It is not our purpose here to analyse the development, content and differences of this new and global social policy paradigm. We should just remind ourselves what its main traits are (acknowledging that this is, of course, a sketchy caricature). The agenda is especially readable from the recommendations made by various experts, particularly within international organizations such as the World Bank, the OECD and (with modification) the EU,[4] but we can outline the main features of these new norms of action, and hence recognize that they now constitute the reform agenda of continental Europe.[5] Whereas social spending was long conceived as favourable to economic growth (under the Keynesian macro-economic paradigm), one of the main new orientations is now to reduce public social spending in order to boost economic activity by bringing back firms' profitability. The reforms should make social protection schemes more conducive to employment by reducing their cost, rather than increasing social spending. The advent of retrenchment policies paved the way to begin seeking new economic functions for social protection. As a rule, the basic philosophy has been to adapt social protection schemes to a supply-side rather than a demand-side macro-economic policy. According to the new norms being developed, the welfare state should be placed in the service of competition (among businesses, states, individuals).

Looked at from this perspective, social programmes are supposed to be more employment-friendly by the linking of benefits to incentives that make it preferable to work rather than to receive social security benefits for doing nothing. Employment and social policies are more and more thought of in terms of incentives (negative, or positive in the case of 'social investment') rather than in terms of rights (or decommodification devices). Employment policies are now focused on stimulating labour supply and activation strategies (Clasen 2000). Increasing female participation in the labour market and thereby facilitating family/work reconciliation is also at the heart of the new social policy paradigms. In pensions, a multi-pillar system which includes both pay-as-you-go and funded schemes (in order to promote investment capacities in the country) is promoted, with an emphasis on the tight link between the level of the pension and the volume of contribution paid (Palier 2003). In health-care systems, the introduction of managed competition has become the main tool for regulation (Palier 2005b).

If these are the main features of the new (global) social policy agenda, then, according to our accounts of the recent reforms, we can say that even the Bismarckian welfare systems have incrementally adopted it. This does not mean that they have been successful in reaching the outcome supposedly associated with this policy agenda, nor that they have totally transformed their ways of thinking and doing. It simply means that they cannot any longer be characterized by blockages, stickiness to the past and 'welfare without work' strategies. Since most of the recent literature has been explaining that conservative corporatist welfare systems were almost unable to adapt to the current economic and social environment or to adopt the new reform agenda, how should we explain the implementation of these changes?

How Did They Change? A Sequential Process of Transformation

Our cases offer no instances of brutal departure from the Bismarckian way of thinking and doing, but rather an incremental and slow shift away from what the first reaction to the crises was. This first reaction was highly determined by the institutional logic of the Bismarckian system (labour shedding and increases in social contribution), but the orientation of the reforms has progressively been changed, by a succession of measures taking into account the consequences of the preceding ones. If we want to understand these systemic changes, we should not be analysing any one (big or small) reform separately from the others but, on the contrary, focusing on the whole 'reforms trajectory', in which each stage closes down some ventures and opens up new opportunities. Our understanding of the changes is thus based on the idea of 'cumulative but transformative' development (Thelen and Streeck 2005; Palier 2005c), a sequential process of change whereby one reform is partly to be explained by the (consequences of the) previous ones, and where learning plays an important role.

All in all, and acknowledging that the actual process varied from one country to another – as well as from one policy field to another – we can discern four main stages to this sequential process of change.[6]

(1) The first reaction to the crises consisted mainly in preserving the most productive male breadwinner's job and social protection by removing all his potential competitors from the labour market. This first phase happened 'before retrenchment', and signified a labour shedding strategy and an increase in social contributions.

(2) However, these measures had the consequence of decreasing the global employment rate and increasing labour costs (through the continuous increase in social contributions): fewer people working had to pay more and more to preserve their social protection and to provide the inactive ones with income. This trend was in great tension with the new economic context of the early 1990s, when the single market was implemented (1992) and the single currency was under preparation (Maastricht criteria adopted in 1993). Hence a second phase of the 'reforms trajectory' can be identified, associated with a lot of decisions aimed at stabilizing if not retrenching social expenditure. However, the retrenchment has been negotiated with the social partners, guaranteeing a relatively low cost for the current 'insiders' (long phasing-in of reforms in pensions, the reactionary recalibration of unemployment insurance benefits [more for those who worked full-time before, less for the precarious careers], the targeting of activation measures at outsiders – including lone mothers) and introducing a new world of welfare through the development of tax-financed, non-contributory benefits.

(3) The political difficulties caused by these attempts at retrenchment (the mid-1990s witnessed strong political opposition to such measures) and their relative failures (social expenditure continued to increase, unemployment to be high), led governments to learn that the institutional setting of the systems had become a problem. They went in for more and more 'institutional reforms', aimed at transforming the very bases of these welfare systems: changes in the financing mechanisms (towards less social contribution and more taxes) as well as in the governance arrangements (weakening of the social partners, privatization or *étatisation*). These changes have weakened the traditional pillars of the Bismarckian welfare systems, thus allowing for further structural changes since the early 2000s.

(4) This last phase has been made of paradigmatic changes, since the objectives and instruments of reform are quite different from what had been the traditional reaction of Bismarckian systems to social problems: the introduction of funded schemes for pensions (as well as reductions in early pensions), the activation of the inactive population (including mothers – even lone mothers), hence the defamilialization of care and the introduction of competition and rampant privatization into health insurance systems. These structural changes mean, first, a shift away from the typical answers to the difficulties of traditional Bismarckian welfare regimes in the 1970s and 1980s, i.e. the 'labour shedding strategy'. Governments are currently trying to escape the 'welfare without work' trap. In the long run, this may also mean

a structural transformation of the Bismarckian welfare systems themselves. So far, we can at least identify ongoing processes of dualization.

In order to provide the reader with a general picture of the policy changes that surround the specific reforms analysed in the various articles, we will now develop these four phases, in showing how much they have been shaped by the typical Bismarckian institutional setting, but also how much the consequences of the first reaction led to further progressive change in the policy agenda.[7]

Before retrenchment, the weight of Bismarckian institutions

The literature has identified several causes of the crisis of the welfare state since the mid-1970s, including socio-economic challenges such as mass and structural unemployment, low fertility and population ageing, rising female labour market participation, increasing capital mobility and intensified competition between economies. Though these trends are important everywhere, the literature on welfare state change has shown that they do not impact in exactly the same way on all countries, since they are filtered by welfare institutions and are influenced by the initial choices (path dependence). 'With its institutionalization, a welfare state becomes a powerful societal mechanism which decisively shapes the future' (Esping-Andersen 1990: 221). Pierson (1994) has shown the importance of welfare programmes in influencing the allocation of economic and political resources, modifying the costs and benefits associated with alternative political strategies, and thus altering ensuing political development. Bonoli and Palier (2000) also stress that welfare institutions structure debates, political preferences and policy choices. They affect the positions of the various actors and groups involved in reform processes. They frame the kinds of interests and resources which actors can mobilize in favour of, or against, welfare reforms. In part, they also determine who can and who cannot participate in the political game leading to reforms. Depending on how these different variables are set, different patterns of support and opposition are likely to be encountered. In order to understand their difficulties and to demonstrate why continental welfare states are the most challenged, a number of analysts refer to the institutional settings of their welfare programmes.

For many analysts, the welfare institutions typical of Bismarckian welfare systems can be said to have long prevented necessary change. Esping-Andersen (1996) has argued that the difficulties met by continental Europe are partly due to the necessity to defend the so-called 'family wage' (thereby excluding the youngest, the oldest and women from the labour market). By family wage, one has to understand the status associated with employment: a salary plus all the social benefits associated with it. Here, Esping-Andersen underlines the problem of a system in which social benefits are mostly linked to work, given to the male breadwinner – and mainly contributory and in cash. It is thus the type of social benefits delivered in continental Europe which helps to explain the specificity of the problems these systems face.

In a similar perspective to Scharpf and Schmidt (2000), Daly (2001) has shown that the Bismarckian welfare states present three specific pressure points in the face of globalization: the funding structure and methods for financing (which create problems of labour costs), the highly legitimate nature of the claim structure (which hampers retrenchment), and the lack of flexibility in a cash benefit-based system (which prevents new social risks being covered). One could thus argue that all the institutional characteristics of the Bismarckian welfare states contribute to its resistance to change: contributory benefits enjoy a particularly high level of legitimacy and are therefore difficult to cut back radically. Transfers are 'paid' by social contributions, so workers assume that they have 'bought' social rights. Benefits are usually generous, so their loss would be more significant than the reduction of a benefit which is already at a low level. People prefer to pay more (contributions) rather than see their benefits (bought by their own work) diminished. Finally, insurance-based transfers are well defended by organized interests, and in particular by trade unions of the different branches corresponding to the different professional schemes.

Looking carefully at the early reaction to the economic crises, during the 1970s and 1980s, one can indeed see the importance of welfare institutions in shaping the responses. In continental Europe, governments have long preferred to increase social contributions rather than cut social benefits. This is counterintuitive from an Anglo-Saxon (and even a Scandinavian) point of view, where the most politically risky thing to do is to raise taxes and where the population prefers some cuts in social programmes to any tax increases.

These differences are due to the differences in the type of benefits and, moreover, in the way in which they are financed. Where a Reagan, a Thatcher or a Major could denounce the excessive weight of taxes and the unwarranted cost of the social benefits delivered to those who do nothing, it was much more difficult for continental European politicians to attack social insurance rights acquired by all the working population through the payment of social contributions. Instead of reducing highly legitimate benefits, it was much easier to raise social contributions, as long as this was to preserve the social rights of all workers and families, and the level of their benefits. On the benefit side, it is also more feasible to reduce flat-rate or means-tested benefits than earnings-related ones. Since earnings-related benefits are often expressed as a proportion of a salary, there is a form of 'automatic' indexation on earnings, which tends to be the most generous form of indexation. In the case of contributory benefits, they remain constant in terms of replacement rates unless cuts in the benefit formula are adopted. These are highly visible and politically difficult to implement.

Whereas, for retrenchment in liberal welfare regimes, the population targeted was usually weak and not well represented – and whereas, in universal regimes, it was the whole population which was to be affected by the reforms – in continental Europe, the beneficiaries of social protection susceptible to cuts are well represented and defended by trade unions. This explains why the state encountered such difficulties in trying to impose retrenchment policies. In most Bismarckian welfare systems, management is shared with trade unions and employers; responsibility tends thus to be diluted, diminishing the capacity of the state to control the development of the social protection system – and particularly its levels of expenditure. Union involvement in the management of social security grants unions a *de facto* veto power against welfare state reforms (Bonoli and Palier 1996).

We see that each trait of Bismarckian welfare institutions works to render welfare retrenchment extremely difficult. Therefore, during the late 1970s and the early 1980s, governments in continental Europe responded to social difficulties mainly by raising the level of social contributions. In recognition of the new problems which they were confronting, governments thus spent more, rather than less. In Germany, '[t]he 80's were not a time of simple retrenchment. Under conditions where neither federal nor state government was obliged to pay the welfare bill, the door was open for increased benefits or expanded entitlements' (Manow and Seils 2000: 279). During the 1980s, while they were decreasing the level of direct income taxation, French governments were raising the level of social contributions paid by employees. As a proportion of taxation, the share of social contribution has increased dramatically (from 39 per cent in 1970 to 46 per cent in 1995) as well as as a proportion of GDP: in 1978, the volume of social contribution equalled less than 20 per cent of French GDP, but had reached almost 23 per cent by 1985 (Palier 2005a). The state was not paying the welfare bill: this was financed by the social contributions given to social insurance funds.

This increase in social spending in the 1970s and early 1980s can be understood in different ways. In part, governments paid the bill for commitments made in an earlier period (see Pierson 2001 for such an explanation). But governments, especially in continental Europe, also increased the generosity of social benefits, notably for those who were particularly hard-hit by the economic crisis (redundant industrial workers, lone parents, poor elderly, long-term unemployed, etc.). In particular, many governments developed benefits aimed at removing jobseekers from the labour market – such as early retirement schemes and invalidity pensions – implementing what Esping-Andersen called the 'labour shedding' strategy and thus paving the way for the 'welfare without work' trap (Esping-Andersen 1996). The point here is that this policy path appeared feasible, since all the related increases in expenditure were offset by politically acceptable increases in social contributions, which occurred repeatedly in these countries during this period. Governments used the instruments already available: their policies consisted mainly of increasing the generosity of existing benefits and increasing the level of existing social contributions.

Retrenchment to save the system: the 1990s

From the early 1990s, a changing context prohibited the continuation of these kinds of policies. Under conditions of economic recession (in the early 1990s), and with the economic constraints of the European Single Market and single currency becoming stronger, continental European governments decided (or rather felt obliged) to opt for retrenchment in the social protection system.

Reforms were introduced which aimed at reducing the level of social benefits while preserving the logic of a given system. One can refer here to the so-called 'consolidation' reforms implemented in Germany at the end of the 1980s and during the early 1990s, or to the French sectorial reforms, aimed at 'rescuing the social security system' (new medical agreements in health care, a new benefit in unemployment insurance and new modes of calculating retirement pensions; cf. Palier 2000: 122–6). One might also refer to the Italian pension reforms of 1991 and 1995, or to similar ones in Spain (included in the Toledo pacts in 1995), and so on.

Such reforms introduced new instruments but remained within the traditional (historical and institutional) logic of Bismarckian welfare systems. The reforms appeared to share certain features, related to the specific institutional settings of these social insurance welfare systems.

First, the retrenchment reforms were not presented as a means of dismantling the Bismarckian welfare state, but of preserving and consolidating it. In the political discourse justifying the reforms one heard that, if reform was necessary, it was not because the system was dysfunctional but because it was suffering the ill-effects of the current situation, where resources were decreasing (because of economic slow-down, unemployment, etc.) and spending was increasing (because of unemployment, ageing, new social demands, etc.). Since it no longer appeared possible to further increase resources, governments had to retrench (a bit). This discourse can be understood if one remembers the high legitimacy of the benefits delivered by this kind of social insurance system and the strong attachment of the population to them. These reforms were not made in the name of criticism of welfare redistribution, but in the name of the crucial necessity to restore their sustainability.

Second, such reforms were usually negotiated, often between different political parties, and almost always with the social partners (for pensions, see Schludi 2005). This can be understood as a consequence of the participation of the social partners in the management of social insurance schemes. Since the systems are financed through social contributions levied on wages (and not through taxation), the representatives of those who pay to and benefit from the systems are central players in the political game concerning social policy reforms. They have a say in the process of reforms, and have the power to eventually block them if they do not agree. Here, the role of these veto players should be understood with reference not merely to the particular political institutions but to the entire welfare state design. France is far from being a consensual political system; however, as in other Bismarckian systems, no social policy reforms could be passed in France without the (at least implicit) agreement of (at least a majority of) the social partners.

Third, the main technique used for reducing welfare benefits in these reforms was to increase the 'contributivity' of the benefits, i.e. to strengthen the link between the amount of contribution and the volume of the benefits (through a change in the calculation formula and/or stricter entitlement rules). This, of course, relied on the already-existing logic of these social insurance schemes (where one gets the right to social benefits by paying social contributions), even though these reforms usually meant a shift away from redistributive (horizontal and vertical) to actuarial principles.

Finally, the acceptance by the social partners of these decreases in benefits was usually based on a quid pro quo (Bonoli 2000), linked to the distinction between what should be financed through contributions and what should be financed through taxation. Retrenchments in social insurance programmes are often accompanied by a clarification of responsibility: the government proposing to the social partners to assume the financing of non-contributory benefits (flat-rate social minima for the elderly, the handicapped, the long-term unemployed; the crediting of contributions for periods out of work because of unemployment, childrearing, etc.) in exchange for decreases in social insurance benefits.

These changes have been based on new instruments (changes in calcula-tion rules, a shift from defined benefits to defined contribution systems, the creation of new state subsidies, etc.), but were perceived as preserving the very nature of social insurance, and sometimes even as reinforcing it (the social partners, for example, often think that making the state pay for non-contributory benefits helps to 'purify' and thus reinforce social insurance). They do not really challenge the principles of social insurance.

Beyond retrenchment: institutional reforms

However, since the early 1990s, the welfare systems based on social insurance have increasingly been perceived as exacerbating economic, social and political difficulties. Before retrenchment, social insurance benefits were used as a support for the victims of the crisis (compensation) and as a tool to counter it (reflation policies, welfare without work strategies). In the following period, when continuous increases in social spending appeared unaffordable, retrenchments were attempted, but essentially to save social insurance, which was perceived as a victim of the crisis (fewer resources, more expenses). However, in the analyses supporting further and deeper reforms, these systems have become part of the cause of the crisis. In France, for example, social insurance has been accused of partly causing a number of economic, social and political problems: the contributory nature of most social benefits is accused of reinforcing social exclusion; the weight of social contributions, of hindering competitiveness and preventing job creation; the participation of social partners in the systems, of weakening the state's capacity to control expenditure and to implement reforms (Palier 2005a). One can see here that, in recent analyses of the problems being met by the Bismarckian welfare systems, the causes of their difficulties seem to be the very characteristics of the systems themselves (contributory benefits, financed by social contribution, managed by the social partners). If this is the case, they need not only to be retrenched but profoundly transformed.

It is not only social scientists who acknowledge the impact of institutions on problems, and their role in shaping, and sometimes preventing, change. Through learning processes, experts and politicians come to recognize these effects – and sometimes therefore to decide to change the institutions. In most of the social insurance welfare systems, (some) structural changes are taking place in order to tackle the structural difficulties.

For instance, in response to growing numbers of jobless people, youth and lone parents or long-term unemployed, new benefits have been created, or former marginal benefits have been developed: these are targeted, flat-rate benefits, usually financed by taxation and run by the state. Governments have also started to develop more active labour market policies (see the article by Clegg). In order to cope with uncontrolled increases in health expenditure, the level of public coverage has been reduced, leaving more room for private insurance (see the contribution by Hassenteufel and Palier). To face demographic ageing, pension reforms have introduced small private top-ups, voluntary and pre-funded pensions over and above the pay-as-you-go mandatory pensions (see article by Bonoli and Palier). To face the new risk of long-term care or the 'dependency of the elderly', new policies have been implemented in the late 1990s (Martin 2003; see also article by Morel).

In all cases, the coverage by social insurance (in terms both of its generosity and its universality) is diminishing, leaving room for other types of social policy instruments – and also goals.

Besides changes in benefits, some other basic pillars of social insurance have been under scrutiny: contribution financing and the involvement of the social partners in the management of social security. Some recent reforms have been aimed at modifying these institutional arrangements. This is certainly the case in France with the increase of exemptions for social contributions, as well as the development of a new tax to finance non-contributory social benefits (the CSG); and with the empowerment of Parliament in the social policy-making process (Palier 2000, 2005a). One could also mention reforms introduced in other Bismarckian countries (for example, the introduction of a 'green tax' in Germany during the 1990s and the switch between recently raised VAT and employers' contribution in Germany). Changes have also marked the governance of the system, usually at the expense of the social partners (see the increasing role of the state in France or Germany, as well as the privatization of employment services in the Netherlands or the creation of a new agency to finance the French long-term care policy; see Martin 2006). These institutional reforms introduce new instruments usually linked to a different logic of welfare (taxation, public or private management of the benefits). They are structural changes which may transform the very nature of the system.

The structural reforms of the 2000s: adopting the new social policy agenda

Since the early 2000s, a new wave of reforms has been developing in continental Europe: the 2003 pension reforms and the 2004 health reforms in France, the Hartz reforms and the 2010 Agenda in Germany, etc. These reforms are not only retrenching social insurance benefits, they are implementing structural adaptations rendered possible by the previous institutional reforms presented above. As all the following contributions show, they signify the adoption of the new social policy agenda mentioned earlier. With regard to pensions, not only are there plans to reduce benefits, but a new basic safety net has been implemented in Germany, and additional, fully funded schemes are proposed for German (Riester funds), French (PERP and PERCO) and Italian citizens. In health, more and more room is being given to competition and private actors, as with the Douste Blazy reform or again through the 2003 German changes. Activation measures are gaining force in the un-employment reforms implemented in France, Germany and other continental

European countries since the early 2000s. Cheaper and more flexible jobs are being created through care policies.

The accumulation of all these recent institutional and structural changes in social insurances, new employment policies (activation, making work pay) and new developments in care policies may signify a general paradigmatic change for the continental welfare states, evincing a shift away from systems aimed at income and status maintenance towards activated and employment-friendly welfare systems. Such structural adaptations may appear marginal in the first place. However, the study of the national cases shows that, however trivial they may appear when introduced (being usually presented as a mere complement to the still central social insurance systems), these policies can develop little by little, eventually to form a veritable 'second world' of welfare within one country (as is the case for the new targeted benefit introduced (RMI) or the new tax (CSG) in France; see Palier 2005c, 2007).

A Dualization of Welfare

The Bismarckian welfare systems are being changed by the current reforms. It is too early to know whether this means a structural transformation of the systems as such. However, we can already identify a process of dualization of the welfare system, as well as of the population protected.

It has become clear that France has now a dual welfare system (Palier 2005a). On the one hand, there are 'national solidarity schemes': family benefits, health care and poverty alleviation, delivering either universal or targeted benefits, mainly financed by taxation and controlled by the state. On the other hand, pensions and unemployment/employment policies have been retained in the social insurance world, even though the meaning of social insurance has changed, becoming more reliant on actuarial and activation principles. Ferrera (1996) has shown that dualization also marked the development of southern European welfare states, and Bleses and Seeleib-Kaiser (2006) speak of the dual transformation of the German welfare state.

This dualization also means that the whole population is not covered any more by the same principles and institutions. When the insiders (with full-time permanent jobs) continue to be insured (relatively 'less well' than before, thus needing to complement their protection with private schemes), a growing part of the population is experiencing the development of 'atypical' jobs, and more people must now rely on other types of social protection than typical social insurance (mainly assistance).

This process of dualization, meaning a change in the welfare system itself, should be understood by the political dynamic created by the Bismarckian welfare institutions themselves. As both Daniel Clegg and Nathalie Morel show so well in their articles, it is in the name of the spirit and practices of typical conservative corporatist social policies that changes are introduced in a segmenting way. As Daniel Clegg puts it: 'Generally, policies have enhanced protection for "insiders" while targeting both benefit cuts and new activation initiatives on "outsiders". After a quarter-century of reforms these are thus neither fully activating nor fully compensatory welfare states, but ones that combine these facets in apparent contradiction. There is a suggestive parallel – and probably a two-way causal link – here with the dualism of labour market regulation increasingly found in much of continental Europe, where precarious employment contracts have been expanded as "exceptions" that simultaneously contradict and reinforce the "rule" of the standard employment relationship for core workers.' In the same vein, Nathalie Morel shows that '[c]are policies have not attempted to modify the traditional gendered division of labour in the household, and the family (or at least a family-like) environment is still considered as the best locus of care. Care policies have also tended to reproduce and reinforce the social stratification dimension of Bismarckian welfare systems: while low-income women have been encouraged to make use of long, low-paid parental leave schemes, and thus to withdraw from the labour market, various measures facilitating the use of private forms of childcare have been developed for higher-income women.'

We see here that everything happens as if the institutions had been changed in order to preserve the social order prevailing in the Bismarckian world of welfare! Does that mean that the future will be like the past? One can hypothesize that this dual way of reforming is the typical (conservative and corporatist) way of adapting to the new economic and social world,[8] and that this segmented pathway is quite robust and will shape the future of continental Europe. Even if the situation was already fragmented and inegalitarian, the recent trend would deepen the divisions towards a more cleft world: a dual labour market, a dual welfare system and a society divided between insiders and outsiders. Some others may think that this period of apparent contradiction in policies (activation *and* compensation, defamilialization, conciliation policies *and* maternal wages) is merely a period of transition, the old world only starting to disappear (hence its remaining traces for the old insiders) while the new one is still young (new schemes and benefits will gain in importance, the new generation will not be treated like the old one was). Since we now better grasp the direction and content of the policy changes, the next research agenda will be to analyse their economic and social outcomes, once these changes will have matured enough to show what their impacts have been.

Notes

1. One can only find isolated national case studies, for example on the Netherlands (Visser and Hemerijck 1997), Italy (Ferrera and Gualmini 2004), Germany (Bleses and Seeleib-Kaiser 2004) or France (Palier 2005a).
2. For a review of the main critiques of Esping-Andersen, see Arts and Gelissen (2002). Esping-Andersen himself considers that the most relevant critiques come from the gender studies which suggest another theoretical perspective and new concepts, like 'defamilialization', to organize the comparison and propose a typology (Lewis 1992; Orloff 1993; Hobson *et al.* 2002).
3. These four articles have been elaborated within the framework of a broader research project: 'The Politics of Reforms in Bismarckian Welfare Systems', led by Bruno Palier, which has been supported by the French Ministry of Social Affairs (DREES-MIRE), Sciences po (Direction scientifique, Cevipof and Centre d'études européennes), the Friedrich Ebert Stiftung, the Fondation Jean Jaurès and the Harvard Center for European Studies.

4. Regarding the World Bank's approach, see, for instance, Palier and Viossat (2001); on the OECD approach, see Armingeon and Beyerler (2004); on the EU, see, for instance, Palier and Pochet (2005).
5. In the recent literature, this new agenda is analysed as having two main versions, the neo-liberal one, and the social-democratic one (then often called the 'social investment' approach by, for instance, Esping-Andersen [2002] or Jenson and Saint Martin [2006]).
6. For a broader presentation of these sequences, see Palier (2006).
7. This part is based on the following section, but also on the analyses of 'national trajectories' provided for the project 'The Politics of Reforms in Bismarckian Welfare Systems'. These analyses will be published in 2008 in a collective book entitled *A Long Good Bye to Bismarck?* published by Amsterdam University Press. It benefited greatly from various comments, including those by Fritz Scharpf, Jonas Pontusson, Peter Hall, Jane Jenson and Karen Andersen, and from discussion within a doctoral seminar co-animated by Kathy Thelen and Bruno Palier; all participants should here be thanked.
8. These dualization processes seem specific to the Bismarckian world, since in liberal countries one speaks more of the squeezing of the middle class and of fragmentation (instead of dualization) of societies, and in Nordic countries, unions, governments and their policies seem to have been able to remain encompassing.

References

Armingeon, K. and Beyerler, M. (eds) (2004), *The OECD and European Welfare States*, Cheltenham: Edward Elgar.

Arts, W. and Gelissen, J. (2002), Three worlds of welfare capitalism or more? A state-of-the-art report, *Journal of European Social Policy*, 12, 2: 137–58.

Bleses, P. and Seeleib-Kaiser, M. (2004), *The Dual Transformation of the German Welfare State*, New York: Palgrave Macmillan.

Bonoli, G. (2000), *The Politics of Pension Reform: Institutions and Policy Change in Western Europe*, Cambridge: Cambridge University Press.

Bonoli, G. (2007), Time matters: postindustrialization, new social risks, and welfare state adaptation . . . , *Comparative Political Studies*, 40: 495–520.

Bonoli, G. and Palier, B. (1996), Reclaiming welfare: the politics of social protection reform in France. In M. Rhodes (ed.), *Southern European Welfare States*, London: Frank Cass, pp. 240–59.

Bonoli, G. and Palier, B. (2000), How do welfare states change? Institutions and their impact on the politics of welfare state reform, *European Review*, 8, 2: 333–52.

Castles, F. G. (2004), *The Future of the Welfare State: Crisis Myths and Crisis Realities*, Oxford: Oxford University Press.

Clasen, J. (2000), Motives, means and opportunities: reforming unemployment compensation in the 1990s, *West European Politics*, 23, 2: 89–112.

Daly, M. (2001), Globalization and the Bismarckian welfare states. In R. Sykes, B. Palier and P. Prior (eds), *Globalization and the European Welfare States: Challenges and Change*, London: Macmillan Press, pp. 79–102.

Ebbinghaus, B. and Manow, P. (2001), *Comparing Welfare Capitalism, Social Policy and Political Economy in Europe, Japan and the USA*, London: Routledge.

Esping-Andersen, G. (1990), *The Three Worlds of Welfare Capitalism*, Cambridge: Polity Press.

Esping-Andersen, G. (ed.) (1996), *Welfare States in Transition: National Adaptations in Global Economies*, London: Sage.

Esping-Andersen, G. (ed.) (2002), *Why We Need a New Welfare State?* Oxford: Oxford University Press.

Ferrera, M. (1996), The Southern model of welfare in social Europe, *Journal of European Social Policy*, 6, 1: 17–37.

Ferrera, M. and Gualmini, E. (2004), *Rescued by Europe? Social and Labour Reforms in Italy from Maastricht to Berlusconi*, Amsterdam: Amsterdam University Press.

Ferrera, M. and Rhodes, M. (eds) (2000), Recasting European welfare states, *West European Politics* (Special Issue), 23, 2 (April).

Hall, P. (1993), Policy paradigm, social learning and the state, the case of economic policy in Britain, *Comparative Politics* (April): 275–96.

Hobson, B., Lewis, J. and Siim, B. (eds) (2002), *Contested Concepts in Gender and Social Politics*, Cheltenham: Edward Elgar.

Huber, E. and Stephens, J. D. (2001), *Political Choice in Global Markets: Development and Crisis of Advanced Welfare States*, Chicago: University of Chicago Press.

Jenson, J. and Saint-Martin, D. (2006), Building blocks for a new social architecture: the LEGO™ paradigm of an active society, *Policy and Politics*, 34, 3: 429–51.

Kautto, M., Fritzell, J., Hvinden, B., Kvist, J. and Uusitalo, H. (eds) (2001), *Nordic Welfare States in the European Context*, London: Routledge.

Leibfried, S. (ed.) (2000), Welfare state futures, *European Review*, 8, 2.

Lewis, J. (1992), Gender and the development of welfare regimes, *Journal of European Social Policy*, 2, 3: 159–73.

Manow, P. and Seils, E. (2000), Adjusting badly: the German welfare state, structural change, and the open economy. In F. W. Scharpf and V. A. Schmidt, *From Vulnerability to Competitiveness: Welfare and Work in the Open Economy*, Oxford: Oxford University Press, vol. 2, pp. 264–307.

Martin, C. (1997), La comparaison des systèmes de protection sociale en Europe: de la classification à l'analyse des trajectoires d'Etat-providence, *Lien Social et Politiques*, 37: 145–55.

Martin, C. (ed.) (2003), *La dépendance des personnes âgées: quelles politiques en Europe?* Rennes: Presses Universitaires de Rennes.

Martin, C. (2006), Prendre soin des personnes âgées dépendantes: le défi européen et le modèle français, *Swiss Journal of Sociology*, 32, 3: 495–509.

Orloff, A. S. (1993), Gender and the social rights of citizenship: the comparative analysis of gender relations and welfare states, *American Sociological Review*, 58: 303–28.

Orloff, A., O'Connor, J. and Shaver, S. (1999), *States, Markets, Families: Gender, Liberalism and Social Policy in Australia, Canada, Great Britain, and the United States*, Cambridge: Cambridge University Press.

Palier, B. (2000) 'Defrosting' the French welfare state. In *West European Politics* (Special Issue, 'Recasting European Welfare States' ed. M. Ferrera and M. Rhodes), 23, 2 (April): 113–36.

Palier, B. (2003), *La réforme des retraites*, 2nd edn (collection Que sais-je?), Paris: PUF.

Palier, B. (2005a), *Gouverner la Sécurité sociale*, 2nd edn, Paris: PUF.

Palier, B. (2005b), *La réforme des systèmes de santé*, 2nd edn (collection Que sais-je?), Paris: PUF.

Palier, B. (2005c), Ambiguous agreement, cumulative change: French social policy in the 1990s. In K. Thelen and W. Streeck (eds), *Beyond Continuity, Institutional Change in Advanced Political Economies*, Oxford: Oxford University Press, pp. 127–44.

Palier, B. (2006), The politics of reforms in Bismarckian welfare systems, *Revue Française des Affaires Sociales* (special issue, 'Social Welfare Reforms in Europe: Challenges and Strategies in Continental and Southern Europe') (January–March): 47–72.

Palier, B. (2007), Tracking the evolution of a single instrument can reveal profound changes: the case of funded pensions in France, *Governance*, 20, 1: 85–107.

Palier, B. and Pochet, P. (2005), Toward a European social policy – At last? In N. Jabko and C. Parsons, *The State of the European Union. Vol. 7: With US or Against US? European Trends in American Perspective*, Oxford: Oxford University Press, pp. 253–73.

Bruno Palier and Claude Martin

Palier, B. and Sykes, R. (2001), Challenges and changes: issues and perspectives in the analysis of globalization and the European welfare states. In R. S. Sykes, B. Palier and P. Prior (eds), *Globalization and European Welfare States: Challenges and Changes*, London: Palgrave, pp. 1–16.
Palier, B. and Viossat, L.-C. (eds) (2001), *Politiques sociales et mondialisation*, Paris: Futuribles.
Pierson, P. (1994), *Dismantling the Welfare State? Reagan, Thatcher and the Politics of Retrenchment*, Cambridge: Cambridge University Press.
Pierson, P. (ed.) (2001), *The New Politics of the Welfare State*, Oxford: Oxford University Press.
Revue Française des Affaires Sociales (2003), The Nordic model, 3, 4.
Scharpf, F. W. and Schmidt, V. A. (eds) (2000), *From Vulnerability to Competitiveness: Welfare and Work in the Open Economy*, 2 vols, Oxford: Oxford University Press.
Schludi, M. (2005), *The Reform of Bismarckian Pension Systems: A Comparison of Pension Politics in Austria, France, Germany, Italy and Sweden*, Amsterdam: Amsterdam University Press.
Swank, D. (2002), *Global Capital, Political Institutions, and Policy Change in Developed Welfare States*, Cambridge: Cambridge University Press.
Sykes, R. S., Prior, P. and Palier, B. (2001), *Globalization and European Welfare States: Challenges and Changes*, London: Palgrave.
Thelen, K. and Streeck, W. (eds) (2005), *Beyond Continuity, Institutional Change in Advanced Political Economies*, Oxford: Oxford University Press.
Visser, J. and Hemerijck, A. (1997), '*A Dutch Miracle*', *Job Growth, Welfare Reform and Corporatism in the Netherlands*, Amsterdam: Amsterdam University Press.
Wilensky, H. (2002), *Rich Democracies: Political Economy, Public Policy, and Performance*, Berkeley: University of California Press.

2
When Past Reforms Open New Opportunities: Comparing Old-age Insurance Reforms in Bismarckian Welfare Systems

Giuliano Bonoli and Bruno Palier

Introduction

Early studies of pension reform in the context of population ageing highlighted the inertia characterizing public pension schemes, especially in Bismarckian countries. Strong attachment by the population, the political influence of the numerous soon-to-retire cohorts of baby boomers, coupled with the absence in many European countries of alternative provision: all suggested that a radical dismantling of pension systems was most unlikely (Myles and Pierson 2001). Even the shift to a multi-pillar pension system combining public and private pensions – like those existing in the Netherlands or Switzerland – was considered out of reach for Bismarckian countries, because of the so-called 'double payment issue' (*ibid.*). (In pay-as-you-go [PAYG] pension systems current generations of workers are financing current pension benefits. A shift to funded provision would entail that one transitional generation would have to pay current pensions through the PAYG system *and* finance their own retirement through a new funded system.) Such a solution was thought highly unlikely, not least because of the political costs associated with it.

In a way, pension systems in these countries represent the quintessence of difficulties to be associated with Bismarckian welfare institutions: benefits being financed by social contributions are as if 'earned through work' and therefore very legitimate and difficult to cut; old-age insurance funds (*Kassen, caisses*, etc.) are managed with the participation of the social partners, and therefore well defended by trade unions. Nevertheless, they are facing the greatest difficulties: being very sensitive to demographic changes, and financed by high levels of social contribution (payroll taxes), which undermine economic efficiency.

However, by the late 2000s, with some hindsight, it has become clear that, even in Bismarckian countries, pension systems are more amenable to reform than had been expected. To be sure, the reform processes have been difficult, and several governments have lost political capital (and sometimes elections) as a result. Nevertheless, some 15 years after the first attempts to reform continental European pension systems, some important changes have taken place. Future pensions are going to be lower in all main Bismarckian welfare states, and several countries have – in various ways – introduced widespread funded pension provision. In most cases, the size of this provision remains small in comparison to the large PAYG schemes, but the trend suggests that one-time 'pure' social insurance pension systems are, slowly, being turned into multi-pillar ones. How did this happen? How did the reformers manage to win against the strong opposition of politically active pensioners and would-be pensioners? How did they find a way out of the double payment problem?

We argue that two elements are crucial to understanding this development:

1. Long phasing-in periods ensure that the large and politically influential cohorts of baby boomers, due to enter into retirement between 2010 and 2030, will be affected only marginally by the reform.
2. The shift towards increased funding takes place in stages, and each stage facilitates the adoption of the next one.

These two features of pension reform processes have immensely facilitated the adoption of otherwise politically suicidal policy packages, and help account for the current shift towards multi-pillarization in social insurance countries. Let us look at each of them briefly.

Long time lags between adoption and full implementation

Pension reforms always have a phasing-in period. It is unreasonable to change the rules determining pension eligibility and levels of pension for people who are only a few years away from retirement. Current workers need time to adapt their saving and work habits to new pension rules. Phasing-in periods can also be politically attractive for reformers (Reynaud 1999). A long transition period may mean that the main losers in a reform will be the current young generations – who are less likely to mobilize against cuts in pensions than the politically powerful baby boomers now approaching retirement. Long time lags do not solve the double payment issue, as the generations to be affected by the cuts will at the same time be expected to pay for current retirees *and* to save for their own retirement. But the gradual adoption of such reform makes its consequences less politically visible than would a sudden shift.

A staged pension reform process

While every country has its own trajectory, it is possible to identify some commonalities in the choices taken. So far, we can identify four stages in the pension reform process:

Stage 1: No retrenchment is adopted. Any shortfall in pension scheme budgets is compensated through contribution increases, or government transfers (often financed through debt). While the timing is somewhat different across countries, this situation prevails until the late 1980s in most of continental Europe.

Stage 2: Concern over rising contribution rates pushes policy-makers to act, and some moderate retrenchment measures are adopted (e.g. a shift to a less generous indexation method). These reforms are perhaps less important for their actual content than for the fact that they bring pension reform, population ageing and the future of pensions into the public debate. They breed a climate of insecurity with regard to future benefits, which prompts some citizens to seek out private individual alternatives.

Stage 3: More radical retrenchment is facilitated by the fact that fewer people are now solely dependent on pay-as-you-go pensions. A second important factor will have been the introduction of funded provision – on a non-compulsory basis, but capable of replacing future income lost because of pay-as-you-go retrenchment.

Stage 4: New reforms are adopted aimed at strengthening the funded element, either through compulsion or stronger incentives.

These four stages refer to an ideal-typical transition from a social insurance to a multi-pillar pension system, and individual countries have followed this pattern to different extents. It must not be understood as a strict sequence of events, but more as a process in which the adoption of given measures facilitates the acceptance of certain options that would otherwise have been politically extremely difficult. If understood in such broad terms, our four-stage roadmap of pension reform helps to make sense of policy developments and to understand why some options which looked unfeasible in the early 1990s have become acceptable in the late 2000s.

Thus in this article,[1] we analyse how incrementalism works in a 'path-dependent' world. If Myles and Pierson (2001) have demonstrated that the menu of options for reform is overdetermined by existing institutional arrangements, we argue that small incremental reforms early in the process generate a new menu of options later on. Individuals as well as political actors come to exploit these new opportunities. By taking these opportunities, they may progressively but dramatically change the whole system.

The cases

The hypotheses presented above make reference to mechanisms inherent in the social insurance character of pensions in Bismarckian countries. Some of them may also exist in multi-pillar pension systems, but we expect both the staging and the delay effects to be particularly important in making reform possible in the hitherto pure social insurance systems. In this article, we test our two hypotheses against evidence collected for three major Bismarckian welfare states: France, Germany and Italy. Though not identical, these three countries display all the features making the pension problem particularly intractable in Bismarckian welfare states. First, pension system-based intergenerational transfers rely almost exclusively on pay-as-you-go pensions, meaning that these welfare states are particularly sensitive to demographic imbalances. Second, these countries share a very low effective age of retirement, resulting in part from policy decisions taken in the 1980s. Third, these countries share some of the lowest employment rates found among traditional OECD countries, especially for older workers. And finally, Germany and Italy are among the fastest-ageing countries in western Europe. All these features put these three countries under strong pressure to retrench in the pensions field.

At the same time, relatively influential labour movements, a population age structure where the cohorts who will enter retirement in the next 20 years are the largest, coupled with strong voter attachment to good public pensions: all make reform in these countries particularly difficult. During the 1990s, all the three countries underwent controversial measures of pension reform which led to the reform's withdrawal and to political defeat. (Witness, in Italy, Berlusconi's first attempt to reform pensions and his subsequent obligation to quit power; the French *Plan Juppé* of 1995 and the subsequent loss of the election in 1997; the 1997 Kohl reform and his government's subsequent loss of the general election.)

The institutional features of old-age insurance help make them particularly difficult to retrench. Owing to the way in which they are financed and calculated, PAYG pensions appear extremely legitimate. For workers, social contributions are different from taxes, they are part of their wage.[2] By paying their social contributions, workers feel they have earned their right to a pension. Therefore, any cut seems particularly unfair for people who have been 'working for their pensions'. Moreover, the way pensions are calculated (pensions are expressed in terms of replacement rates of former wages in Bismarckian systems) reinforces the feeling that the pension is a continuation of the wage: what you get in exchange for your work. Any cut in pension would thus be particularly visible, since the level of pension is individualized (with reference to one's own wage) and the loss in purchasing power would be immediately evident.[3]

This situation of strong contrasting pressures leaves little room for manoeuvre for governments. They cannot resist the pressures to retrench, as this would have disastrous economic (and subsequently political) consequences. At the same time, if they retrench, they expose themselves to the risk of electoral punishment. In this context, the strategy adopted by seemingly all social insurance countries has been a combination of blame avoidance, procrastination and incremental change. Blame avoidance techniques have been well documented in the literature (Weaver 1986; Pierson 1994), and consist mostly of the obfuscation of retrenchment, via changes in complicated formulas, the effects of which will be unclear to most voters. A second strategy that has clearly been used is that of delaying the impact of reform. This has most notably been the case in Italy, where the reform adopted in 1995 does not fully come into force until 2035. Most current workers are either not affected by the changes or are concerned only marginally. In this case, delaying the impact of the reform has proved an effective strategy for avoiding mass protest and electoral punishment (Ferrera and Jessoula 2005). The third strategy has been to implement incremental changes, through the layering (Thelen 2004) of funded voluntary schemes on the top of compulsory PAYG schemes.

Trajectories of Pension Reform in France, Germany and Italy

An ideal-typical transition from a Bismarckian to a multi-pillar pension system is likely to follow the four-stage process outlined above. While this frame of analysis does not perfectly fit actual developments in our three countries, it captures remarkably well the broader trends which have emerged over some two decades. We are not, of course, implying the existence of any long-term master plan behind this staged process. Our contention is rather that each stage opens up new reform opportunities, by changing the political context in which pension reform takes place. These new opportunities are taken up by the various actors concerned in pension reform – who may not necessarily have themselves been present in the previous phase.

We should also point out that we understand the staging of pension reform trajectories primarily as a logical rather than (necessarily) a chronological sequence. From a logical point of view, as argued above, countries will follow the sequence outlined here. In reality, the various stages may not be organized exactly in the same way, or new stage 3 reforms may be adopted after a stage 4 reform.

Stage 1: contribution increases

Initially, pension scheme problems were dealt with via increases in contributions. This was the 'automatic' adjustment mechanism built in to Bismarckian pension systems. In Germany, the combined employer–employee contribution rate went from 14 per cent in 1960 to 18 per cent in 1980 and to a peak of 20.3 per cent in 1998 (Hinrichs 2005). In France, between 1985 and 1991, while the social contribution paid by employers to the compulsory general scheme (offering a replacement rate of 50 per cent of the reference wage) remained stable (at 8.20 per cent), the old-age insurance contributions paid by salaried workers increased from 4.7 to 6.55 per cent of wages (up to a ceiling) (Palier 2003b). In Italy, until the late 1980s, the adjustment took the shape of higher transfers from the general budget into the pension scheme, which contributed significantly to high public deficits and debt in that country (Ferrera and Jessoula 2005).

Stage 2: the first wave of reform: adjusting to (moderate) pressures

Adopted in the early 1990s, first-wave pension reforms have a number of elements in common. First, they tend to contain only moderate retrenchment, and nearly no action is taken to extend funded provision. Sometimes additional elements are also introduced, such as more government funds for pension schemes. Second, first-wave pension reforms tend to be rather consensual. Partly because of their moderate character, partly because they balanced retrenchment with concession to the trade unions, these reforms have generally not resulted in mass demonstrations or electoral punishment.

However, first-wave reforms put concerns about future pensions high on the political agenda and into public debate.

Italy: the 1992 Amato reform.   Until the early 1990s, Italy had one of the most generous and costly pension systems in Europe. The state scheme provided pensions equal to 70 per cent of the last five years' average salary from the age of 55 or 60, for women and men respectively. In addition, the system made extremely generous provision for early retirement, in the shape of the so-called seniority pensions, available after 35 years of service in the private sector and after only 20 in the public sector. Financial pressures on the scheme intensified in the late 1980s, when the government budget deficit and debt reached worrying proportions. A first attempt at containing pension expenditure was made in 1992. On that occasion the statutory age of retirement was increased to 60 for women and 65 for men, and the reference salary was changed from the last salary (or the average of the last five years) to the average of the last ten years. These moderate cuts concerned those already in employment. For those entering the labour force after the adoption of the reform, the reference salary was to be calculated over the whole career. In addition, eligibility conditions for the seniority pensions were tightened and harmonized across occupational groups. Finally, some provision facilitating the setting-up of supplementary pension funds was introduced (Ferrera and Jessoula 2005).

The 1992 Italian reform was accepted with little resistance, even though it reduced future benefits quite dramatically. The extreme generosity and the inequalities of the system probably made it difficult for the losers to defend what looked like privilege rather than social rights. In addition, many of the most radical changes were to be introduced over long periods of time, most notably, the shift to career earnings as the reference for benefit calculation was to start affecting benefits some 40 years after the adoption of the reform. This extreme generosity, coupled with long phasing-in periods, made reform politically possible. Its effectiveness in containing future pensions expenditure was by the same token limited.

Germany: the 1992 pension reform.   The 1992 pension reform is considered the last act of a decades-long 'pension consensus'. Since the 1950s, in fact, pension policy had been somewhat isolated from partisan politics, and important decisions were taken with the support of the main political parties. The 1992 reform, adopted in 1989 by the Christian democratic government headed by Chancellor Kohl, was supported by the main opposition party, the SPD. The consensus was underpinned by a wide-ranging policy network which included social insurance experts and favoured very much the preservation in Germany of the traditional pension arrangement. Cross-party consensus and agreement among experts meant that the 1992 reform was largely a depoliticized exercise (Hinrichs 2005). The need to prepare for demographic transition was generally accepted, as were the moderate cuts envisaged.

The key measures adopted included an increase in the federal subsidies paid into the scheme, the introduction of a permanent deduction for pensions claimed before the standard age of retirement, the phasing-out of subsidies for early retirement (until 2012) and a shift in the indexation method from gross to net wages. This last measure was justified by reference to the need to keep the net replacement ratio constant. In fact, indexation on gross wages – in the context of higher contribution rates due to population ageing – would have meant higher net replacement rates. The expected result of the reform was a reduction by some 10 percentage points in the contribution rate required to finance the scheme (Hinrichs 2005).

The 1992 reform soon came to be seen as insufficient. In part this was due to the increased social costs of unification. Industrial restructuring in the East meant high rates of unemployment and high inflows into early retirement programmes. As a result, contribution rates were rising faster than expected. On the other hand, the 1990s also saw a change in the dominant policy paradigm in social policy, and while in the late 1980s it had been considered acceptable to have eventual pension contribution rates in the region of 25 per cent, this was not the case any longer, especially in the context of the single market (where firms try to lower costs) and preparation for the single currency (where governments try to reduce public spending and deficits rather than increasing social contributions). The way was open for a second wave of reform.

France: the 1993 pension reform. The pension reform issue has been almost permanently on the agenda over the last two decades in France. The popularity of the pension system, the divisions within the labour movement and the fact that some of its most radical sections are not inclined to collaborate with any government-sponsored retrenchment initiatives have made the reform of pensions a particularly thorny issue. Governments of different political persuasion have been equally fearful of the potential political consequences of pension reform, and have tended to procrastinate over policy change.

Following more than a decade of reports and commissions, a newly elected (1993) right-wing government managed to push through a pension reform with surprisingly little opposition. The government favoured the adoption of measures suggested in an earlier White Paper published by their socialist predecessors in 1991. The reform was restricted to employees in the private sector. For them, the number of contribution-years needed to qualify for a full pension of 50 per cent of the reference salary was to be increased from 37.5 to 40. At the same time, the 'reference salary' was to be the average revalued salary of the best 25 years (instead of 10 years). Third, the indexation of benefits currently in payment was to be shifted from gross wages to prices. The overall impact of this series of measures, as eventually adopted, was a reduction in benefits (by almost a third) and possibly also an increase in the age of retirement, since employees qualified for a full pension 2.5 years later than under the previous legislation.

These proposals – which were clearly unacceptable to the trade unions – were accompanied by plans to set up an 'old-age solidarity fund' (*Fonds de Solidarité Vieillesse*), financed through general taxation (as opposed to contributions), with the task of paying for the non-contributory elements of the insurance-based pension schemes. The new fund takes financial responsibility for minimum pensions (which are granted on the basis of an income-test and regardless of contribution record) and for contribution credits to be given to unemployed people, those serving in the army, and to parents. Before the 1993 reform these non-contributory benefits had been to some extent financed by employment-related contributions. In fact, the shift in the financing of the non-contributory elements away from contributions to taxation had been a key demand of the labour movement.

The French 1993 reform was not adopted consensually. The Socialist Party and the main union federation were officially against it, but there were no attempts by either opponents to challenge the reform by calling strikes or by setting up informal protests and demonstrations. Bearing in mind what happened to subsequent attempts at cutting pensions, the 1993 reform stands out as one that generated little opposition. In fact, there was a clear quid pro quo between the unions and the government. Retrenchment was made more acceptable through the introduction of the old-age solidarity fund (which basically meant more funds for pensions) and recognition of the management role being played by the social partners in the French system (Bonoli 2000; Palier 2005). In 1995, Juppé tried to apply the same kind of reform to the public sector, but without any negotiation. As a consequence of his method, a high level of protest was triggered and the government lost the election in 1997. During its mandate, the socialist government of 1997 to 2002 continued to procrastinate over pension reform.

Stage 3: more radical departures in the second wave of reform

The problem with first-wave reforms is that they have only a limited impact, and shortly after their adoption it becomes clear that even the reformed pension systems will probably not be able to withstand the expected demographic pressures. Yet there are probably further reasons for the emergence of a second wave of reform. Globalization, the spread of liberal ideas in the field of social policy, makes it easier for reformers to tackle the issue of a shift to a partly funded pension system. Moreover, people themselves have started to 'save' for their pension, trying to compensate by themselves for announced reductions in future pension provision. This explains why, only a few years after the adoption of pension reforms, which were sometimes perceived and presented as major achievements, work starts on a new, second wave of reforms.

Italy: the 1995 Dini reform. The 1992 reform was widely considered insufficient. For this reason, by the mid-1990s pension reform was back on the political agenda. First, in 1994 a right-of-centre government headed by Silvio Berlusconi tried to put through a series of cuts in pensions without seeking external support. The response of the trade unions was to call a general strike, which persuaded the government to abandon its plans. By contrast, in 1995, a 'technical' government, which had the support of the left in parliament, managed to push through a more fundamental reform. The key modification was a shift from a defined-benefit system, where benefits are expressed as a proportion of earnings over a given number of years, to a defined-contribution system. Benefits now depend on the total amount of contributions paid by workers, which upon retirement is converted into an annuity whose value depends on the age of the person, on how the country's economy is performing and on the number of pensioners. The last two parameters are meant to allow the government to keep pension expenditure under control. The reform will most likely result in lower benefits (Natali 2002; Ferrera and Jessoula 2005).

From the first stages of the preparatory work for the 1995 reform, it was clear that it was going to be essential for the government to obtain the support – or at least the acquiescence – of the labour movement. Berlusconi's previous failure to retrench pensions unilaterally, coupled with the weakness of the 'technical' government (which did not have its own majority in parliament, but was supported externally by a small number of centre-left parties), provided powerful incentives to seek consensus. The starting point for the negotiations was even a document drafted by trade union experts.

The 1995 reform was adopted with the support of the trade unions, who, in return for their approval, obtained a fairly long phasing-in period for the new system, which is due to affect people retiring from 2013 onwards. The key constituencies of the Italian trade union movement – current pensioners and older workers – were not affected by this reform. The unions also obtained equalization of treatment between the different occupational groups (under the previous legislation, some groups – civil servants, but also some self-employed – had been entitled to more generous treatment). More specifically, contribution rates for public sector workers were increased to the same level as those paid by private sector employees (20 per cent of earnings). Those paid by the self-employed were also increased, though to the lower rate of 15 per cent of earnings. In addition, the reform increased the incentives for saving into a pension fund, first introduced in the previous reform.

Germany: the 2002 and 2006 reforms. Shortly after the adoption of the 1992 reform, pensions were back on the political agenda in Germany. The Kohl government introduced a more radical reform in 1997 which, through a demographic weighting of benefits, would have reduced pension levels and contained costs for the medium to long term. But the pension consensus hitherto reigning in Germany was gone. The Kohl reform was repealed by the social democratic government which came to power in 1998. Under pressure to deliver an alternative policy, the social democrats adopted a pension reform modifying the pension formula so as gradually to reduce replacement rates from a current 70 per cent for a full contribution record to around 64 per cent by 2030. Together with these cost containment measures Germany has also introduced provision for a fully funded private pension, to which private sector employees can voluntarily contribute tax-free up to 4 per cent of their earnings (up to a ceiling), known as the *Riester Rente*. The reform includes also a commitment to reduce expenditure if a joint employer and employee contribution rate of over 20 per cent of gross wages is required by 2020 (or over 22 per cent by 2030) (Hering 2004; Hinrichs 2005). The new funded provision is supposed to compensate for the reduction in benefits agreed on this occasion.

Pushing through this reform proved extremely difficult for the government. Because pension politics had become adversarial, it was unreasonable to aim for a consensual solution. The social democratic government had to deal both with internal opposition and with union dissatisfaction. Substantial opposition from the left wing of the SPD could only be overcome via skilful policy-making by Schröder himself, based on the isolation of opponents rather than on their inclusion in policy-making (Hering 2004). The 2002 German reform none the less did contain some expansion measures. Most notably it introduced a means-tested benefit of last resort for older people who had not managed to build up a contribution credit sufficient to generate an adequate pension. Germany had in fact been an exception in Western Europe, for not having had this kind of provision before within the pension system. Older people with insufficient income had been forced to rely on their adult children or, if this was not possible, on general social assistance (Hinrichs 2005).

Soon after the formation of the second Grand Coalition government (between the Christian democrats and the Social democrats) in late 2005, pension reform was back in the political debate. Pessimistic projections concerning the rise in the equilibrium contribution rate pushed the leaders of the new government to agree on a substantial pension reform: an increase in the standard age of retirement from 65 to 67. This is expected to be phased in gradually between 2012 and 2029. A two-year rise in retirement age is a major cut in pension generosity, even though the effect of this is somewhat moderated by the fact that, with longer contribution records, retirees will obtain a higher pension.[4] This measure – never mentioned during the 2005 election campaign – generated surprisingly little opposition. The fact that the two main parties were behind it and that the opposition consisted only of smaller parties arguably facilitated its adoption.

France: the 2003 reform. Nine months after having been elected the Raffarin government launched a second big pension reform: the same one that was repelled under Juppé (in 1995) and procrastinated over by Jospin (from 1997 to 2001). The new reform aimed first at aligning the situation of the public to the private sector. The government announced that public sector employees would have to contribute over 40 years, just like private sector employees, for a full pension. Second, it aimed at expanding the length of contributions payment required for a full pension. Indeed, the period of contributions payment was to be increased for everyone (public and private sector) to 41 years in 2008 and almost 42 years in 2020. It was also announced that the revalorization of pensions would be made for everyone on prices (pensions for civil servants had been indexed on wages). A new system of incentives for delaying retirement for as long as possible was also created: a bonus (*surcote*) was to be implemented for those retiring after the legal age and a sanction (*décote*) in case of retirement before this age – or in case of missing years of contributions.

The announcement of these measures having sparked fierce opposition and a lot of demonstrations from the trade unions, the government came up with some concessions: such as guaranteeing a replacement rate of 85 per cent of SMIC (the minimum wage) for the lowest pensions (the average rate of replacement in France being 74 per cent in 2003). It also announced that people who had begun work more than 40 years before the age of 60, and who had begun to work between 14 and 16 years old, could retire at 58. It further announced the creation of a supplementary regime meant to take into account the bonus in the calculation of civil servants' pensions. It announced there would be an increase of 0.2 per cent in the social contributions rate after 2006, in order to finance retirements before 60 – and counted on a decrease in unemployment to finance the deficit of the pension systems. In fact, these measures would only cover one-third of the future deficit – leaving room for further reforms, planned for 2008.

Finally, the reforms planned to help the development of 'saving' through tax exemption. Two systems of voluntary saving were supported, one individual (PERP: *plan d'épargne retraite populaire*, which can be proposed to individuals by any bank or private insurer), and PERCO: *plan d'épargne retraite collective*, to be organized within firms or at the branch level by the social partners. In both these cases, the government was explicit that people should try to compensate for future decreases in compulsory PAYG pensions, by saving for themselves.

Stage 4: expanding funded provision

The first and the second waves of pension reform in Bismarckian countries reduced the level of future public pension benefits, sometimes quite substantially. In France, according to projections, the replacement rate for standard workers will decline from the pre-reform level of 74 per cent on average to 66 per cent (according to projections released by the government in 2003). In Italy, the replacement rate of the public pension scheme, typically around 70 per cent before the reform, is expected to decline to 48 per cent. After some further changes since 2002, the replacement rate is also due to be reduced dramatically in Germany. These massive reductions in the replacement rates of public pension systems will need to be compensated through private and/or occupational provision. The experience of multi-pillar countries, when their pension system was based on one single scheme providing replacement rates in the region of 40–50 per cent of the average wage, was that second-pillar provision developed very unevenly if it was voluntary. This conclusion is further reinforced by observation of the UK and US cases, where occupational pensions cover only about 50 per cent of the workforce.

Yet, implicitly or explicitly, the reforms adopted in Bismarckian countries expect younger workers to join pension funds and begin to save for their own retirement, on a voluntary basis. Government projections of future combined replacement rates (for both public and private/occupational cover) are based on the assumption that current working generations will start making substantial contributions into their own pension accounts. This was clearly the case for Italy, where the Ministry of Welfare predicts a more or less constant replacement rate of around 65–70 per cent until 2050 – but by that year, some 17 per cent of previous earnings will have to come from a second-pillar pension (Ferrera and Jessoula 2005). In Germany, according to official projections, the 7 percentage point decline in public pension replacement rates will be more than compensated for by regular payments and subsidies paid into the new *Riester Renten*.

However, in order to compensate for declining public pensions, it is essential that the take-up of new second-pillar pension schemes be high; indeed, in younger cohorts, it should approach 100 per cent of the working population. Yet, in reality, this is nowhere the case. In Italy, the take-off for second-pillar pensions was particularly slow, partly because the incentives introduced in the first reform were insufficient. While these were introduced in 1993 it was not until 1998 that the first company pension fund was set up. By 2003 there existed over 100 funds, covering approximately 1,000,000 workers; but the take-up rate remains low, at 15.4 per cent of potential participants. Take-up is particularly low among younger workers, i.e. those due to face reduced benefits when they retire (Ferrera and Jessoula 2005). The situation is not so dissimilar in Germany, where by 2003 the new *Riester Renten* had been taken up by only 12 per cent of employees (Hinrichs 2005). The difference is, of course, that there, cuts in the basic pension had been less dramatic. In France, the development of PERP is still embryonic, even though the existence of 'life insurance' has long been used as a means of preparing for old age. If one can see any development in saving for pensions in France, less than a third of the population is so doing (Palier 2003a).

It is clear that funded provision is not developing quickly enough to make up for the shortfall in pensioner income that will result from decisions taken in the 1990s. Younger workers, who still have to pay high pension contributions to finance existing PAYG schemes, are evidently reluctant to forgo additional consumption in order to finance their own retirement. As a result – and in a way in line with what happened in multi-pillar countries in the 1960s and 1970s – an expansion of compulsion in second-pillar pension provision is increasingly being considered in Bismarckian countries.

Italy is the country which has moved furthest in this direction, arguably because of the pre-existence of an employment-related saving system used to finance severance payments (TFR – *trattamento di fine rapporto*). In 2004, in the third big pension reform in 12 years, after having considered the compulsory transfer of TFR into a pension fund, the government introduced legislation allowing this to take place automatically – unless the employee explicitly objects (Ferrera and Jessoula 2005).

Discussion

The above accounts of pension policy developments highlight the uniqueness of national trajectories – influenced by initial institutional structures and domestic political factors – as well as the existence of some common features. As anticipated in the introduction, we can identify two such commonalities: long phasing-in periods and the staged processes of reform.

Long phasing-in periods

The various reforms adopted in the three countries covered have all had relatively long phasing-in periods. To some extent, this is inevitable, because

Table 1

Year of reform, full implementation date and time lag for major pension reforms in
France, Germany and Italy

	Year of reform	Full implementation	Time lag
France	1993	2004	11
	2003	2020	17
Germany	1989	2012	23
	1999	2025 approx.	26 approx.
	2006	2029	24
Italy	1992	2032	40
	1995	2035	40

workers need time to adapt to changes in legislation. On the other hand, the
longer the phasing-in period, the less effective the reform will be in containing
future pension expenditure. It is difficult to assess precisely the extent to
which this strategy has been adopted, because reforms typically happen in
different stages and combine old and new calculation methods on a pro rata
basis. This makes it extremely complicated to summarize information
concerning the length of phasing-in. A simpler way to compare reforms in
relation to how long they shift the cost of change into the future is to look at
the full implementation, i.e. the year in which people entering retirement will
begin to receive pensions calculated entirely on the basis of the post-reform
rules. Table 1 sums up this information for our three countries.

The length of the phasing-in period of a pension reform is a crucial
parameter in determining its political chances. It tells us much more than
when a policy will be fully in force. The duration of the phasing-in period
determines who will be affected by the reform, in terms of age groups. As a
result it tells us how old the first persons to be affected by the new rules are
today, but it also it shows us how numerous the cohorts affected are in
comparison to the older ones that will manage to reach retirement unaffected
by the reform. These two pieces of information are essential for assessing the
political chances of a proposed pension reform.

Younger voters, first, are less likely than their older counterparts to be
concerned with the future of their pensions, partly because retirement age is
so far away into the future for them and partly because they have more
pressing issues to deal with (labour market, family situation, and so forth). As
a result, a long phasing-in period means that the first 'victims' of the reform
are, when the decision is taken, in their twenties or thirties, and thus less
likely to mobilize against cuts. The analysis of phasing-in periods highlights
a paradox in current pension politics. Those who are most interested in
pension policy, pensioners and working-age individuals approaching the age
of retirement, are the least likely to be personally affected by reform. In
contrast, the younger voters who will be hit by the changes are less interested
and less likely to mobilize in this field. The concept of 'retirement pension'

Table 2

Proportion of the voting age population directly affected by a pension reform,
depending on the length of the phasing-in period, 2001

Length of phasing-in	France (%)	Germany (%)	Italy (%)
10 years	58	74	55
20 years	40	47	38
30 years	21	27	19
40 years	4	10	3

Population aged between 18 and the age of the first cohort to be affected by the reform,
calculated on the basis of a retirement age of 60 for France and Italy and 65 for Germany.
Source: Recalculation of data obtained from national statistical offices (www.insee.fr;
www.destatis.de; www.istat.it).

is associated with old age, but long phasing-in periods in pension reforms mean that, in reality, these are issues for younger people.

Second, the length of the phasing-in period determines the relative size of the groups who will be affected by a reform and those who will manage to enter retirement without seeing their entitlements cut. The relative size of these two groups of voters is obviously a key determinant of the political chances of a reform. If the actual losers constitute a sufficiently small group of voters, then reform can be expected to succeed. Analyses of referendum voting behaviour on pension policy issues in Switzerland have shown a very strong tendency for age groups to vote on the basis of their own interest. For example, voters aged over 65 have been consistently opposing reductions in the age of retirement (Bonoli and Häusermann 2005). This can be understood with reference to the fact that by opposing a lower age of retirement older voters restrict the total number of retirees and hence the number of competitors for (scarce) pension resources. We can thus expect older voters, unaffected by future cuts, to be supportive of proposed retrenchments in pension provision.

Table 2 shows the potential reduction in the proportion of voting-age individuals directly affected by a reform as a result of different phasing-in periods. While the information provided is clearly an approximation, it shows how powerful a long phasing-in period can be in dramatically reducing the number of directly affected voters, and hence of potential opponents.

The length of the phasing-in period seems to be a crucial factor in determining the chances of a pension reform. Earlier studies of pension reform highlighted the effectiveness of division as a tool to facilitate the adoption of reform (Pierson 1998; Bonoli 2000; Myles and Pierson 2001). Reforms affecting only parts of the electorate, for example private sector employees and not civil servants, were seen as more likely to be adopted, because the potential opposition was divided. Long phasing-in periods can be seen as a different way of dividing the electorate: longitudinally instead of cross-sectionally. Its effects are probably stronger, because they are reinforced by two behavioural features unevenly distributed between the age groups: interest in pensions (as seen above) and the likelihood of participating in elections (Norris 2002).

A staged reform process

None of the countries covered has reformed its pension system via one single overhaul. Instead, pension reform has so far been a process spanning at least two decades. This feature of pension reform signifies much more than that it is an incremental process, whereby hard-to-swallow policies are administered in small doses over relatively long periods of time. The way in which we suggest the staging of pension reform should be understood is to focus on changes in the context of reform between one stage and the next. Our claim is that each pension reform facilitates the adoption of the next one. This hypothesis does not necessarily require Machiavellian assumptions with regard to policy-makers' intentions. We do not think that those who conceived the first reform had a precise plan as to where they wanted matters to lie some two decades later. But it is undeniable that each wave of pension reform has had an impact on working-age people's expectations and behaviour with regard to their own retirement, and that this has successively opened up new opportunities for reform.

The series of cuts in promised future pension entitlements has gradually reduced people's expectations with regard to their own retirement pensions. Public opinion data from Eurobarometer surveys show how the proportion of the population which is confident that there will be a decent pension waiting for them has declined quite dramatically over the 1990s and early 2000s (see table 3). It is unfortunate that different surveys have asked different questions – making the comparison of results across time difficult. Nevertheless there is a striking difference in the proportion opting for the most optimistic answers in 1992 as against early 2000. The drop in confidence is particularly strong in Germany.

The period covered by table 3 happens also to be a decade characterized by the downward redefinition of pension rules. In a way, one could say that a majority of respondents to the Eurobarometer surveys have probably answered correctly: given the series of pension reforms adopted in our three countries between 1989 and early 2000, fewer people will have access to decent benefits when they retire.

But a perceived decline in future pension benefits has uncertain direct consequences for the politics of pensions. On the one hand, we might assume there will be a reduced propensity to mobilize politically in defence of something that is withering away, anyway. On the other hand, we might also expect the attachment to at least a subsistence-level pension to be stronger, and hence the degree of mobilization to be stronger against future attempts to cut pensions. The preference for one or the other of these two hypotheses must be based on empirical analysis, but currently available evidence does not support either claim.

In fact, the impact of declining confidence in pension systems on pension politics is probably stronger, but indirect. As working-age individuals realize

Table 3

Pension optimists among working-age individuals
(percentage answering the items underlined)

Year (survey)	Question	France	Germany (west)	Italy
1992 (EB 37.1)	Do you think that the pensions you will receive when you retire will be – Completely adequate/Just about adequate/ Somewhat inadequate/Very inadequate	44.5	70.6	52.7
1999 (EB 51.1)	In the future there will be more elderly than there are now. Do you think that people will get less pension for their contributions? Yes/No/Don't know	11.5	24.4	24.9
2001 (EB 56.1)	Do you think that the state pension you will receive when you retire will allow you to get by – With great difficulty/with difficulty/ easily/very easily	24.4	23.3	13.8

Source: Own calculation on the basis of Eurobarometer surveys.

that their pensions will be lower than those of previous generations, they will, to the extent that their financial situation makes it possible, turn to private, individual alternatives. Since the early days of capitalism, to be able to rely on a decent income stream in old age has been an extremely powerful aspiration for the vast majority of current workers. Both in the past and in countries where such an income stream is not guaranteed by the state, those who can, choose to provide for themselves privately. We can thus expect workers who have seen their projected future pensions scaled down, and have adjusted their expectations in response, to turn to the private sector, for example by buying life insurance cover.

Figure 1 shows the impressive rise in life insurance liabilities (the 'promises' they make to their customers) or assets (for Germany and Switzerland). The increase has been spectacular in France and in Germany, but it is clear that in all these countries working-age people are preparing for their retirement on the basis of lower expectations with regard to state pensions. These are countries, especially Italy, where life insurance has never been traditionally widespread. By way of comparison, figure 1 also includes the trajectories followed by two multi-pillar pension systems: Switzerland and the Netherlands. While an increase in life insurance liabilities has occurred everywhere, it is clear that it has been much stronger in the traditional Bismarckian countries. Moreover, we can assume that people also try to compensate for future pensions lower than expected by investing in housing, thus explaining, perhaps, the continuous increase in real estate prices in continental Europe.

Figure 1

Financial liabilities of life insurance companies, in million euros
(assets for Germany and Switzerland)

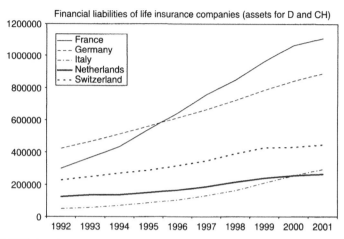

Financial liabilities of life insurance companies (assets for D and CH)

France
Germany
Italy
Netherlands
Switzerland

Source: OECD (2005).

Conclusion: The Logics of Reform

Contrary to the expectations of the early 1990s, policy-makers in Bismarckian countries have managed substantially to scale back levels of pension entitlement. In the late 2000s, less than two decades after the beginning of the reform process in Bismarckian pension systems, future entitlement levels have been dramatically reduced, to far below what could have been imagined in the early 1990s. Several factors help explain this unexpected development, not least the persistence of budgetary problems, low economic growth and low levels of employment in the three countries covered in this article. But high problem pressure alone does not, in our view, explain the totality of the gap between the predictions made in the early 1990s and the reality we now know.

In this article, we have argued that radical retrenchment in pensions has been possible for two reasons. First, long periods of phasing-in have targeted the cost of the reform on small minorities in current electorates (the young), who, in addition, are less inclined to mobilize politically in general and on pension issues in particular. Long phasing-in periods are thus indicative of much more than simply 'putting off' the consequences of tough decisions. They are more akin to the divisive strategies already mentioned in the pension reform literature of the early 1990s (Pierson 1994). Long phasing-in periods allow politicians to exploit longitudinal divisions in the electorate rather than cross-sectional ones.

Second, pension reform processes have proceeded in stages. Countries have started with moderate reforms – combined with encouragements to make private additional provision – and have adopted tougher reforms in subsequent stages of the reform process. During the time elapsed between these steps, working-age generations have adapted their own expectations, and hence behaviour, by turning massively to private alternatives (to public pensions) for the provision of income in retirement. The animosity and hostility to cuts in pensions, so visible in the early 1990s and which brought so many governments down, has seemingly been replaced by personal strategies geared to caring for an individual's own retirement. Using the twin concepts of voice and exit developed by Hirschmann (1970), we can argue that people's reaction to threats to their pension entitlements has shifted from voice to exit.

In Bismarckian countries, working-age individuals in the early 1990s took to the streets when their pensions were threatened. However, through the 1990s they have reduced first their expectations concerning future pension benefits and then their dependency on public pensions, so that pension reforms unthinkable fifteen years ago are now a reality.

Notes

We would like to thank John Myles for his very helpful comments.
1. As John Myles suggested to us.
2. In France, pensions are seen as a deferred wage, and pension cuts are, as a result, perceived as a fundamentally unjust act (Palier 2005).
3. For instance, any French person can understand the size of cuts planned by the 2003 reforms when the minister announces that the replacement rate will go from 74 per cent on average to 66 per cent.
4. Thanks to Karl Hinrichs for pointing this out to us.

References

Bonoli, G. (2000), *The Politics of Pension Reform: Institutions and Policy Change in Western Europe*, Cambridge: Cambridge University Press.
Bonoli, G. and Häusermann, S. (2005), New socio-structural conflicts in social policy issues: evidence from Swiss referendum votes. Paper presented at the 3rd ESPAnet annual conference, Fribourg, Switzerland, 22–24 September.
Ferrera, M. and Jessoula, M. (2005), Reconfiguring Italian pensions: from policy stalemate to comprehensive reforms. In G. Bonoli and T. Shinkawa (eds), *Ageing and Pension Reform around the World*, Cheltenham: Edward Elgar, pp. 24–46.
Hering, M. (2004), Turning ideas into policies: implementing modern Social Democratic thinking in Germany's pension policy. In G. Bonoli and M. Powell (eds), *Social Democratic Party Policies in Contemporary Europe*, London: Routledge, pp. 102–22.
Hinrichs, K. (2005), New century new paradigm: pensions reform in Germany. In G. Bonoli and T. Shinkawa (eds), *Ageing and Pension Reform around the World: Evidence from Eleven Countries*, Cheltenham: Edward Elgar, pp. 47–73.
Hirschmann, A. (1970), *Exit, Voice and Loyalty: Responses to Decline in Firms, Organizations and States*, Cambridge, MA: Harvard University Press.
Myles, J. and Pierson, P. (2001), The comparative political economy of pension reform. In P. Pierson (ed.), *The New Politics of the Welfare State*, Oxford: Oxford University Press, pp. 305–33.

Natali, D. (2002), *La ridefinizione del welfare state contemporaneo: la riforma delle pensioni in Francia e in Italia*, Department of Political and Social Sciences, Firenze: European University Institute.

Norris, P. (2002), *Democratic Phoenix: Reinventing Political Activism*, Cambridge: Cambridge University Press.

OECD (2005), *Institutional Investors' Yearbook 2004*, Paris: OECD.

Palier, B. (2003a), Facing pension crisis in France. In N. Whiteside and G. Clarke (eds), *Pension Security in the 21st Century: Redrawing the Public–Private Divide*, Oxford: Oxford University Press, pp. 93–114.

Palier, B. (2003b), *La réforme des retraites* (Collection Que sais je?), Paris: PUF.

Palier, B. (2005), *Gouverner la sécurité sociale: Les réformes du système français de protection sociale depuis 1945*, Paris: Presses Universitaires de France.

Pierson, P. (1994), *Dismantling the Welfare State? Reagan, Thatcher, and the Politics of Retrenchment*, Cambridge: Cambridge University Press.

Pierson, P. (1998), The politics of pension reform. In K. G. Banting and R. Boadway (eds), *Reform of Retirement Income Policy: International and Canadian Perspectives*, Kingston, ON: Queen's University, pp. 272–93.

Reynaud, E. (ed.) (1999), *Réformes des retraites et concertation sociale*, Geneva: Bureau International du Travail.

Thelen, K. (2004), *How Institutions Evolve: The Political Economy of Skills in Germany, Britain, the United States and Japan*, Cambridge: Cambridge University Press.

Weaver, K. (1986), The politics of blame avoidance, *Journal of Public Policy*, 6, 4: 371–98.

3

Towards Neo-Bismarckian Health Care States? Comparing Health Insurance Reforms in Bismarckian Welfare Systems

Patrick Hassenteufel and Bruno Palier

Introduction

The specificities of health policies – as against welfare policies in general – have often been remarked on, because of the role of health professionals (especially doctors) on the one side and of the medical industry on the other. The collective protection of risks and the promotion of solidarity are not the only policy issues in the health care sector; professional and economic issues also play a great role. This is why 'health care politics are more than a subset of welfare politics and the health care state is more than a subsystem of the welfare state' (Moran 1999: 4).

Despite these specificities, our purpose here is to show that it is highly relevant to analyse health policies as an important component of Bismarckian welfare systems for three main reasons. First, health insurance is historically at the core of these systems. In Germany, mandatory health insurance – created in 1883 – was the first social insurance to be established. In France the social security system is still identified with the health insurance system: for most French people *sécurité sociale* signifies public coverage for their health expenses. Second, the various systems of health insurance share some very important Bismarckian traits: access to health protection based on work, financing based on social contributions paid by employee and employer, administration by para-public structures governed by social partners: the sickness funds. Hence health insurance systems can clearly be distinguished from the national health services characterizing social democratic and liberal welfare states. Third, it is these institutional similarities which help explain the common problems and trajectories of reform since the end of the 1970s.

We will be dealing with the following questions in this article. What explains the common trajectories of health care reform in Bismarckian countries? How far are the reforms really changing the health insurance systems? Is there a growing realignment with national health systems? Are the changes blurring national differences between Bismarckian health insurance systems?

In order to address these issues, we will analyse three cases: Germany, France and the Netherlands. The first two countries represent the two main examples of health insurance systems in Europe but they also have some important differences: the French system is far more centralized and controlled by the state than is the German one, which represents the most typical Bismarckian case because of its historical origins and the greater autonomy of the sickness funds (Bandelow and Hassenteufel 2006). The Dutch health protection system is not strictly Bismarckian because of the existence of a first universal component (AWBZ), created in 1967, which is partly financed by taxes and covers mainly long-term care and mental health care. However, the second component clearly has Bismarckian characteristics: this compulsory (for 65 per cent of the population) health insurance system (ZFW), created in 1941 and financed by contributions, represents the biggest part of health risk coverage in the Netherlands.

The article is organized in three sections. The first section provides a general overview of the characteristics of health insurance systems compared to national health services. The second reviews the different aspects of cost containment policies, corresponding to the retrenchment sequence of reforms and highlighting the role of policy-learning processes. The third examines the structural changes occurring in the post-retrenchment sequence of reforms, which have been dominated by issues of governance.

Common Features and Problems: Health Insurances Are Social Insurances

In this section, we contrast the two ways in which health care can be organized, in order to highlight the social insurance traits of health insurance systems.

Main historical characteristics of health insurance systems

The history of health care systems in the developed countries indicates that at various periods all countries shared similar health care objectives (first to aid the sick on low incomes, then to guarantee a substitute income for salaried workers suffering from illness and, for Europeans after the Second World War, to ensure access to health care for all), but that they chose different solutions. These differences originate especially from the types of institutions assuming the cost of health care (the role of the state, of the mutual insurance societies and private insurance companies), from the way in which the health care supply was organized (the importance of public or private hospitals, the role played by general practitioners, etc.) and the way the development of the medical professions had been organized in the past (the importance of the liberal practice of medicine). These differences also reflect the different priorities held by each system: for some, universal health cover, for others the maintenance of liberal medicine, and for yet others the resilience of private insurances.

In Europe, one can find two types of health care systems.

1. *The national health systems* (Sweden, Norway, Denmark, Finland, Great Britain, Italy, Spain, and in part Portugal and Greece) ensure almost free access to health care for all citizens in order to guarantee universal cover for illness. The supply of health care is organized mainly by the state and

funded by taxes. Some of these systems depend on a highly centralized organization (as is the case in Great Britain) while others have decentralized their organization and management (as is the case especially in the Nordic countries).

2. *The health insurance systems* (Germany, France, Austria, Belgium, Luxembourg, and to a lesser extent the Netherlands, Switzerland, and most of the countries in central and eastern Europe). The supply of health care is partially private (primary or ambulatory health care, certain hospitals or clinics), and partially public (in particular a proportion of hospital services) and most often guarantees the patient's free choice of doctor, as well as the status of the liberal practice of medicine. Expenses are mainly assumed by the different health insurance funds and financed by social contributions. The French system is centralized while the German and the Dutch systems are more decentralized.

The national health systems generally ensure a large degree of equality of access to health care and relatively low levels of health spending; but they may provide a questionable quality of treatment and are known especially for extremely long waiting lists before access to specialist care might be possible. By contrast, health insurance systems – in which the supply of health care is often plentiful – allow for patient choice, comfort and often quality of care to be guaranteed, but most often at the cost of high health spending, and occasionally inequality of access to health care.

How do health insurance systems traditionally operate? In order to stress the importance of welfare arrangements and institutions for understanding the politics of welfare reform, we will refer to the four main institutional dimensions – rules of access, types of benefits, financing and management arrangements – in order to analyse how particular health insurance systems operate. We will show (1) how access to the health system is organized; (2) what types of services the latter guarantees; (3) how expenditure on health is financed; and (4) how the entire system is organized and regulated. We will then be able to show how these traits partly imply the kinds of problems and kinds of reforms these systems have been subjected to.

Access: who has the right to benefit from the health system? National health systems are open to all those residing legally within a country, without any particular conditions, whereas health insurance systems were first intended for employees and their dependants. In Europe, they have been extended to cover everyone, via free personal insurance for the most deprived. In Germany and the Netherlands over a long period, the richest had not been obliged to sign on within the compulsory system of health insurance and had been privately insured (30 per cent of the population in the Netherlands, 10 per cent in Germany). However, the 2005 reform (in the Netherlands) and the 2007 reform (in Germany) made health insurance compulsory for all.

Access to health care providers: If countries with a strong Bismarckian tradition have chosen not to go in for public national health systems, it is partly because it appeared important to keep choice and freedom as a central feature of the health care system. Health insurance systems most often ensure quite a large

Table 1

Proportion of public expenditure, out of total health-care expenditure, 2004 (%)

United Kingdom	86.3	Italy	75.1
Sweden	84.9	Spain	70.9
Norway	83.5	Austria	70.7
Denmark	83.0	*Netherlands*	*62.3*
Japan	81.5 (in 2003)	Switzerland	58.4
France	*78.4*	United States	44.7
Germany	*76.9*		

Source: OECD (2007).

liberty of choice of doctor for the patient, who may go directly to a specialist (accessible via the ambulatory care sector), consult several doctors on the same pathology, or even be admitted directly to hospital (as is the case in France). By contrast, the majority of national health systems try to control the circulation of patients inside the system. The patient's freedom to choose his or her doctor, appreciated by French or German patients, creates competition between doctors, which encourages them to write numerous prescriptions in order to satisfy the client and prevent him or her from consulting other doctors (French patients consume twice the quantity of drugs as their European counterparts).

The nature of the benefits: Sick pay is covered by health insurance systems: originally, it was the main purpose of health insurance to replace income lost because of illness. Today, however, most of the health expenditure goes on covering the cost of treatments (70 per cent of health expenditure is for the remuneration of professionals). No health system covers the full expenditure on health care. National health systems are those in which the difference between public expenditure and total health care expenditure is the smallest. By imposing only a very limited co-payment, they offer the most generous assumption of the costs of treatment and thus guarantee the best access to health care for all (cf. table 1). In the case of Germany and the Netherlands, the relatively low figures for proportionate public expenditure can be attributed in part to the fact that not all the population was covered by the obligatory system.

In all the health care systems of western Europe, the costs of the most expensive treatments, required for treatment of the most serious illnesses (cancer, cardiovascular diseases, AIDS, diabetes, etc.) and for long-term illnesses (degenerative disease), are extremely well covered. Indeed, the costs that these treatments represent are very high and account for the majority of health expenditures. It is in the health insurance systems that you find the highest share of public spending devoted to inpatient care. However, less expensive but more frequent treatments, connected to less serious conditions and usually treated by practitioners in the ambulatory care sector, are met to a greater or lesser degree depending on the system in question. In Great

Britain, as well as in Germany up until 2003, ambulatory medicine consultations are almost free, but dental care and glasses are not well covered. France is the exception for her poor coverage of ambulatory health care (only 60 per cent of ambulatory treatment is covered by obligatory health insurance). This is why complementary insurance is so well developed in France (about 85 per cent of French people having mutual society or complementary health insurance to cover part of the expenses for which they are left to pay). In the Netherlands 90 per cent of the population has taken out supplementary insurance, though this represents only a small fraction of overall health expenditure (Cohu *et al.* 2006: 208). By comparison, only 1 per cent of Swedes have supplementary health insurance, 11 per cent of Britons and 25 per cent of Germans (those hitherto above the threshold of obligatory health insurance, along with those who wish to supplement their health cover).

Financing: the financing of the systems: The national health systems favour taxation while the health insurance systems have for a long time favoured social contributions charged on salaries (payroll taxes). When health care systems first started up, it seemed logical to fund health insurance expenditure through contributions charged on salaries, since the main objective was to guarantee sick pay for those who were too ill to work.

Remuneration of the producers of health care: In order to ascertain how to distribute the money collected to the different health care agents, national health systems favour an *a priori* financing of the system. Each year they define the total amounts that will be spent on health, and allocate them to the different agents, who must thus manage a budget set in advance. By contrast, in health insurance systems ambulatory health care is financed *a posteriori*: it is the demand for treatment which comes first, the total amounts spent being dependent on doctors' activity and on the prescriptions they write: a system which works like an open ticket office. This type of financing does not lend itself to control of the level of health expenditure.

In France and Germany (until recently), countries in which the liberal practice of medicine predominates, most physicians are paid on the basis of fee for service in the ambulatory sector. In the Netherlands this is only the case for privately insured patients, the mandatory-insured being paid for on a capitation basis. In Sweden, all doctors draw the main part of their income (at least 60 per cent) from salaries. In Great Britain hospital doctors are salaried, whereas general practitioners working in the ambulatory sector, under contract with the NHS, are paid mainly on a capitation basis.

The organization and regulation of the system: National health systems are much better at organizing the supply of health care, but the extent of the supply is more limited than in insurance systems.

In national health systems (in the UK and Nordic countries at least), ambulatory care is primarily general medicine, most often carried out in groups, in practices in Great Britain, in health centres in Sweden. In these cases primary health centres are often the key expression, since other health professionals such as nurses or kinesiologists work alongside the doctors. In France, the Netherlands and Germany, on the other hand, ambulatory care includes both general practitioners and specialists. It is in France and in

Germany, countries where numerous specialists are found in the ambulatory sector (60 per cent of ambulatory doctors are specialists in Germany, and 49 per cent in France), that the compartmentalization between ambulatory and hospital medicine is the most marked, with the risks of a lack of coordination, of redundancy or even of contradictions in treatment. These risks are all the greater since it is these two countries which still offer the highest proportional amounts of hospital care. For all that this decreased sharply during the 1990s, the number of hospital beds remains extremely high in Germany (6.4 beds for acute cases per 1,000 inhabitants) and in France (4.3 beds).[1]

Who makes the decisions and regulations? Each type of health system seems to have its own particular model of regulation. National health systems are strictly regulated by the public authorities alone, national in the British case, predominantly local in the case of the Nordic countries or those of southern Europe.

Health insurance systems are based more on negotiation between the managers of health insurance funds and representatives of the medical professions, as the German case shows. The principle of self-administration (*Selbstverwaltung*) by management and labour has enabled the German system to function on a basis of permanent negotiation. Within this framework, the doctors – who assert their identity as liberal practitioners – have agreed to assume some of the responsibility for the management of public money. All self-employed doctors are compulsory members of the doctors' unions (*Kassenärztliche Vereinigungen*), and since the 1980s these doctors' representatives have taken part in the negotiation of the budget given over to health expenditure, the amount of the fees being adjusted in accordance with the total activity of physicians within this limited budget. The doctors have also accepted that there should be regulation and control of their practices, provided that this is carried out by a body made up of doctors and which represents them (the regional doctors' union). Doctors' unions thus carry the double task of controlling their members and representing their interests. In France the negotiation between sickness funds and numerous and divided doctors' trade unions also concerns the amount of fees, but it is more controlled by the state (no agreement – *convention médicale* – can be signed without the approval of the state, which participates in the negotiation through the director of the health insurance, a senior civil servant nominated by the government).

Specific problems of health insurance systems

In health as in other sectors (such as pension or unemployment insurance), institutional differences explain most of the divergent developments. The health care systems of France, the Netherlands or Germany on the one hand, and the British or the Swedish ones on the other, have been challenged by distinct, if not opposite, problems in recent decades. In the UK and Sweden, health care is altogether a state service, and thus it was relatively easy for the government to control the development of expenditure for health, basically by freezing the budget of the National Health Service. The main problem remains: how do you achieve an efficient and adequate health care system with the limited resources the government makes available? By contrast, in

Table 2

Evolution in health expenditure

	Total health expenditure as percentage of GDP			
	1980	1990	2000	2004
Canada	7.1	9.0	8.9	9.9
Denmark	9.1	8.5	8.3	8.9
France	7.6	8.6	9.2	10.5
Germany	8.7	8.5	10.3	10.6
Italy	–	8.0	8.1	8.7
Japan	6.4	5.9	7.6	8.0 (2003)
Netherlands	7.5	8.0	7.9	9.2
Norway	6.9	7.7	8.5	9.7
Spain	5.4	6.7	7.2	8.1
Sweden	8.8	8.2	8.4	9.1
United Kingdom	5.6	6.0	7.3	8.1
United States	8.7	11.9	13.3	15.3

Source: OECD (2007).

France, the Netherlands and Germany, the government does not directly control health care expenditures. There are no budgetary limits or freezes; rather there is a system of reimbursing the health care expenditures first incurred by an insured person. The problem here is an uncontrolled upward trend in health expenditure. The problems confronted by these health care systems are at polar opposites: while in the UK waiting lists are the key issue, in France, the Netherlands or Germany health insurance deficits and cost containment are on the top of the agenda.

Although they fail to record the best results for the health of their population, the health insurance systems give rise to higher total health expenditure (cf. table 2). Table 2 underlines that Sweden is the country where the evolution in health spending between 1980 and 2004 was the best controlled.

Having shown how important the institutional settings of the health care systems are for understanding its functioning and problems, we will now turn to the processes of reform in France, Germany and the Netherlands, in order to see how they have coped with their specific problems.

The reforms decided and implemented since the mid-1970s can be summarized into three main issues that form the policy agenda for health insurance systems. The financial and the cost containment issues are specific for health insurance systems, as we have just mentioned. The third issue (governance) has much more in common with national health services, but was differently implemented in Bismarckian systems. However common the agenda is, responses have been specific, as table 3 summarizes and as we will show in the next two sections.

Table 3

The reform agenda in health care and its implementation in
Bismarckian health insurance systems

Policy issues	Policy measures in health insurance systems
Financial issues	• Raising social contributions
	• Financing by taxes
Cost containment	• Reduction of reimbursement rates and
(retrenchment in health care)	co-payment for patients (silent privatization)
	• Global volume envelopes
	(negotiated cost containment)
	• Capped budgets for health expenditures
	• Controlling medical practice
	(therapeutic norms and evaluation)
Governance	• Competition
(managed competition)	(between health suppliers/between health insurers)
	• Managerialism
	• Creation of state agencies
	• Reorganization of medical care (GPs as keepers,
	health networks, integrated care, etc.)
	• Institutional reforms of sickness funds
	(hollowing out the role of social partners)

The three issues correspond to three main sequences (which partly overlap in time) in the reform of Bismarckian health insurance systems: a 'before retrenchment' sequence (starting in the mid-1970s), which mainly dealt with financial issues by rising social contributions; a 'retrenchment' sequence (starting in the early 1980s) characterized by the predominance of cost containment policies and, eventually, a 'restructuring' sequence (starting in the mid-1990s) focused on governance issues in order to increase the efficiency of health insurance systems.

Retrenchment in Bismarckian Health Insurance Systems

Containing costs in health insurance systems

Since the beginning of the 1970s, in France, Germany and the Netherlands, health care expenditures increased much faster than the economy grew. As for pension or unemployment insurance, the first main response to this trend has not been retrenchment, but to increase social contributions paid to health insurance funds (meanwhile, in national health systems, budgets have been controlled through rationing services, giving rise to waiting lists and waiting times). By the mid-1980s, increasing the social contribution appeared an economic dead end for the Bismarckian countries, and attempts were made to limit the growth of health insurance expenditure and to reduce the deficits of the health insurance funds.

Cost containment policies in Bismarckian health insurance systems have two main aspects: the introduction of a capped budget for health expenditures and a decrease in health risk coverage.

Limiting the health budget. Budgeting logic was introduced to the Netherlands in the early 1980s. In 1983 an open-ended hospital reimbursement system was replaced by a global budgeting system for hospital operating expenses. In 1984 the scope of the general budgeting system was extended to all other inpatient-care institutions. Acquisition of expensive technologies was also restricted, fees and salaries were limited and a complex system for planning the development of hospital facilities and the geographical distribution of specialists was launched (Harrison 2004: 135). At the end of the 1980s the government also tried to introduce global expenditure caps for medical specialists – with the threat of fee reduction for cases of excessive prescription. In the 1990s medical specialists' payments were progressively integrated into hospital budgets. In 2000 a legal basis was provided for integrating hospital specialists' fees also into the hospital budget. Since then medical specialists have had to negotiate their fees with hospital management rather than with the health insurers (Schut and Van de Ven 2005: 63). Meanwhile, from 1996, the Drug Prices Act enabled the state to impose price limits on the prescription drugs covered by the health insurance system.

In Germany, cost containment policies followed the historical pattern of self-administration, being negotiated between sickness funds and the doctors' unions (Hassenteufel 1996). Yet as early as 1975–6 unions signed agreements with the sickness funds which included a limitation on price rises for medical acts. In 1985 the unions accepted the implementation of 'global volume envelopes', according to which physicians continued to be remunerated on a fee-for-service basis, but each service rendered carried not a fixed monetary value, but a fixed point value. Each trimester the sickness funds were to distribute a fixed-sum global envelope to the unions, who were then to divide the amount of money by the number of treatment points submitted by doctors. Increasing services should then no longer increase expenditure, since the 'value' of each service was set to diminish to the extent that the volume of its provision increased.

But neither these negotiated envelopes nor the health reform act of 1988 (the Blüm reform), which introduced therapeutic classes for pharmaceuticals in order to restrain their prices, had the hoped-for effects on the financial situation of the health insurance system. In 1990–1 the average growth of health costs was 5 per cent and in 1991 the health insurance system again showed a deficit of 5.5 billion Deutschmarks. A new reform seemed called for in the context of German unification and a structural law on the health system was voted at the end of 1992. Many changes were here decided on, in the effort to curb overall health care expenditure.

1. The hospital financing system was completely reformed from a per-bed, per-diem basis to global budgets based upon standard illness categories. These budgets would not be permitted to increase more than the average rate of German wage increases from 1993 through to 1995.

2. The activity and number of physicians became restricted: the overall body of doctors was given a strict aggregated prescription budget of 24 billion DM (being the total cost of prescriptions in 1991); the global volume envelope for physician reimbursement was maintained (since 1989 the unions had been trying to negotiate its abolition); the number and type of physicians who could practise within each regional division was limited.

3. The state would exert a stronger control on negotiations between sickness funds and unions, on the functioning of these institutions, and obtained the right to intervene directly if the actors of the self-administration system did not implement the law.

Meanwhile, in France, in the 1980 conventional negotiation, the minister of social affairs tried to impose a 'global volume envelope', as in Germany, in order to try to link the growth of expenditure in ambulatory care to economic growth. This goal was accepted by the sickness fund (CNAM), which then negotiated with the medical unions in exchange for the creation of the so-called 'sector 2' (*secteur* 2). Doctors in this sector are able to charge higher fees than those reimbursed by the sickness funds, the difference being paid directly by the patient. But only one medical union, the FMF – representing mostly specialists from large cities (being those most favoured by this sector 2) – accepted this system. The CSMF, the biggest union, was clearly against it. Because of this opposition, the global volume envelope was never implemented. In 1983 a global budget for hospitals was introduced in an attempt to control costs in this sector.

After the 1988 presidential election the new government, headed by Michel Rocard, wanted to negotiate regulation, as in Germany. This strategy also corresponded to a reorientation of regulation away from a financial to a medicalized logic, based on the medical evaluation of therapeutic activities. It was only introduced in the new *convention* signed in October 1993. An objective of cost growth was fixed (3.4 per cent), as were 'medical references'. If a doctor did not conform to these therapeutic norms he could be penalized. But these changes were limited. The main point is that doctors could not be penalized automatically if the target fixed rate was overshot.

The limited effects of such negotiated cost containment policies in France explain the introduction of a capped budget for all health insurance expenditures in the 1996 reform (the *Plan Juppé*) which imposed an annual vote on national health spending objectives (ONDAM) on every sector of the health insurance system (ambulatory and hospital care).

Reducing mandatory health insurance coverage. The other aspect of retrenchment, also typical of Bismarckian health insurance systems, has been the reduction of the health risk coverage. In France, the public coverage of health expenditures clearly decreased between 1980 and 2002, from 79.4 to 75.5 per cent, because of the reduction of reimbursement rates for patients and of the creation of direct patient co-payments for health care services (creation of the hospital flat-rate co-payment in 1982, patients' co-payment for medical consultation, drugs and medical analysis). The 2004 reform again raised the co-payment for patients: €1 annual growth of the hospital flat rate, a new €1 co-payment for medical consultation, de-reimbursement of drugs. Unless you are under acute care (and then almost fully covered), the level of patient co-payment was raised to 30 per cent for medical consultation, to 40 per cent for drugs and to 20 per cent for hospitalization.

In Germany, this trend began with the 1988 health care reform act, which introduced patients' co-payments for pharmaceuticals, hospital inpatient stays, physical therapy and spa cures. It was pursued in 1997 (but the main measures were withdrawn shortly after the change of government in 1998). The reduction of health risk coverage has again been more visible since 2003. The law for the modernization of the health insurance system increased the level of co-payment and created an 'office fee' for patients in the ambulatory sector. Hospital fees went up to €10, patients have to pay 10 per cent of the price of each drug (with a minimum charge of €5 and a maximum of €10) and an 'office fee' of €10 per trimester and per pathology for certain visits to a specialist (if not following a family doctor's consultation). Moreover, voluntary private health insurance is now supposed to cover for teeth prostheses, and some benefits are not covered any more – such as thermal cure, drugs without prescriptions, sterilizations, medical transports, dental prostheses and glasses. Meanwhile, individual health expenses have been limited to 2 per cent of annual revenue (1 per cent in the case of chronic sickness).

In the Netherlands the latest reforms have also excluded several benefits from the sickness fund scheme, so these have to be covered by out-of-pocket payments by patients.

Explaining cost containment policies: policy failures and policy learning

In our three countries, the main aim of cost containment policies is the stability of the social contributions rate in order to stabilize labour costs and maintain economic competitiveness. The deficits of health insurance, added to the financial constraints linked to the Maastricht Treaty, explain the common retrenchment policies in Bismarckian health care systems. But the evolution of cost containment policies from negotiated policies to more constrained policies imposed by the state can be explained by a policy learning process based on policy failures, as the German health care structural reform act of 1992 (the 'Seehofer Reform') and the French *Plan Juppé* in 1996 clearly show.

In 1990/1 the German government faced a growing fiscal crisis because of the costs of German unification and the recession. The high level of German wage costs made it necessary to curb the evolution of health insurance contributions paid by employees and employers. The political strategy followed by the new health minister Horst Seehofer is a good example of a policy learning process: he was state secretary under Blüm (minister of social affairs) and experienced the failure of the health insurance reform of 1988. Seehofer negotiated with the main opposition party, the SPD (social democrats). He took their claims into account (especially the centralization and strengthening of the sickness funds). As a result the SPD backed the reform. This allowed the approval of the law by the second Chamber, the *Bundesrat*, which has a veto power on this topic (because hospitals are a *Länder* prerogative) and where the SPD had the majority. It also allowed Seehofer to outmanoeuvre the Liberal Party (FDP), which traditionally defended the interests of physicians and those of the pharmaceutical industry.

The 1996 French reform is also a consequence of a policy learning process. Three main failures of previous cost containment policies had been identified in several public reports on the health insurance system since the beginning of the 1990s:

- The lack of constraints on doctors that the reform addressed by introducing global budgets for the reimbursement of doctors with financial penalties if the fixed rate for budget increases was overstepped.
- The limits of imposing fixed budgets on hospitals. The need to restructure the supply of hospital beds (reduction of the number of beds, changing from short-stay to long-stay beds, and so on) had often been mooted. The reform addressed this by creating regional hospital agencies in order to implement this restructuring.
- The lack of control by the state, leading to extending state power in the health insurance system with the vote in Parliament on national health spending objectives (ONDAM) and greater intervention in the negotiation of collective contracts between doctors' organizations and the health insurance funds.

Yet none of these reforms was successful in the long term. As table 2 shows, in France health expenses continued to grow very fast and the deficit still grew. The target of the national health spending objective (ONDAM) was temporarily reached in 1997, but never again in the years after. These budgets were ineffective because of the failure of the sanction mechanism (Hassenteufel 2003). Doctors led a successful juridical battle against penalties, which were finally abandoned. Since 1996 health expenditure has always exceeded budgets, without any sanction against doctors. Moreover, in 2002, France's GPs actually went on strike for higher fees (€20). The raising of the fees was accepted by the new minister of health, at a time when the deficit of the health insurance system was already growing!

In 2004 a new law on health insurance was voted by the French parliament in the context of a huge deficit in the health insurance system (€10.6 billion in 2003, €11.6 billion in 2004; €8.3 billion expected for 2005). This last reform was accepted by the main physician trade union (the CSMF) – which was not very surprising, since this law embodies no new constraint on doctors (for their activity, for prescriptions or for installation) and gives specialists the right to get higher fees when patients go directly to them, without being referred by a GP. The main effort is being asked from patients, in the form of raising co-payments and taxes. This evolution is also clear in the German case, where the modernization law of 2003 (Hassenteufel and Palier 2005) introduced patient co-payments for medical consultation in ambulatory care (as we have already mentioned) and at the same time planned the end of regional budgets for doctors.

In the Netherlands cost containment policies were more successful (see table 2) but led to new problems during the 1990s, especially the increase in waiting lists. This policy failure created a new window of opportunity for market-oriented reforms (Helderman *et al.* 2005: 203).

The Dutch case illustrates how the reform agenda slowly moved from cost containment issues to more structural ones, aimed at changing the governance of the system. The reforms adopted since the mid-1990s have led to structural changes which are partly blurring the difference between health insurance and national health systems.

The Transformation of Bismarckian Health Insurance Systems

At first glance structural changes introduced by the reforms adopted in the last decade seem to follow similar patterns to national health services. But a closer look underlines their links with the specific problems we have analysed previously. These changes also led to specific health insurance system trajectories: the silent privatization of health care coverage, the limits imposed on financing by social contributions, the lack of regulation of the health care supply.

The hybridization of Bismarckian health insurance systems

It is possible to characterize as path-breaking some of the changes that occurred from the 1990s, since they introduced new principles and new instruments to the health insurance systems, some of them being close to the national health service systems (especially to the British one – Hassenteufel 2001), namely, more universal coverage, more taxes to finance health expenditure, the development of New Public Management devices and more control over the patient's circulation within the system.

Towards universal coverage for health care. As we have already noticed, a first universal component was created in 1967 in the Netherlands and since then extended, and the 2005 reform made the second component compulsory for the whole population. In France the 'silent privatization' processing of health risks (due to co-payments) increased the role of optional supplementary health *mutuelles*, that not all the population could afford. Therefore, introducing a new form of coverage for the poorest appeared necessary. The *Plan Juppé* included the idea of the creation of universal medical coverage. This measure was not implemented immediately, but was taken up again by the Jospin government: the universal health coverage (*Couverture Médicale Universelle* – CMU) was created at the end of 1999. Every person residing lawfully in France, irrespective of his or her employment status or contribution record is insured for health risks. In 2003 complete CMU coverage was made available to about 7 per cent of the population, who benefited from a basic package of health services. Meanwhile in Germany concerns have recently been raised over there being an increasing number of uninsured people (with estimates ranging from 80,000 to 300,000), who are mostly jobless and not eligible for unemployment insurance and/or the owners of small businesses (Greß *et al.* 2006). The 2007 reform tackles this issue by guaranteeing insurance for people who may have lost their private insurance (which may concern 200,000 people) and by establishing the principle of universal obligation for health insurance. Therefore, the total population is now covered in Germany (whether by private or public health insurance schemes).

More taxes to finance public health expenditure. The deepening of economic competition within the Single European Market put pressures on those welfare systems mainly financed by social contribution. Inasmuch as health care systems no longer restrict their cover to those with jobs (who therefore pay contributions), and since health spending today is mainly to fund health treatment (with no connection to income from employment), it seems more appropriate to finance this expenditure through income or consumption taxation rather than through payroll taxes. For these reasons, one structural reform of health insurance systems has been to change their mode of financing, from social contribution to taxation. This has gone relatively far in France especially, since most of the social contribution paid by employees was replaced by a general tax on revenue in 1998. The French pay a specific tax of 5.25 per cent for health insurance on all their income from salaries and capital. This tax, called CSG (*contribution sociale généralisée*), funds approximately 30 per cent of expenditure on health care. The pharmaceutical industries pay a tax on their sales and advertising expenditure. The taxes on tobacco and alcohol (representing most of the cost of these products) are partly allocated to the general social security system and account for 3.4 per cent of its revenues.

Health expenditures are financed only to the extent of 8.4 per cent by income taxes in Germany, though this was increased in the reform of 2003 by adding specific taxes: cigarette prices were raised by €1 per packet to enhance the tax financing and it was also decided that wage compensation in the case of sickness was no longer to be financed by employers but by the contributions of employees. In consequence, the contribution rate is no longer shared equally between employers and employees, since the latter pay 0.9 percentage points more. Taxes (especially on tobacco) are supposed to cover expenditures deemed not to conform to the actuarial foundations of the health insurance system (the so-called *versicherungsfremde Leistungen*). Moreover, the sickness funds are cross-subsidized from social security schemes covering old-age and unemployment risks (Altenstetter and Busse 2005: 124).

Even more important, the central debate on the future of health insurance in Germany is over its financing. Both the two main political parties (SPD and CDU) are trying to move away from a system of insurance financed by payroll taxes. The concept of the SPD, the so-called *Bürgerversicherung* (citizen's insurance), would place all citizens under the same health system, thereby ending the distinction between public and private health insurance and broadening the financing base by including all incomes. This system would in fact be close to that of a tax-based one, since all citizens would be covered *per se* – and there would in turn be a levy on all sorts of incomes. On the other hand, in the model envisaged by the CDU (called *Kopfpauschale* and copied from Switzerland), every person would have to pay a flat-rate contribution to the health system of about €160 to €200 per month. In this conception, the idea of progressively taxing incomes would be limited to the actual tax system, whose progressiveness should be strengthened accordingly (Grabow 2005). Both proposals thus differ from an insurance system based on work-related contributions; nevertheless, the new governmental coalition between the CDU–CSU and the SPD had great difficulty in trying to reach a compromise agreement between the two conceptions. This is why a bipartite commission was created in the spring of 2006. After almost one year of negotiation a new law was passed in February 2007, but this did not radically transform the financing of the system, which still relies on employer and employee contributions. Nevertheless three significant changes were introduced: the planned creation of a health fund (*Gesundheitsfonds*) in 2009 to fix a unified payroll contribution rate for every sickness fund; the possibility for sickness funds to charge enrollees with a uniform lump-sum premium; the coverage of children to be financed out of general tax revenue (a change to be progressively introduced).

Comparable developments have been even more obvious in the Netherlands because of the introduction, in 2005, of a flat-rate contribution for every insured person, to cover about 50 per cent of health insurance expenditures.[2] The state here offers financial help for low-income contributors – and cover for children.

Managerialization of the hospital sector and the creation of new state agencies. In France this managerialization process began with the 1991 law. The purpose of the law was to make hospital regulation take into account the real activity of hospitals (importing into France the 'diagnosis-related group' method from the USA). With this reform each hospital's budget was to depend upon an evaluation of its activity and its prospective development, both to be negotiated with the state. Since the beginning of the 1990s, two new tools for evaluation have been introduced: the 'programme of medicalized information systems' (geared to evaluating the activity of each hospital and to introducing payment systems based on diagnosis-related groups) and 'medical references' for ambulatory care (containing therapeutic norms and norms for prescription). The 1996 reform further promotes and generalizes the evaluation of therapies in the health insurance system with the creation of a National Agency for Accreditation and Evaluation in Health (ANAES), recently incorporated within the new top authority on health (*Haute Autorité en Santé*) created in 2004. They have been introduced to increase economic and medical efficiency (Robelet 1999) and to make competition work between hospitals. Regional hospital agencies (*Agences Régionales d'Hospitalisation*) have also been created to achieve this goal by distributing budgets between hospitals, based on an evaluation of the performance of every hospital. These agencies also have the right to close inefficient hospitals after an accreditation enquiry. Such changes have led to the rise of 'managerialism' among hospital directors (Pierru 1999).

The same pattern of evolution has occurred in Germany and the Netherlands since 2000. The financing system changed with the introduction of flat-rate reimbursement for hospitals. Diagnosis-related groups (DRG) systems in which fees are reimbursed after the evaluation of diagnosis and treatment – rather than length of stay – were set up. In Germany an *Institut für Qualität und Wirtschaftlichkeit im Gesundheitswesen* was also established for the diffusion of therapeutic norms and tools for evaluation, especially in respect of drugs (checking which medicine is most efficient and has the best price/effect ratio).

Reorganization of ambulatory care. We know that health insurance systems guarantee great freedom of choice for the patients. It is, however, contemplated more and more that the movement of patients within these systems should be controlled, as in the national health services; this is both to limit ineffective expenditure and to improve the monitoring of the patient and the coordination of treatment. Thus it is sought to make the general practitioner or 'family doctor' play the role of 'referring doctor' (who must be seen before any specialist consultation), to have a medical file circulated between all those involved in the treatment of a patient, and to institute health care channels or networks (e.g. teams of practitioners brought together by the same insurer). The implementation of such new practices represents a restriction on the freedom of choice and, often, a more important role for the general practitioners.

In France the 1996 reform made it possible for GPs to act as gatekeepers for patients who agree to contract with them (*médecins référents*). However, this system was replaced by another (*médecin traitant*) in 2004, geared to making GPs the 'drivers' of patients in the health system. All French insured persons now have to choose their *médecin traitant* (it is usually a GP, but it can be a specialist). It will cost them more if they consult a specialist directly without being referred by their main GP. In Germany the 2003 reform developed the system of the 'family practitioner', to take the role of piloting the patient towards specialists. It also made possible the creation of medical centres in place of a single doctor's consulting practice, in order to promote cooperation between doctors and other health professionals. In the Netherlands the sickness funds have the right to create health networks and day-surgery hospitals.

Even so, despite the similarities in the instruments utilized, these evolutions have not ended the gap between health insurance and national health service systems. Some institutional specificities still remain, especially with regard to the role of the sickness funds – the main issue for governance reform.

Sickness funds between competition and state control

The role of sickness funds in relation to the governance structure of the health insurance systems has followed two different paths: growing competition between health insurance funds in Germany and the Netherlands, growing state control in France.

Competition for German and Dutch health insurance funds. In the Netherlands, competition between insurers was developed in two main stages: the Simon Plan in 1991 and the reform of 2005. Regulated competition was progressively introduced for the second and the third compartment of health insurance because of the lack of incentives for efficiency and innovation in the prevailing health insurance system (Schut and Van de Ven 2005: 65–7). The starting point of the structural transformation process was the market-oriented model of managed competition developed by the Dekker Commission (appointed by the government) in 1987. This model was progressively introduced from the beginning of the 1990s by the successive centre-right and centre-left governments. In 1991 enrollees in the compulsory health insurance systems got the right to choose their fund. The 2005 reform abolished the difference between public and private insurances: competition was extended to the whole of the second compartment (former ZFW, see the Introduction, above) and – in consequence – private companies are now offering most of the care coverage. On 1 January 2006, the Dutch population gained the power to choose and change their own health insurers (25 per cent of the population did so forthwith). Meanwhile sickness funds and private insurers received the power to negotiate the price, quality and volume of hospital treatments and to selectively contract with health care providers. In order to make competition work, a thorough system of risk adjustment was developed, based on age, gender, region, disability, employment status, pharmacy cost groups and – since 2004 – on diagnostic cost groups. The reform has tried to combine the social nature of health insurance with the achievement of efficiency via a competitive market environment (Hemerijck and Marx 2006). The state has a clearly regulatory role: defining the framework of the health market and supervising the balance between competition and solidarity.

In Germany, the 1992 'Seehofer Reform' planned to progressively introduce competition between public health insurance funds by giving insurants a free choice between them. As services were not allowed to differ beyond legislatively fixed limits, price competition was supposed to incite funds to compete by merging and slimming down their administrative staff (the number of health insurance funds has indeed dramatically diminished, from more than 1,000 to 250). The sickness funds have increasingly been influenced by orientations derived from private business (Bode 2004). They conceive their organizations as market players racing for new members and as enterprises facing business partners and customers. Sickness funds offer more and more special advantages to their members (especially after the 2003 reform): counselling, health checks, packages with complementary insurance, reductions on contributions for enrollees' participation in health-improving activities, refunding of contributions in case of the non-consumption of reimbursed services. In 2003, the reform even made a first step towards the transformation of sickness funds into health care purchasers. They can differentiate the range of services available to their enrollees by selective contracting with networks of local providers and by developing prevention or disease management programmes. The latest reform, adopted in February 2007, offers the further possibility of contracting with single providers. The 2006 law on drug provision allows sickness funds to negotiate special prices with producers of pharmaceuticals and to provide their members with cheaper drugs (Bode 2006).

All such changes in Germany since the mid-1990s can be subsumed under an attempt to render the insurance system more efficient, while guarding its essential features. The health reform of 2003 did not differ much from this logic; it inscribed itself in the 'Agenda 2010' (the many reforms in social protection planned by Gerhard Schröder in the early 2000s) and its overall aim was to reduce contributions without abolishing the assurance system or its corporatist functioning. At the same time the competition logic is still growing, as the name of the latest reform shows: *Wettbewerbs Stärkungs Gesetz* (law for the improvement of competition). Inter-fund competition is broadening, but at the same time the planned implementation in 2009 of a *Gesundheitsfonds*,[3] directly linked to the federal state – in order to fix a centralized contribution rate for health insurance[4] and to combine solidarity and competition – can be interpreted as a further step in the direction of a regulatory health state, challenging the autonomy of leading actors in the traditional health care system: especially doctors and social partners in the German case (Moran 1999). The frequency of state intervention in this self-regulatory health care system increased from the early 1990s with the implementation of sectoral budgets and the stronger control of contribution rates. The 'shadow of state hierarchy' (Wendt *et al.* 2005: 22), based on the threat of state intervention, has broadened.

However, the trend towards a regulatory health care state has been even more obvious in France.

'Etatisation' in France. In France, even if competition was favoured in the hospital sector and has been characterizing the ambulatory sector ever since the late 1920s (the *médecine libérale*), a different trend is now in evidence: the strengthening of the state. This *étatisation* of French health insurance (Hassenteufel and Palier 2005) really started with the 1996 reform, which gave new institutional tools to the state in order to increase its control over the whole health insurance system. In the hospital sector the new regional state agencies have taken over the previous powers of the sickness funds. In the ambulatory sector the scope of collective bargaining between sickness funds and doctors' organizations has been reduced and the state has been allowed to replace the social partners when the latter are not able to reach an agreement. The 1996 reform also obliged parliament to vote a national health spending objective (ONDAM) every year, which sets targets for financial limits for health insurance expenditure. Given this reform, the government can more easily go in for cost containment every year, since it is now a constitutional obligation (the parliament being in France strongly controlled by the government).

The 2004 reform furthered this trend by creating a national union of sickness funds (UNCAM) to be directed by a senior civil servant, him/herself to be nominated by the government. This 'director' has the power to nominate the directors of local sickness funds and now heads negotiations with the different medical professions – hitherto the role of the Chair of the now disappeared administrative board of the fund, as representative of the social partners. Indeed, the law has replaced this administrative board of the social partners by advisory boards on which both users and parliament have representatives. The institutional model behind this change is clearly the state agency model.

New policy elites: different forms of regulatory health care state. The differences in health insurance trajectories can be explained by differences between the emergent new policy elites in health policy. Non-medical (especially economic) expertise is playing a growing role in the reforms. It is one important aspect of the decline of the health care state (Moran 1999). In the French case, since the beginning of the 1980s, we have been able to observe the constitution of a group of senior civil servants, specialists in health insurance policies and occupying strong positions (especially in the cabinets of the ministry of social affairs and of the prime minister) (Hassenteufel *et al.* 1999). They played a growing role in the decision-making process, not merely in the case of the Juppé reform (Hassenteufel 1997) but in respect of other decisions also: the global budget for hospitals, hospital performance evaluation, global volume envelopes, therapeutic norms for ambulatory care, hospital management, and so on. This new 'welfare elite' wants to raise the efficiency of the health insurance system through the strengthening of the state. They have been trained in French elitist (and statist) *grandes écoles* rather than in universities and have therefore fewer links with academic expertise or to international debate.

The situation is rather different in Germany (Döhler and Manow 1997) and the Netherlands, where academic expertise (especially with regard to questions of economics and public health) plays a growing role. The expertise is more internationalized than in France, which partly explains why there has been more policy transfer of competition mechanisms, inspired by foreign examples – and, in short, which explains that the international diffusion of market tools in health care has more impact in Germany and the Netherlands than in France. Academic experts, especially health economists, are now embedded in the health policy networks of Germany especially, as the example of Karl Lauterbach shows.[5] Indeed, expertise in health insurance policy was institutionalized in Germany through the creation, in the mid-1980s, of the Advisory Council for Concerted Action in the Health Care System (renamed the Advisory Council on the Assessments of Developments the Health Care System – *Sachverständigenrat zur Begutachtung der Entwicklung des Gesundheitswesen*), which has a role in setting the agenda and framing the policy debate for health care, and sometimes even prepares policy decisions (Brede 2006: 441).

In the Netherlands the first proposals for regulated competition were made in 1986 by a government-appointed committee headed by W. Dekker, chairman of the board of the Philips Corporation; and the 1991 and 2005 reforms[6] were inspired by these proposals.

One might also mention that in Germany elected politician members of the social and health commissions have won autonomy from interest groups (Trampusch 2005). Political actors (the minister of health, the state secretaries for health, the health policy speakers of the leading political parties, the health ministers of some *Länder*, deputies, members of the health commission) are playing a greater role in the health policy decision-making process, as the creation (in April 2006) of a bipartite commission (charged to elaborate a new reform project) composed of 16 political actors, coming from the parliaments and the *Länder* and belonging to both parties of the governmental coalition, bore out. The new policy elite in German health policy is composed of experts, political actors and the so-called political civil servant (*politische Beamte*), at the top of the federal health administration and discretionarily nominated by the health minister. Politicians also played an important role in the last Dutch reform, whose ideological dimensions were geared to promoting competition and privatization. In the Netherlands the locus of power has shifted since the mid-1990s, with the revision of the corporatist decision-making structure[7] coupled with the growing autonomy of individual health providers and insurers (Helderman *et al.* 2005: 200).

The role of such new policy elites underlines the 'non-incidental' nature of the structural reforms so far remarked on. Rather, they follow a reform design elaborated by programmatic actors who have the capacity partially to redefine the policy frameworks for health care (Hassenteufel 2007). Nevertheless, the implementation of these reforms will be incremental, as befits a middle-term learning process.

Conclusion

Up until now and despite the institutional reforms, continental health insurance systems have remained Bismarckian (they are still mainly financed by social contributions, managed by health insurance funds, delivering public and private health care, and freedom is still higher than in national health systems). This is due to the incremental strategy chosen for the introduction of structural change. Those changes are embedded in the existing institutions. The aim of the reforms is more to change the logic of institutions than to change the institutions themselves; they follow a 'conversion' type of change (Streeck and Thelen 2005). Hence, structural changes occur without revolution in the system. The new 'regulatory health care state' (Hassenteufel 2007) that we have seen emerging in Germany, France and the Netherlands can be said to be 'neo-Bismarckian'. Health insurance systems are combining universalization through the state and marketization based on regulated competition; they associate more state control (directly or through agencies) with more competition and market mechanisms.

Acknowledgements

We would like to thank the many participants in the various 'Bismarck' conferences for their helpful comments and questions, and more specifically Rosemary Taylor and Claus Wendt for their careful reading and very interesting suggestions.

Notes

1. It is more limited in the United Kingdom (3.9 beds), the Netherlands (3.5), and relatively low in the United States (2.9) and in Sweden (2.4) (source: OECD 2003).
2. Only the employer's share is now calculated in relation to the employee's income.

Patrick Hassenteufel and Bruno Palier

3. And of a federal union for all sickness funds headed by a former SPD deputy. The German governance reforms are partly inspired by the Dutch reforms, which explains the new similarities between the two systems, especially the competition between sickness funds and the compensation of risks through a centralized fund.
4. Up until now each fund has had the power to fix its contribution rate.
5. Professor for health economics after a PhD at Harvard University, he was the main adviser to the Health Minister Ulla Schmidt from 2000 until 2005.
6. The 2005 reform was recommended by the Dutch Social and Economic Council in its 2004 report on health insurance reform (Cohu et al. 2006: 212).
7. In the annual survey of the most powerful people in the Dutch health care system, the minister of health and the national director of the health insurance are at the top of the list (Top 100 Medische Macht, *Mednet Magazine*, 12 January 2006: 18).

References

Altenstetter, C. and Busse, R. (2005), Health care reform in Germany: patchwork change within governance structures, *Journal of Health Politics, Policy and Law*, 30, 1–2, 121–42.
Bandelow, N. and Hassenteufel, P. (2006), Mehrheitsdemokratische Politikblockaden und verhandlungsdemokratischer Reformeifer: Akteure und Interessen in der französischen und deutschen Gesundheitspolitik, *Kölner Zeitschrift für Soziologie* (Special Issue no. 46, *Soziologie der Gesundheit*): 320–42.
Bode, I. (2004), Die Regulierung des Gesundheitssystem in Frankreich und Deutschland: Ähnliche Debatten, aber unterschiedliche Reformperspektiven. In W. Neumann (ed.), *Welche Zukunft für den Sozialstaat? Reformpolitik in Frankreich und Deutschland*, Wiesbaden: Verlag für Sozialwissenschaften, pp. 87–118.
Bode, I. (2006), Fair funding and competitive governance: the German model of health care organization under debate, *Revue Française des Affaires Sociales*, 2–3: 183–206 (English version).
Brede, F. (2006), Politikberatung in der Gesundheitspolitik. In S. Falk, D. Rehfeld, A. Römmele and M. Thunert (eds), *Handbuch Politikberatung*, Wiesbaden: Verlag für Sozialwissenschaften, pp. 436–48.
Cohu, S., Lequet-Slama, D. and Volovitch, P. (2006), The Netherlands: reform of the health system based on competition and privatisation, *Revue Française des Affaires Sociales*, 2–3: 207–26 (English version).
Döhler, M. and Manow, P. (1997), *Strukturbildung von Politikfeldern*, Opladen: Leske and Budrich.
Grabow, K. (2005), Fighting with Goliath: the reform of the public health care insurance scheme in Germany, its potential to increase employment and alternative models of reform, *German Politics*, 14, 1: 51–73.
Greß, S., Walendzik, A. and Wasem, J. (2006), Hartz IV und gesetzliche Krankenversicherung-Nichtversicherte als gesellschaftliches Problem, *Sozialer Fortschritt*, 55.
Hall, P. (1993), Policy paradigm, social learning and the state: the case of economic policy making in Great Britain, *Comparative Politics*, 25, 3: 275–98.
Harrison, M. (2004), *Implementing Change in Health Systems: Market Reforms in the United Kingdom, Sweden and the Netherlands*, London: Sage.
Hassenteufel, P. (1996), The medical profession and health insurance policies: a Franco-German comparison, *Journal of European Public Policy*, 3, 3: 57–74.
Hassenteufel, P. (1997), *Les médecins face à l'État, une comparaison européenne*, Paris: Presses de Science-Po.

Hassenteufel, P. (2001), Liberalisation through the state: why is the French health insurance system becoming so British? *Public Policy and Administration*, 16, 4: 84–95.

Hassenteufel, P. (2003), Le premier septennat du plan Juppé: un non-changement décisif. In J. De Kervasdoué (ed.), *Carnet de santé de la France 2003*, Paris: Dunod, pp. 122–47.

Hassenteufel, P. (2007), New policy elites and the growth of the regulatory health care state in Europe. ECPR Joint Sessions, Helsinki.

Hassenteufel, P. and Palier, B. (2005), Les trompe-l'oeil de la 'gouvernance' de l'assurance maladie: contrastes franco-allemands, *Revue Française d'Administration Publique*, 113: 13–28.

Hassenteufel, P., Bachir, M., Bussat, V., Genieys, W., Martin, C. and Serré, M. (1999), *L'émergence d'une 'élite du Welfare'? Sociologie des sommets de l'État en interaction. Le cas des politiques de protection maladie et en matière de prestations familiales*, research report, MIRE.

Helderman, J.-K., Schut, F., Van der Grinten, T. and Van de Ven, W. (2005), Market-oriented health care reforms and policy learning in the Netherlands, *Journal of Health Politics, Policy and Law*, 30, 1–2: 189–209.

Hemerijck, A. and Marx, I. (2006), Redirecting continental welfare in Belgium and the Netherlands. Conference 'A long Goodbye to Bismarck? The politics of reform in Continental Europe', Harvard University, Center for European Studies.

Moran, M. (1999), *Governing the Health Care State*, Manchester: Manchester University Press.

OECD (2003), *Data on Health*, Paris: OECD.

OECD (2007), *Data on Health*, Paris: OECD.

Palier, B. (2004), *La réforme des systèmes de santé*, Paris: PUF.

Pierru, F. (1999), L'hôpital-entreprise: une self-fulfilling prophecy avortée, *Politix*, 46: 7–47.

Robelet, M. (1999), Les médecins placés sous observation: mobilisations autour de l'évaluation médicale en France, *Politix*, 46: 71–97.

Schut, F. and Van de Ven, W. (2005), Rationing and competition in the Dutch health-care system, *Health Economics*, 14, 1: 59–74.

Streeck, W. and Thelen, K. (2005), *Beyond Continuity: Institutional Change in Advanced Political Economies*, Oxford: Oxford University Press.

Trampusch, C. (2005), From interest groups to parties: the change in the career patterns of the legislative elite in German social policy, *German Politics*, 14, 1: 14–32.

Wendt, C., Rothgang, H. and Helmert, U. (2005), *The Self-regulatory German Health Care System between Growing Competition and State Hierarchy*, Transtate Working Papers no. 32, University of Bremen.

4
Continental Drift: On Unemployment Policy Change in Bismarckian Welfare States

Daniel Clegg

Introduction

In much comparative welfare state research Bismarckian welfare institutions – encompassing but status-maintaining social insurances, financed from social contributions and co-managed by social actors – are portrayed as a source of policy stability. Where substantive policy shifts *have* been identified in Bismarckian welfare states, they are usually likened to the reforms under way in other welfare state contexts, and their adoption related to domestic factors exogenous to and autonomous from welfare state institutions, especially the opportunity structures offered by political conditions and institutions or instances of political entrepreneurialism. Policy change is thus seen as somewhat unusual in Bismarckian welfare states, and both its extent and content have been mainly explained without reference – and often in contradistinction – to the impact of welfare institutions.

Focusing on the development of unemployment policy in Belgium, France, Germany and the Netherlands since the early 1980s, this article tells a somewhat different story. It shows, first, that these policies have changed considerably right across continental Europe over the last quarter-century. It argues, second, that unemployment policy reforms adopted in Bismarckian welfare states share certain features that set them decisively apart from reforms adopted in this policy sector in other welfare institutional contexts. It suggests, finally, that although there are some differences in the degree and substance of unemployment policy reforms adopted in the cases examined, these are as much related to differences in the exact structure of their Bismarckian welfare state institutions as they are to any of the manifold other variations in their policy-making environments. In sum, the article demonstrates that welfare institutions are an important part of the story of social policy change, and not merely stasis, in continental Europe.

The story told here lends some support to recent institutionalist theorizing on incremental-but-transformative change. The sequential manner in which considerable – if often unnoticed – shifts have occurred in continental European unemployment policy highlights the pervasiveness of 'drift' and 'layering' as mechanisms of substantive policy change within stable institutional frameworks. However, by uncovering an apparently systematic relationship between the possibility frontier for unemployment policy change and specific institutional features of welfare states, the article also raises some questions that the broader institutional change literature has to date left unanswered. In so doing, it offers a more nuanced perspective on the scope for and resistance to social policy change in continental Europe.

The article is organized in four main sections. The first section provides a general overview of labour market changes in developed countries and the labour market policy reform agendas they are driving. The second briefly elaborates on some of the main arguments that have been made regarding the scope for and determinants of labour market policy change in Bismarckian welfare states specifically. The longer third section reviews 20 years of unemployment policy development in Belgium, France, Germany and the Netherlands, highlighting the partial alignment of these four cases on a similar, but distinctively unorthodox, package of policy changes. The final section examines the specific role of welfare institutions in explaining both the similarities in and differences between the four countries' reform trajectories, and discusses the style and the scope of the changes that have occurred.

Labour Market Transformations and Unemployment Policy Reform Agendas

The development of advanced economies over the last quarter-century has placed unemployment policies, traditionally geared to income replacement and support during temporary labour market transitions, under multiple and contradictory strains. Most basically, the incidence of unemployment has been consistently higher in the last two decades than at any time since the Second World War. At the same time, though, the nature of the unemployment risk has changed, with the growing importance of the service sector in developed countries' economies, and the related shift to more flexible employment relationships. The expansion of previously 'atypical' forms of work and increased churning at the bottom end of the labour market mean it is often difficult for workers to establish full eligibility for contributory unemployment protection to cover future periods of joblessness. This applies particularly to women, who tend to be over-represented in atypical and service employment, and to have the most irregular employment trajectories. The protective capacity of contributory unemployment insurance also appears increasingly inadequate for job-starters, who often face a prolonged period of unemployment early on in their working lives. Similarly, having been designed to cover the risk of short-term cyclical or frictional unemployment, unemployment insurance benefits that are normally time-limited are ill-adapted to the problem of long-term unemployment, considerably more prevalent today than at any time before the 1970s, particularly among those with low or no professional qualifications.

For all these reasons, there has been a strong case for 'more' unemployment policies over the last two decades. Economic considerations, however, have simultaneously pointed to an equally pressing need for 'fewer' or at least 'different' unemployment policies. In the golden age of welfare state expansion, active management of the economy relied to a large extent on the use of macro-economic, demand-side stimuli, leaving labour market policies to play a supportive role. As Keynesian regulation has fallen into discredit, an increasing emphasis has once again been placed on the need to stimulate the supply side of the economy in general and of the labour market specifically. One interpretation is that the best way to promote international competitiveness, growth and the generation of new jobs is to limit the fiscal and regulatory constraints that social protection arrangements – including unemployment protection – impose on economic actors. A somewhat different slant is that collective intervention remains necessary at the work–welfare interface, but must be more oriented to economic adjustment goals – and notably must intervene more proactively in the (re)integration of those without work into available jobs. The incentive problems potentially caused by the collision of old unemployment insurance systems and the increasingly flexible labour market are also held up in favour of a reorientation of unemployment policies, both by those who believe it should be tackled through fewer rights-based unemployment policies, and those in favour of fewer unemployment policies *tout court*.

Clearly, then, no stable consensus has emerged in recent years around a single recipe for adapting unemployment policies to the changed social and economic context. The cross-cutting and contradictory pressures referred to above have nonetheless seen policy-makers across developed economies turn, at least rhetorically, towards an increasingly standardized basket of policy ingredients or agendas (cf. Clasen and Clegg 2006a, 2006b), also promoted by international actors such as the OECD and the European Commission's Social Affairs Directorate. Though it is useful for analytical purposes to distinguish these, it should be noted that they are seen as complementary and mutually reinforcing components of a 'fundamental reform' in which changes are explicitly implemented across a range of policy dimensions to activate policy complementarities (cf. Coe and Snower 1997).[1]

Given the massive increase in the incidence of unemployment and the more general context of permanent austerity (Pierson 1998), concern with *cost containment* has provided the backdrop for many recent reforms in unemployment policy. Partly this is a case of expenditures on the un-employed being caught up in a more general turn to retrenchment, or at least to restricting the growth of public expenditure. But under conditions of mounting unemployment, automatic (i.e. rights-based) expenditure on the unemployed is also uniquely vulnerable to a scissors effect, where costs rise and receipts diminish in tandem, resulting in growing deficits. In this context cost containment in unemployment policy has suggested itself almost naturally, in the name of good accounting.

More sensitive to the changing profile of employment-related risks, another orientation in unemployment benefit policies is the *recalibration* of benefit rights. It is increasingly perceived to be necessary to gear unemployment protection systems to the risks borne by the growing number of workers with non-standard employment biographies, mainly by relaxing contributory conditions for benefit eligibility that are often premised on long periods of full-time labour market participation. Given fiscal constraints, however, it appears inevitable that any such relaxation of the employment terms on which access to benefits is possible for some will necessarily have to be counterbalanced with reductions in entitlements for others. Arguments about the overprotection of certain groups under existing benefit arrangements are made to point to areas in which such compensatory cuts could be made. The basic idea is thus to simultaneously correct both 'overreach' and 'undershoot' in existing benefit provisions, leading to a system that offers less extensive protection to 'insiders' but extends basic protection to 'outsiders'.

A third agenda in recent unemployment policy reforms is captured by the notion of *activation*. In general terms, activation initiatives seek to move unemployed individuals off social benefits and into more productive activities. A first set of instruments includes measures concerned with the regulation of benefit receipt, such as tighter job-search requirements, more extensive definitions of suitable employment and more effective benefit sanctions in the event of non-compliance. A second set includes instruments that more directly adapt unemployed workers to the labour market or vice versa, through the provision of skills training for the jobless or the creation or subsidization of earmarked 'springboard' jobs. Cutting across both is the formalization of the relationship between the jobseeker and the collectivity in a written 'agreement' or 'plan', detailing the rights as well as the responsibilities of both parties over the course of an unemployment spell (cf. Dufour *et al.* 2003).

A final important thrust in contemporary unemployment policy reform discourses and initiatives concerns *integrative administrative restructuring* of the policy sector. Though this agenda commands less media attention, it is in many ways the procedural precondition for the successful introduction of new substantive orientations. This is particularly true of two partially over-lapping reform dynamics, namely the harmonization of separate tiers of benefit provision for the unemployed (e.g. insurance-based and assistance-based provisions), and the rapprochement or even fusion of institutions charged with the delivery of cash benefits and the public employment services (PES). Such reforms are intended to reduce overlap and boundary disputes at the level of policy coordination, improving the coherence and efficiency of public policies for the unemployed. At the delivery level, they seek to facilitate the creation of 'single gateways' to all labour market services for all jobseekers (cf. Clasen *et al.* 2001), reducing the complexity of the unemployment policy system for its users while at the same time allowing delivery agents to effectively support and/or monitor their efforts to move from welfare to work.

These four agendas are summarized in table 1, intended to capture the thrust both of the main recommendations by international organizations and of the concrete reforms that have been implemented in the countries where unemployment policy has been most 'fundamental' and high-profile.

With respect to both, this presentation downplays the considerable scope for differences in the mix and setting of different instruments within the broad reform agendas, where distributive issues are often at stake. The

Daniel Clegg

Table 1

Agendas and measures of 'orthodox' unemployment policy reform

Reform agenda	Policy measures
Cost containment	• Cuts in benefit levels • Cuts in benefit durations • Stricter eligibility requirements
Recalibration	• Enhanced/safeguarded protection for those with no/atypical work histories • Reduced protection for those with long work histories • More needs-based benefit entitlements
Activation	• Stricter job-search/acceptance requirements with effective sanctions • Increased investment in training/job creation for the unemployed • Development of reintegration plans/contracts for benefit recipients
Integrative administrative restructuring	• Closer policy harmonization of different benefit tiers • Closer integration of benefit and employment administrations • Development of 'single gateways' to services

emphasis placed on 'levelling up' and 'levelling down' in benefit recalibration could vary significantly, as could the mix between 'negative' (job-search-based) and 'positive' (training- and employment-based) forms of activation. Furthermore, different policy choices have implications for the cost-containment potential of reform, or at least for the time horizon within which cost containment is set. Precisely these kinds of variations have been repeatedly identified in comparative analyses of unemployment policy reform, with a contrast between the neo-liberal British trajectory and the neo-social democratic Danish trajectory particularly recurrent (cf. Torfing 1999; Barbier 2004). A parallel contrast can be drawn between the distributive slant of the work–welfare recommendations of the OECD and the EU respectively (Casey 2004). The point here is not to refute the importance of such variations, but to emphasize the underlying structural features of 'orthodox' unemployment policy reforms of all stripes. This also provides a benchmark against which the hypotheses regarding the scope for and determinants of unemployment policy change in continental European welfare states can be re-evaluated.

Shared Stasis and Divergent Dynamism: Perspectives on Unemployment Policy Reform in Continental Europe

Much recent writing about Bismarckian welfare states has been relatively gloomy about the prospects for policy reform of any kind. Esping-Andersen famously dismissed them as 'frozen welfare landscapes' where 'the cards are very much stacked in favour of the welfare status quo' (1996a: 27). Pierson (2001) was only moderately more optimistic in his assessment, noting the existence in continental Europe of a large and, in comparative context, unique anti-reform constituency.

Much of the Bismarckian welfare states' apparent resistance to change is argued to follow directly from their institutional arrangements. Palier (2002: 205) has suggested that because social protection in continental Europe is largely contribution-financed, and social contributions are not perceived by voters as taxes, policy-makers can opt for revenue adjustment measures rather than cost containment without risking political backlash. Furthermore, this policy response is likely to face far less opposition than cutting benefits as, thanks to the strong insurance principle on which access to benefits rests in continental Europe, benefit entitlements are more readily perceived as 'acquired rights'. Even if many voters fail to mobilize on the issue of unemployment, these 'institutional appropriateness' arguments will serve as useful rhetorical resources for those who do have a direct material interest in framing a campaign against retrenchment. This would include trade unions, which thanks to another important feature of Bismarckian welfare institutions – the involvement of the social partners in the governance of benefits – also have some institutionalized influence over policy development.

The obvious limit to a simple revenue adjustment policy seems to be the upward pressure that it places on contribution rates, and thus non-wage labour costs. Here, however, the strictly welfare institutional explanation for Bismarckian policy stability is bolstered by a broader argument from institutional political economy. In Bismarckian countries, employers' competitiveness strategies have – in part because they have internalized the constraint of relatively high non-wage labour costs – often focused less on the reduction of labour costs and flexibility than on the continual search for productivity increases, including by laying off workers for whom the productivity/cost ratio is lowest. As restructuring initiatives of these kinds are actually facilitated by the availability of generous social benefits, the latter should enjoy support not just from organized labour but also from organized capital. Facilitated once again by the social partners' role in the governance of unemployment insurance and related social protection schemes, the adaptation of continental European economies to enhanced international competitiveness has thus, it is argued, relied on welfare expansion to facilitate 'labour shedding' (cf. Esping-Andersen 1996b; Hemerijck et al. 2000; Ebbinghaus 2000) rather than welfare adaptation to embrace flexibility and the development of low-end service employment. In such a context, cost containment, recalibration and activation reforms have no obvious 'functional' relevance.

When analysts have focused on the role of welfare state structures in mediating unemployment policy development, the diagnosis has therefore been one of a 'stasis bias' shared by all countries with Bismarckian institutional profiles. Increasingly, however, this interpretation has been challenged by scholars holding up examples of more fundamental shifts in unemployment and other social policies in continental European countries. Yet the challenge has been a partial one. By emphasizing the importance of features of the background policy-making environment that allow reformers to sporadically nullify or circumvent the influence of welfare institutions, these analyses have actually reinforced the impression that this influence essentially works against policy change.

Such analyses of individual instances of unemployment and social policy change in continental Europe are too numerous to review here, but it is possible to summarize some of the pro-change factors that this body of work has identified. Prominent among these are contextual features of the broader political environment of the welfare state, either contingent or structural. Left-party incumbency has come to be seen by many as a precondition for change (e.g. Levy 2001). Somewhat similarly, Pierson (2001: 448–51) argues that in continental Europe explicitly negotiated reform offers the only viable alternative to 'standing pat'. But the likelihood of negotiated reform, he emphasizes, depends crucially on more structural features of the political context, including the power resources of pivotal actors, either parties or unions, and their vulnerability to 'poaching' from rivals. Particularly based on a comparison of the Dutch 'miracle' and the German *Reformstau*, other scholars have stressed the strategic importance of a strong executive, capable of casting a 'shadow of hierarchy' over social actors, as a condition for reform-oriented social pacts (Ebbinghaus and Hassel 1999; Hemerijck *et al.* 2000). Yet others have pointed to the need for reformers to be able to frame a plausible 'crisis narrative', a function both of objective social conditions and of the institutional resources at their disposal (Cox 1999; Kuipers 2006). Finally, some have called attention to the reform possibilities offered by tactical political manoeuvring and skilful exploitation of windows of opportunity for reform, such as that offered to German chancellor Schroeder by the scandal around accounting procedures in the German public employment service (cf. Vail 2003).

What these rather diverse accounts of policy change in Bismarckian welfare states all share is a stress on the non-welfare variations between the countries of continental Europe. Together they suggest that, although these welfare states can experience major policy shifts, they will do so to very differing extents and at very different times, depending on how certain contingent and structural variables line up. It is thus a picture of 'divergent dynamism' they put forward, apparently far removed from the 'shared stasis' thesis, but in fact sharing many of its assumptions. As we will see below, neither fits very well with the reality of unemployment policy development in Belgium, France, Germany and the Netherlands over the last 25 years.

Unemployment Policy Change in Belgium, France, Germany and the Netherlands

These four countries represent an interesting test case for the different hypotheses regarding the scope for and determinants of unemployment policy change in Bismarckian welfare states. All four countries clearly fit the latter characterization, both on the basis of convention and through examination of the institutional profile of their welfare arrangements. Despite some non-negligible differences, which will be returned to below, their unemployment policy systems were in the early 1980s all centred squarely on compensatory insurance, and all corresponded fairly closely to Leisering's (1996: 409) definition of Bismarckian arrangements, where social insurances are managed by 'autonomous parastatal institutions with their own budget, financed by social contributions of workers and delivering benefits calculated on the basis of prior individual earnings'.

At the same time, these four countries have manifold economic, political and social differences. France and Germany are G7 members, Belgium and the Netherlands smaller, more export-oriented, economies. Where socialist-led governments held power in France for over three-quarters of the 1980s and 1990s, this was a period of conservative ascendancy in Germany, while the Netherlands and Belgium were both ruled by broader coalitions, though with rather greater stability in the Dutch case than the Belgian. France and the Netherlands are two unitary states, while German and Belgian governments must operate in a context of federalism and, in Belgium, of increasing tensions between regional and linguistic communities. The strength of organized labour also varies considerably, with rates of union membership over 50 per cent in Belgium, beneath 10 per cent in France, and somewhere between these extremes in Germany and the Netherlands. Finally, as a result of the wage moderation and working time reductions negotiated in the now famous Wassenaar agreement of 1982, the Dutch economy has enjoyed a somewhat healthier macro-economic situation and much stronger employment growth than the other countries (cf. Visser and Hemerijck 1997), where equivalent social pacts have been much debated but never to date successfully implemented.[2]

On the basis of the currently dominant theoretical perspectives, we would thus expect unemployment policies in these four countries to be either equally immobile or very unequally dynamic. It is surprising, then, that the story is rather one of both considerable change *and* of some striking parallels between the four cases.

The evidence concerning the extent of cost containment initiatives in the four countries is complex. Over the period from 1985 to 2003, expenditure on unemployment benefits did remain globally stable (Belgium) or increase somewhat (France, Germany and the Netherlands), even after correction for unemployment rates. But it would be wrong to infer that cost containment has not been on the unemployment policy agenda. Very early on in some cases (Germany and the Netherlands) and everywhere since the early 1990s, tightening benefit eligibility and/or cutting benefit entitlements has been a salient feature of the continental European experience. If this fails to show up clearly in expenditure data it is because these cuts have been offset by selective expansions of entitlements for particular groups within the unemployed, particularly the older unemployed and/or those with the longest contribution histories. Put the other way round, expansionary measures to facilitate 'labour shedding' – on which much of the literature has focused – have been accompanied by, and probably actually necessitated, contractions in other parts of the benefit system. We can speak of a qualified expansionary dynamic and, equally legitimately, of a *qualified* concern with cost containment.

These apparently conflicting agendas of expansion and contraction have been reconciled by the particular form that the recalibration of benefit rights

Daniel Clegg

has taken in continental Europe. Despite insurance-oriented systems offering apparently plentiful scope for an equalitarian rebalancing of rights between 'insiders' and 'outsiders' (Levy 1999), the reality of continental European unemployment policies appears to have been more one of reinforcing the rights of insiders and reducing those of outsiders. This could be called a *reactionary* recalibration, because it apparently works against rather than with the grain of contemporary labour market changes. It has often taken place through a reinforcement of the 'contributiveness' of unemployment insurance, that is, by linking access to and levels and duration of unemployment benefits more closely to employment history/contribution record and seniority. Unemployment insurance systems have, in short, often distanced themselves from the management of 'bad risks'.

Though the contribution principle has a long pedigree in German social policy, it was not hugely reflected in unemployment benefits in the early 1980s. This changed in the second half of the decade, initially in largely expansionary ways. Successive reforms in the mid-1980s tied the duration of unemployment insurance (ALG) entitlement much more to prior contributions, ultimately increasing it for some (older) workers from 12 months to a maximum of 32 (Clasen 2005: 64–5). For the conservative government of the time, one major motivation was to head off the risk of long-term unemployment swelling the tax-financed unemployment assistance (ALH) caseload. For the social partners, the reform allowed ALG to become a passage to early retirement (Trampusch 2005: 210–11; Reissert 2004). Since the end of the post-reunification boom, however, the equivalence principle has been turned to more restrictive ends. During the 1990s 'original ALH', for those without prior ALG receipt, was first cut and then scrapped, forcing more people on to social assistance (*Sozialhilfe*). And though the Hartz reforms of the early 2000s did introduce cuts across the board, by far the deepest were concentrated on those without entitlement to ALG, notably through the merging of ALH and *Sozialhilfe* into a new ALG II, a general assistance scheme for those capable of work. German unemployment protection thus 'continues to distinguish between a better-off, but shrinking, core clientele, for whom there has been relatively little retrenchment, and a growing periphery which has been affected much more, with the gap between the two groups widening' (Clasen 2005: 53).

The French case shows striking parallels (Daniel 2000). The reforms of 1982–4, which separated a contribution-financed insurance system for 'good contributors' and the shorter-term unemployed from tax-financed assistance (or 'solidarity') systems for bad contributors and the longer-term unemployed, set the tone. A 1992 reform then considerably tightened the work requirements for access to unemployment insurance, especially for those with shorter work records. As the main tax-financed unemployment assistance scheme for the long-term unemployed (ASS) also had relatively strict work-related eligibility criteria, and the system for 'bad contributors' (AI) had been all but scrapped, the result was a sharp rise in claims for the general assistance provision (RMI) created by the socialist government in 1988. Though access to unemployment insurance was relaxed, particularly for those with short contribution records, during the period of strong economic growth at the turn of the new century, it has subsequently been retightened in the reforms of 2002 and 2005, the latter of which in particular followed the now 'classic' logic of unemployment insurance agreements in recessionary times (Vericel 2006a).

In the Netherlands, the introduction of the New Unemployment Insurance Act (NWW) in 1987 ended all tax-financing of unemployment insurance and restructured the benefit considerably. Under the new system, receipt of benefit for over six months became much more highly dependent on work record and, particularly, age (Boekraad 1998: 735; Green-Pedersen 2002). The amendment of the system in 1995, with the 'purple' Lib–Lab coalition now in power, tightened the eligibility requirements for basic benefits and extended benefits yet further, but compensated for this through the introduction of a new short-time benefit, paid at 70 per cent of the minimum wage, for those who had worked for at least 26 of the last 39 weeks. The most recent reforms to Dutch unemployment insurance, adopted in 2005, then greatly weakened the reference to seniority in the calculation of benefit eligibility and hence the age-bias of the system (EIRO 2005). In the Netherlands there is thus evidence of an at least partial retreat from the more reactionary logic of unemployment benefit recalibration that has characterized French and German reforms, as well as the earliest Dutch ones.

It is the Belgian case that is the real outlier with respect to the way that the unemployment benefit system has been recalibrated in the face of cost-containment pressures. This is not because the expansionary aspects of Belgium's unemployment policy reform trajectory have not followed 'labour-shedding' ends. On the contrary, after the expansion of the *prépension* and 'benefit top-up' systems for older workers in the 1980s, by the early 1990s nearly half of all unemployment expenditures in Belgium were devoted to 'non-job-seeking activities' (Kuipers 2006: 73; De Lathouwer 2004). And though there is growing awareness of the unsustainability of this approach (Burnay 2005), the blockages encountered in recent negotiations around a new 'intergenerational contract' (cf. EIRO 2004a; Moulaert 2006) suggest that it will be difficult to reverse. It is more the corresponding treatment of 'regular' unemployment benefits that sets Belgium apart. Rather than a general turn towards enhanced contributiveness, eligibility requirements have remained largely unchanged, as has the unlimited duration of insurance benefits – unique in the developed world. The system has accordingly maintained an exceptionally high coverage rate, making recourse to assistance benefits very marginal in comparative perspective (De Lathouwer 2004). Cost pressures have instead been managed by a progressive abandonment of the wage protection function of unemployment insurance and a *de facto* targeting of benefits on the basis of individual, household or family need (Marx 2007: 127–32). Since the second half of the 1980s maximum benefits have been only moderately uprated, narrowing the gap separating them from minimum benefits. For 'cohabitees' – a group comprising essentially married women and young people living with their parents – even minimum benefits have been allowed to stagnate (*ibid.*). Across the board, benefits have become ever more modest, and what growth of social assistance receipt there has been among the unemployed is largely accounted for by a growing need to supplement inadequate insurance benefits (Vanheerswynghels 1999).

Turning to activation, we see a similar picture of considerable parallels between the four cases in the ways this agenda has been integrated in a somewhat distorted form in recent unemployment policy reforms. Attempts to mainstream activation have faced considerable resistance, even though this has weakened in the more recent period. Rather than no activation at all, however, what we see in continental Europe is the *selective* development of activation, concentrated at the margins of the unemployment benefit system and/or directed to those without earnings-related support.

This is perhaps clearest in France. Specific governmental employment measures have been systematically directed to groups excluded from unemployment insurance, and particularly young people (Daniel and Tuchszirer 1999; Enjorlas *et al.* 2001). At the same time, contractual approaches to benefit delivery were pioneered not in the insurance core of the unemployment benefit system, but rather at its assistance margins, in the name of the fight against social exclusion. The most obvious example is the RMI, which since its introduction in 1988 has carried an explicit obligation to promote social or professional *insertion* as a condition for benefit receipt. Only since 2000, with, first, the introduction of a 'return to work plan' (PARE) for unemployment benefit recipients and, more recently, the development of graduated benefit sanctions for all the unemployed, has the logic of activation developed more widely.

In Germany activation also came on to the policy agenda, mainly through a caseload-driven reawakening of the long-standing but largely dormant right of local authorities – who manage the benefit – to impose work requirements on *Sozialhilfe* recipients (Voges *et al.* 2001). This was partly pragmatic – it allowed beneficiaries to build up rights to contributory benefit, and local authorities to shift the cost of providing support back on to the social insurance system – but partly also reflected a sea-change in attitudes (Annesley 2002). This has to an extent impacted on ALG recipients subsequently, for example with the 1997/8 law on the reform of employment support, which increased the unemployed individuals' share of the burden of proof for job search and somewhat broadened employment suitability criteria (Clasen *et al.* 2006: 142). But in the recent period the activation logic has above all been further reinforced for assistance recipients. The Hartz reforms vastly expanded the range of wage subsidies open to the longer-term unemployed and – simultaneously – essentially abolished suitability criteria and introduced tougher sanctioning rules for recipients of the new ALG II (Ludwig-Mayerhofer 2005).

Even in Belgium, where the unemployed social assistance caseload is less than a tenth of all the unemployed (De Lathouwer 2004), the most decisive activation reforms have concerned the Minimex assistance scheme: first the introduction of 'Integration Conventions' for recipients aged under 25 (Lemaigre 2000: 217), and more recently its transformation into a new *Revenu d'Intégration Sociale* (RIS), placing greater emphasis on measures to help with the return to work (Gilson and Glorieux 2005). Though activation measures have more recently been proposed for the unemployed in general, they have met with considerable resistance. This was the case of the 2004 'plan for the activation of the search behaviour of the unemployed'. Its content was significantly watered down after vigorous protests from the trade unions, and measures based on it are now being developed only very progressively, limited in the first place to workers aged between 25 and 30 who have already experienced long durations of unemployment (cf. EIRO 2004b; Faniel 2005).

The Dutch case deviates somewhat from this pattern. For a long time, comprehensive activation measures were also here focused primarily on the growing assistance clientele. The late 1980s saw the introduction of 'reorientation interviews' for the long-term unemployed, organized around cooperation agreements between local social services departments and the placement offices of the national employment service (Boekraad 1998: 756). The 'stimulating function' of benefit administration was further reinforced by a new law on social assistance in 1989 and then the New National Assistance Act (NABW) of 1996 which imposed an explicitly contractual approach on assistance claimants (Westerveld and Faber 2005: 170). The Jobseekers Employment Act (WIW) of 1997 finally created communal employment funds out of pre-existing special employment measures for the young and the long-term unemployed, facilitating the more seamless and explicit linkage of the latter with the communally administered social assistance system. Unlike in the other cases, however, activation has eventually become an organizing principle for the whole Dutch benefit system, including unemployment insurance. After a series of reforms initiated in the mid-1990s, the programmatic integration of employment policy and social security was largely complete by 2001 – and the basis for obligatory profiling interviews for all the unemployed had been laid (Hemerijck 2003: 260).

With respect to the administrative reorganization of the policy sector, the main trend emerging across the cases is one of few integrative changes and, accordingly, of continued complexity. Far from encouraging the closer harmonization of benefit systems for the jobless, the refocusing of unemployment insurance on good risks often seems to push in exactly the opposite direction. Fostering closer cooperation between unemployment benefit systems and the PES has also been delicate, as the Belgian and French cases show. In the framework of constitutional reforms decided in 1980, the Belgian PES was separated from benefit administration and became a competence of the regions (Brussels, Flanders and Wallonia) and communities (for the Germanophones). Since that time this institutionalized divorce has been seen as a major brake on the development of more comprehensive activation policies in Belgium (OECD 1996), but nothing more than building on the 'cooperation accords' first piloted in the late 1990s has to date been possible. In France, relationships between the national employment agency (ANPE) and the unemployment insurance institution, Unedic, have always been strained (cf. Marimbert 2004; CERC 2005). The reform creating the PARE in 2001 failed to live up to the expectations vested in it largely because – not being accompanied by organizational reforms – it required a close cooperation between these two institutions that proved less than forthcoming (Cour des Comptes 2006). In recognition, the drive to effect a more fundamental administrative reform has since been stepped up, firstly with the 2005 'law on social cohesion' and then with the tripartite convention of 2006 between the state, the ANPE and Unedic. Again privileging new cooperations, neither reform has, however, done much to address the underlying problem of institutional complexity (Vericel 2005, 2006b).

In Germany a single institution has long managed unemployment insurance and job placement services, and concern about policy coordination problems has focused on cost-shifting games within the multi-level (local, federal) responsibility structure for benefits. The 2000 'law to improve cooperation between employment services and providers of social assistance' and particularly the creation of ALG II have addressed this to a certain extent. At the same time, though, the distinction between ALG I and ALG II has been institutionalized through the creation of quite separate organizational circuits (Ludwig-Mayerhofer 2005), signalling the continuing limits on truly integrative organizational change.

Once again, it is the Dutch case that bucks the continental European trend. In the period since the 1993 publication of a highly critical report by a Parliamentary inquiry into the administration of workers' insurances, successive reforms have fundamentally restructured the administration of benefits and services for the unemployed. The reform path has been complicated, not to say confused (cf. Wierink 2000; Hemerijck 2003: 253–5). But particularly since 1999, when the government rejected the advice of the powerful social and economic council (SER) and called for 'an integral return to public competence in the administration of benefits' (Wierink 2000: 33), the integrative dynamic at work has become very clear. Though separate benefit tiers in the Netherlands remain, these are increasingly seen as part of the same system, and connected to work-related measures in similar ways. At the delivery level this is reflected in the central role of the public Centres for Work and Income (CWI), which now serve as the first point of access to all benefits and services for all the unemployed.

The foregoing discussion is summarized in table 2. It identifies what can be seen as a distinctively Bismarckian trajectory of unemployment policy change, based on a modification of 'orthodox' agendas and a typical mix and setting of policy measures to reflect this.

Furthermore, the last two columns show that the policies enacted in Belgium, France, Germany and the Netherlands over the last quarter-century map quite consistently on to this, notwithstanding a certain number of non-confirmatory cases. Rather than either shared stasis or divergent dynamism, then, what we see is a largely shared dynamism in continental European unemployment policy, but a dynamism that is of a particular, unorthodox, kind.

Discussion: Continental Drift

Whether emphasizing 'shared stasis' or 'divergent dynamism', conventional perspectives on social protection systems in continental Europe all emphasize the underlying self-reproducing tendencies of Bismarckian welfare institutions. What the above analysis demonstrates, though, is that such institutional self-reproduction is in no way as inimical to policy change as has been suggested, at least in unemployment policy. Many of the policy changes reviewed above have actually helped to preserve the integrity of insurance-based, contribution-

Table 2

Agendas and measures of 'Bismarckian' unemployment policy reform

Modified reform agenda	Bismarckian policy measures	☑	☒
Qualified Cost containment	• Selective expansion • Cuts in benefit levels • Cuts in benefit durations • Stricter eligibility requirements	B, F, D, NL	
Reactionary Recalibration	• Reduced protection for those with no/atypical work histories • Enhanced/safeguarded protection for those with long work histories • More *contributiveness* in benefit entitlements	F, D, NL95	B, NL95+
Selective Activation	• Stricter job-search/acceptance requirements with effective sanctions *in SA* • Increased investment in training/job creation for the *unprotected* unemployed • Development of reintegration plans/ contracts for benefit recipients *in SA*	B, F, D, NL95	NL95+
Little Integrative Administrative Restructuring	• Closer policy *coordination* of different benefit tiers • Closer *cooperation between* benefit and employment administrations • Development of *front-line* 'single gateways' to services	B, F, NL95 (D)	NL95+ (D)

Key: B = Belgium; F = France; D = Germany; NL95 = Netherlands until mid-1990s; NL95+ = Netherlands after mid-1990s; ( ) = uncertain positioning.

financed and managerially autonomous unemployment protection arrangements, heading off pressures for more fundamental institutional change. Qualified cost containment and reactionary recalibration have combined to help make selective expansions compatible with the limitation of deficits on which the self-regulatory basis of Bismarckian social insurance arrangements rest. Activation at the margins has allowed insurance arrangements to *de facto* renounce their responsibility for 'bad risks' without undermining the normative primacy of the employment basis of rights to guaranteed income replacement on which the survival of Bismarckian social insurances depends (cf. Clegg 2002). Unemployment policies in continental Europe have changed not in spite of attempts to preserve the institutional *status quo*, but rather because of them.

It is thus the self-reproducing dynamics of their similar institutional frameworks for unemployment policy that explain the largely analogous and distinctly

Figure 1

Incremental and non-incremental change in continental
European unemployment policy

	Time X	Time X + 1	Time X + 2	Time X + 3	Time X + N
Cost containment	Qualified	Qualified	Qualified	Qualified	Less qualified
Recalibration	No	Reactionary	Reactionary	Reactionary	Less reactionary
Activation	No	No	Selective	Selective	Less selective
Integrative administrative reform	No	No	No	Limited	Less limited

'Meta-policy reform'

unorthodox changes in unemployment policies witnessed over the last quarter-
century in the four continental European countries analysed here. Logically,
too, some of the small deviations from this general continental European
reform trajectory are best explained by small differences in these institutional
frameworks. Thus, if a basic protection orientation has been privileged over
a more reactionary recalibration of unemployment insurance in Belgium, it
is arguably because of the unusual 'Ghent-like' features of the Belgian unemployment insurance system, in which trade unions alone administer benefits
and receive federal funds for each beneficiary. This gives unions a strong
financial and organizational incentive to keep the unemployed 'inside' the
system through the maintenance of unlimited benefits, and to pursue
institutional reproduction through a different mechanism – the progressive
levelling down of all benefits – from that which has been used where institutional incentive structures differ.

Although these welfare states are usually associated with policy stability,
unemployment policy change has nowhere been marginal. Though core
institutional arrangements have been preserved, their distributive impact and
logic and their effect on the labour market have been decisively altered. If
this change has often gone unheralded in the existing literature, it is probably
because it has been effected through a stepwise incremental process, with
small shifts on one policy dimension creating the need and conditions for
further reforms down the line. This pattern of change is captured by cells
Time X to Time X + 3 in figure 1. Qualified pressures for cost containment
build up and lead in time to a reactionary recalibration of unemployment
insurance, which results in the expansion of the claimant reservoir for
assistance measures. This creates an opening for activation measures at the
margins of the system, which in turn raises the question of the articulation

between income protection and help with return to work, leading to at least limited attempts at integrative administrative reforms. Though very different in style from 'fundamental reforms' of the type seen or promoted elsewhere, the cumulative effect of this 'reform cascade' is quite significant change across a number of policy dimensions. This would seem to equate it with the kind of 'incremental change with transformative results' that Streeck and Thelen (2005) have recently placed at the top of the agenda of institutional analysis. The trajectory of unemployment policy change in continental Europe seems specifically to owe much to the dynamics of 'drift' – where old institutions are not adapted to new social conditions – and 'layering' – where change is initially implemented at the margins, in the name of patching up existing arrangements – that have been identified by these and other authors (*ibid.*; Hacker 2004; Palier 2005).

However, if the analysis presented here thus lends some support to recent theorizing on the scope for incremental change in dense institutional environments, it also raises some questions about it. This literature has usefully shown that significant policy change can occur in a context of institutional stability, and implicitly suggests that such change could be just as transformative as that brought on by institutional crisis or discontinuity. Parts of the foregoing analysis of unemployment policy reform in continental Europe suggest that the latter claim might be overly optimistic. Across a number of reform dimensions, the major outlier in our analysis is the Netherlands in the period since the mid-1990s – that is, precisely since the time when a major institutional reconfiguration of the Dutch workers' insurances was launched, ultimately culminating in total exclusion of the social partners from their governance role in the system (Wierink 2000: 33; Kuipers 2006: 147–8). Though this change could not be equated with a 'dramatic disruption like war or revolution' (cf. Streeck and Thelen 2005: 5), it is hard to see it as simply incremental either, fundamentally and frontally challenging as it did a key pillar of the Bismarckian institutional framework. As figure 1 suggests, it is possible that the transformative potential of 'continental drift' has limits everywhere, and a similar 'meta-policy reform' – a reconsideration of how to make policy itself (cf. Dror 1968), notably concerning, as in the Netherlands, the respective role of the social partners and the state – will be a precondition for further change (transition to cell *Time X + N*) in the other three cases too.

The contrast is instructive here between the Bismarckian welfare states and countries like Denmark and the UK. No significant 'meta-policy' reform – and far less a revolution – occurred in either of those cases, and yet it appears to have been possible to enact rather more fundamental unemployment policy reforms than has been the case in much of continental Europe. This has analytical implications, notably for understanding which mechanisms of incremental change are likely to prevail in different (welfare) institutional contexts (cf. Hacker 2004: 246–8), and what this implies for the possibility frontier of policy change. More importantly for present purposes, it underscores that, while unemployment policies are far from frozen in Bismarckian welfare states, neither are they – for better or worse – as readily mutable as in other welfare state contexts.

Conclusions

Despite their popular image as 'frozen landscapes', this article has shown that Bismarckian welfare states have witnessed considerable change in the domain of unemployment policy over the past quarter-century. Furthermore, across the four cases examined, the trajectory of change is often strikingly similar, notwithstanding their considerable social, political and economic differences. Bismarckian welfare institutions are therefore crucial for understanding changes to the unemployment policies of continental European countries, and not merely for explaining their supposed inertia.

Policy change in continental European unemployment policy has been coextensive with, and derivative of, the process through which existing policy institutions have been reproduced. This has shaped its content decisively, and made it diverge from more orthodox recipes. Generally, policies have enhanced protection for 'insiders' while targeting both benefit cuts and new activation initiatives on 'outsiders'. After a quarter-century of reforms these are thus neither fully activating nor fully compensatory welfare states, but ones that combine these facets in apparent contradiction. There is a suggestive parallel – and probably a two-way causal link – here with the dualism of labour market regulation increasingly found in much of continental Europe, where precarious employment contracts have been expanded as 'exceptions' that simultaneously contradict and reinforce the 'rule' of the standard employment relationship for core workers.

Though they have not blocked unemployment policy change entirely, Bismarckian welfare institutions have therefore influenced it and probably also constrained it. The article has shown that unemployment policy reforms in continental Europe have occurred incrementally, through an accumulation of small changes. But it has also suggested that there are limits to the transformative potential of this 'continental drift', and that pushing the possibility frontier of unemployment policy reforms out further may require the kind of 'meta-policy' reform, and abandonment of Bismarckian institutions, witnessed in the Dutch case. Whether such a potentially conflictual reform will actually prove feasible in given national contexts is another matter, and here variables of a broader social, economic and political variety may well prove relevant. But understanding the nature and extent of transformations that have already occurred will help us to better specify the terms of the strategic choices that unemployment policy actors in continental European countries face as they look to the future.

Notes

The author gratefully acknowledges support from the European Commission Marie Curie Fellowships Programme for the award (MEIF-2003-500835) which funded the research for this article.

1. Relaxation of Employment Protection Legislation (EPL) is increasingly seen as an integral part of this fundamental reform, linking the unemployment policy reform agendas addressed more fully here to the pursuit of a so-called 'flexicurity' policy (cf. European Commission 2006).

2. The high rate of employment in the Netherlands today owes much, however, to the development of part-time employment in the 1980s and 1990s. In full-time equivalents, the Dutch employment rate in 2003 was equivalent to the German, somewhat higher than in Belgium but actually somewhat lower than in France.

References

Annesley, C. (2002), Reconfiguring women's social citizenship in Germany: the right to Sozialhilfe, the responsibility to work, *German Politics*, 11, 1: 81–96.

Barbier, J.-C. (2004), Systems of social protection in Europe: two contrasted paths to activation, and maybe a third. In J. Lind, H. Knudsen and H. Jørgensen (eds), *Labour and Employment Regulation in Europe*, Brussels: Peter Lang, pp. 233–54.

Boekraad, B. (1998), Un modèle de polder en pleine évolution: histoire récente et réorganisation de la sécurité sociale aux Pays-Bas, *Revue Belge de Sécurité Sociale*, 40, 4: 723–67.

Burnay, N. (2005), Travailleurs âgés: d'une politique de réduction de chômage à une politique du vieillissement actif. In *L'Etat social actif: vers un changement de paradigme?* Brussels: PIE–Peter Lang, pp. 209–32.

Casey, B. (2004), The OECD Jobs Strategy and the European Employment Strategy: two views of the labour market and of the welfare state, *European Journal of Industrial Relations*, 10, 3: 329–52.

CERC (2005), *Aide au retour à l'emploi*, Rapport du CERC no. 6, Paris: La Documentation Française.

Clasen, J. (2005), *Reforming European Welfare States: Germany and the United Kingdom Compared*, Oxford: Oxford University Press.

Clasen, J. and Clegg, D. (2006a), Beyond activation: reforming European unemployment protection systems in post-industrial labour markets, *European Societies*, 8, 4: 555–81.

Clasen, J. and Clegg, D. (2006b), New labour market risks and the revision of unemployment protection systems in Europe. In K. Armingeon and G. Bonoli (eds), *The Politics of the Post-Industrial Welfare State*, London: Routledge, pp. 192–210.

Clasen, J., Davidson, J., Ganssmann, H. and Mauer, A. (2006), Non-employment and the welfare state: the United Kingdom and Germany compared, *Journal of European Social Policy*, 16, 2: 134–54.

Clasen, J., Duncan, G., Eardley, T., Evans, M., Ughetto, P., Oorschott, W. van and Wright, S. (2001), Towards 'single gateways'? A cross-national review of the changing role of employment offices in seven countries, *Zeitschrift für Ausländisches und Internationales Arbeits- und Sozialrecht*, 15, 1: 43–63.

Clegg, D. (2002), The political status of social assistance benefits in European welfare states: lessons from reforms to provisions for the unemployed in France and Great Britain, *European Journal of Social Security*, 4, 3: 201–25.

Coe, D. and Snower, D. (1997), *Policy Complementarities: The Case for Fundamental Reform of the Labour Market*, CEPR Discussion Paper no. 1585, London: CEPR.

Cour des Comptes (2006), *L'évolution de l'assurance chômage: de l'indemnisation à l'aide au retour à l'emploi*, Rapport Public Thématique, March.

Cox, R. (1999), The social construction of an imperative: why welfare reform happened in Denmark and the Netherlands but not in Germany, *World Politics*, 53, 3: 463–98.

Daniel, C. (2000), L'indemnisation du chômage depuis 1974: d'une logique d'intégration à une logique de segmentation, *Revue Française des Affaires Sociales*, 54, 3–4: 29–46.

Daniel, C. and Tuchszirer, C. (1999), L'activation des dépenses passives: un habit neuf pour une idée ancienne. In B. Gazier *et al.* (eds), *L'Economie sociale (XIXe journées de la AES)*, Paris: L'Harmattan, pp. 373–82.

De Lathouwer, L. (2004), Reforming policies and institutions in unemployment protection in Belgium. Unpublished manuscript.

Dror, Y. (1968), *Public Policymaking Re-examined*, San Francisco: Chandler.

Dufour, P., Boismenu, G. and Noel, A. (2003), *L'aide au conditionnel: la contrepartie dans les mesures envers les personnes sans emploi en Europe et en Amérique du Nord*, Brussels: PIE–Peter Lang.

Ebbinghaus, B. (2000), *When Labour and Capital Collude: The Varieties of Welfare Capitalism and Early Retirement in Europe, Japan and the USA*, Working Paper PSGE no. 00.4, Cambridge, MA: Center for European Studies, Harvard University.

Ebbinghaus, B. and Hassel, A. (1999), Striking deals: concertation in the reform of continental European welfare states, *European Journal of Public Policy*, 7, 1: 44–62.

EIRO (2004a), *Employers Demand End to Early Retirement and a 40-hour Week*, EIRO record no. BE0408301N.

EIRO (2004b), *New System of Monitoring Unemployed People Introduced*, EIRO record no. BE0402302F.

EIRO (2005), *Government Accepts SER Recommendation on Social Insurance Reform*, EIRO record no. NL0506102F.

Enjorlas, B., Laville, J.-L., Fraisse, H. and Trickey, L. (2001), Between subsidiarity and social assistance – the French republican route to activation. In I. Lødemel and H. Trickey (eds), *An Offer You Can't Refuse: Workfare in International Perspective*, Bristol: Policy Press, pp. 41–70.

Esping-Andersen, G. (ed.) (1996a), *Welfare States in Transition*, London: Sage.

Esping-Andersen, G. (1996b), Welfare states without work: the impasse of labour shedding and familialism in continental European social policy. In Esping-Andersen, G. (ed.), *Welfare States in Transition*, London: Sage, pp. 66–87.

European Commission (2006), *Employment in Europe 2006*, Luxembourg: Office for the Official Publications of the European Communities.

Faniel, J. (2005), Réactions syndicales et associatives face au 'contrôle de la disponibilité des chômeurs'. In *L'Année Sociale 2004*, Brussels: ULB, pp. 133–48.

Gilson, S. and Glorieux, M. (2005), Le droit à l'intégration sociale figure comme première emblématique de l'Etat social actif: quelques commentaires de la loi du 26 mai 2002. In P. Vielle, P. Pochet and I. Cassiers (eds), *L'Etat social actif: vers un changement de paradigme?* Brussels: PIE–Peter Lang, pp. 233–55.

Green-Pedersen, C. (2002), *The Politics of Justification: Party Competition and Welfare State Retrenchment in Denmark and the Netherlands from 1982 to 1998*, Amsterdam: Amsterdam University Press.

Hacker, J. (2004), Privatizing risk without privatizing the welfare state: the hidden politics of social policy retrenchment in the United States, *American Political Science Review*, 98, 2: 243–60.

Hemerijck, A. (2003), A paradoxical miracle: the politics of coalition government and social concertation in Dutch welfare reform. In S. Jochen and N. Siegel (eds), *Konzertierung, Verhandlungsdemokratie und Reformpolitik in Wohlfahrstaat*, Opladen: Leske and Budrich, pp. 232–70.

Hemerijck, A., Manow, P. and Van Kersbergen, K. (2000), Welfare without work: divergent experiences of reform in Germany and the Netherlands. In S. Kuhnle (ed.), *The Survival of the European Welfare State*, London: Routledge, pp. 106–27.

Kuipers, S. (2006), *The Crisis Imperative: Crisis Rhetoric and the Reform of Social Security in Belgium and the Netherlands*, Amsterdam: Amsterdam University Press.

Leisering, L. (1996), Les limites de l'Etat d'assurance sociale? Les mutations sociales ou le défi des garanties de revenu publiques. In MIRE (ed.), *Comparer les systèmes de protection sociale en Europe*, vol. 2, Paris: MIRE, pp. 403–37.

Lemaigre, T. (2000), Mesures d'activation: coup d'accélérateur. In *L'Année sociale 1999*, Brussels: ULB, pp. 215–21.

Levy, J. (1999), Vice into virtue: progressive politics and welfare reform in continental Europe, *Politics and Society*, 27, 2: 239–73.

Levy, J. (2001), Partisan politics and welfare state adjustment: the case of France, *Journal of European Public Policy*, 8, 2: 265–85.

Ludwig-Mayerhofer, W. (2005), Activating Germany. In T. Bredgard and F. Larsen (eds), *Employment Policy from Different Angles*, Copenhagen: DJOF, pp. 95–112.

Marimbert, J. (2004), *Rapport au Ministre des Affaires Sociales, du Travail et de la Solidarité sur le rapprochement des services de l'emploi*, Paris: Ministère des Affaires Sociales, du Travail et de la Solidarité.

Marx, I. (2007), *A New Social Question? On Minimum Income Protection in the Postindustrial Era*, Amsterdam: Amsterdam University Press.

Moulaert, X. (2006), Conférence sur la fin de carrière: véritable négociation ou tentative de légitimation de l'action gouvernementale? *Chronique Internationale de l'IRES*, 100: 35–44.

OECD (1996), *Le service public de l'emploi: Belgique*, Paris: OECD.

Palier, B. (2002), *Gouverner la sécurité sociale: les réformes du système français de protection sociale depuis 1945*, Paris: Presses Universitaires de France.

Palier, B. (2005), Ambiguous agreement, cumulative change: French social policy in the 1990s. In W. Streeck and K. Thelen (eds), *Beyond Continuity: Institutional Change in Advanced Political Economies*, Oxford: Oxford University Press, pp. 127–44.

Pierson, P. (1998), Irresistible forces, immovable objects: post-industrial welfare states confront permanent austerity, *Journal of European Public Policy*, 5, 4: 539–60.

Pierson, P. (2001), Coping with permanent austerity: welfare state restructuring in affluent democracies. In P. Pierson (ed.), *The New Politics of the Welfare State*, Oxford: Oxford University Press, pp. 410–56.

Reissert, B. (2004), Germany: a late reformer. Unpublished a manuscript.

Streeck, W. and Thelen, K. (2005), Introduction: institutional change in advanced political economies. In W. Streeck and K. Thelen (eds), *Beyond Continuity: Institutional Change in Advanced Political Economies*, Oxford: Oxford University Press, pp. 1–40.

Torfing, J. (1999), Workfare with welfare: recent reforms of the Danish welfare state, *Journal of European Social Policy*, 9, 1: 5–28.

Trampusch, C. (2005), Institutional resettlement: the case of early retirement in Germany. In W. Streeck and K. Thelen (eds), *Beyond Continuity: Institutional Change in Advanced Political Economies*, Oxford: Oxford University Press, pp. 203–28.

Vail, M. (2003), Rethinking corporatism and consensus: the dilemmas of German social protection reform, *West European Politics*, 26, 3: 41–66.

Vanheerswynghels, A. (1999), Chômage et minimex. In *L'Année Social 1998*, Brussels: ULB, pp. 197–98.

Vericel, M. (2005), La réorganization du service public de l'emploi ou la difficile mise en œuvre d'une réforme, *Droit Social*, 12: 1174–8.

Vericel, M. (2006a), Le nouvel accord sur l'assurance chômage pour *2006–08*, *Droit Social*, 2: 129–33.

Vericel, M. (2006b), La convention Etat-ANPE-Unedic du 5 mai 2006: un accompagnement renforcé des demandeurs d'emploi mais pas de véritable réorganization du service public de l'emploi, *Droit Social*, 9/10: 900–4.

Visser, J. and Hemerijck, A. (1997), *A Dutch Miracle: Job Growth, Welfare Reform and Corporatism in the Netherlands*, Amsterdam: Amsterdam University Press.

Voges, W., Jacobs, H. and Trickey, H. (2001), Uneven development: local authorities and workfare in Germany. In I. Lødemel and H. Trickey (eds), *An Offer You Can't Refuse: Workfare in International Perspective*, Bristol: Policy Press, pp. 71–103.

Westerveld, M. and Faber, K. (2005), Client contracting in social security in the Netherlands. In E. Sol and M. Westerveld (eds), *Contractualism in Employment Services: A New Form of Welfare Governance*, The Hague: Kluwer, pp. 167–87.

Wierink, M. (2000), Réforme des structures de la protection sociale et révision de la place des partenaires sociaux, *Chronique Internationale de l'IRES*, 64: 26–38.

5

From Subsidiarity to 'Free Choice': Child- and Elder-care Policy Reforms in France, Belgium, Germany and the Netherlands

Nathalie Morel

Introduction

As has been argued by various authors (cf. Daly and Lewis 2000), care policies provide a fruitful point of entry for analysing welfare state change. Indeed, care policies represent in most cases a relatively new responsibility for the welfare state and are in fact one of the most dynamic areas of welfare state expansion (cf. Daly 1997). As such, care policies are part and parcel of the restructuring of the welfare state. This restructuring involves both a recasting of the overall set of relationships between family, market and state, and a transformation of gender relations and norms.

The aim of this article is to examine this process of reform and restructuring in the Bismarckian or 'conservative corporatist' welfare systems. Basing our inquiry on a comparison of France, Belgium, Germany and the Netherlands, we seek to draw out the impact of the specific nature of Bismarckian welfare state institutions on the nature and timing of the reform trajectories in childcare and elder-care policies implemented over the past 25 years.

The choice of these countries may at first sight seem problematic. Indeed, while it has become common for comparative welfare state analysts to speak of welfare state clusters, there has been some considerable debate as to which criteria are most relevant for identifying these clusters. These debates have mostly been spurred by Esping-Andersen's 1990 tripartite welfare regime typology.

Various scholars have called into question this typology, often by pointing to important intra-regime variations along one or more specific variables. In this respect, the conservative regime is perhaps the one that has elicited most criticism, not least from gender theorists who have argued that Esping-Andersen's predictions in terms of the low levels of services and of female labour-market participation associated with the conservative welfare regimes hardly hold true in the case of France or Belgium, which both display fairly high public childcare coverage for children aged 3 and above. Similarly, various works have highlighted important intra-regime differences with respect to employment levels for women or lone mothers, or regarding poverty rates among single-headed families, and with respect to other gendered patterns of inequalities (Lewis 1992; Sainsbury 1996; Bussemaker and van Kersbergen 1999). Thus, it has often been argued that France and Belgium are not properly 'conservative' countries to the same extent as Germany or the Netherlands, and various other classificatory attempts have tended to separate these countries into different clusters.

Without discarding the theoretical and social importance of looking more closely at the gendered outcomes of different welfare arrangements, my approach here is to look at the specific policy contents and reform trajectories rather than outcomes for defining 'families of nations'. I suggest that when attention is directed towards both childcare and elder-care policies, there is a much stronger case to be made for grouping these countries together than if one looks just at childcare, which has usually been the focus in gender studies.

Indeed this article shows that patterns of reform in care policies in Bismarckian welfare systems share similar logics and trajectories. I argue that it is the shared conservative and corporatist traits of Bismarckian labour markets and welfare state institutions – and their impact on labour market adjustment possibilities and preferences – that have driven care policy reforms. These reforms have been very closely linked to specific employment strategies, and the politics of welfare without work and subsequent attempts to shift away from such a labour-shedding strategy go a long way in explaining both the nature and the timing of child- and elder-care policy reforms in Bismarckian welfare systems. Care policies have been used during the 1980s and early 1990s to reinforce the traditional male-breadwinner model that characterizes Bismarckian countries but, in the late 1990s, when low employment rates became widely regarded as the key problem for the sustainability of these welfare states, care policies were used to raise female employment levels. This change therefore marks a real U-turn in the role assigned to women, who are now expected not only to care but also to work – a 'farewell to maternalism' which Ann Orloff (2006) has shown to characterize other countries also. However, the reforms implemented here bear the imprint of the conservative corporatist legacy of these welfare states in terms both of reform trajectories and policy design.

In the next section I draw out the key institutional characteristics of the postwar model in conservative welfare states, and discuss briefly how the strong emphasis on the male-breadwinner model, and the resulting welfare without work syndrome, has exacerbated the welfare state crisis in these countries – a diagnosis that became widely shared in the late 1990s.

The next section describes the policy reforms implemented in these four countries in the fields of childcare and elder care and the policy logic that has underpinned them. Two phases of policy reforms can be distinguished. The first set of reforms, in the 1980s and up to the late 1990s, based on a (female) labour-shedding strategy, has sought to reinforce the traditional male-breadwinner model as a way to combat unemployment, while the second

set of reforms, starting in the late 1990s, has aimed at raising employment
levels, and especially female employment rates. In the four countries, however,
a focus on promoting 'free choice' has justified the introduction of measures
that have simultaneously reinforced social stratification in terms of access to
the labour market – meaning that some women have much more 'free choice'
than others – and weakened certain labour market rigidities. Indeed, we
argue that care policy reforms have provided a backdoor for the introduction
of labour-cheapening measures and for increasing employment flexibility in
otherwise very rigid labour markets.

The third section offers a concluding discussion of the specific rationale
and trajectory of care policies in Bismarckian welfare systems.

Characterizing Bismarckian Welfare Systems

A conservative corporatist postwar social contract

As far as care issues are concerned, three main characteristics of Bismarckian
welfare systems should be emphasized. First, of crucial importance is, of
course, their strong reliance on the male-breadwinner model and strong
support of the traditional family. Various policies and tax disincentives have
traditionally discouraged women's participation in the labour market or
encouraged their withdrawal after marriage or childbirth, so that female
participation rates have generally been low. In this model, men are expected
to work full-time and women to care full-time for children and the elderly.
This reliance on a male breadwinner in a system based on employment-
related social insurance means that women have generally lacked individual
social entitlements and have instead received benefits through their husband.

Another defining characteristic is the principle of subsidiarity: intervention
should not take place at a level higher than necessary; when an individual is
in need of care, help should be sought first from the family or local community, or from voluntary associations – the state steps in only as last resort (this
is particularly true of Germany and the Netherlands). The belief is that the
family is the best possible provider of care and that substitutive policies by
the state might undermine the family. Family policies therefore offer generous
financial transfers to families to support them in their role of primary welfare
providers but little in terms of substitutive social services. Bismarckian countries
are thus very transfer-heavy and service-lean. The 'freedom of choice' rhetoric
that later developed and which has guided care policy reforms fits well with
this principle of subsidiarity.

Active labour market policies have typically been underdeveloped and
this is even more apparent with regard to policies to promote women's employment. In the 1960s, when faced with labour shortages, Germany, France and
Belgium chose to bring in foreign 'guest' workers rather than draw on the
domestic reserve of female labour – thereby also reinforcing the male-breadwinner
model (Esping-Andersen 1996; Bussemaker and van Kersbergen 1999).
Scandinavian countries chose instead to bring women into the labour market,
which prompted the development of childcare services and other policies to
help parents reconcile work and family life as early as the early 1970s.

The crisis of the male-breadwinner model

Taken together, these various characteristics help to account for the situation of 'welfare without work' which Bismarckian countries found themselves in after the economic crisis of the mid-1970s. In a system where the family is dependent on the male breadwinner, protecting the employment and 'family wage' of this male worker has been a central concern of trade unions. As a result, it has been nearly impossible for Bismarckian countries to implement 'labour-cheapening' strategies of flexibilization and labour market deregulation as in the liberal countries. The Nordic public employment strategy (which prompted the rapid increase in female labour market participation) has not been followed either. Instead, Bismarckian welfare states sought to maintain productivity via a labour-shedding strategy, which typically took the form of early retirement schemes and/or an expansion of disability policy (Esping-Andersen 1996; Bussemaker and van Kersbergen 1999). This labour-shedding strategy also involved discouraging female labour market participation.

Such a strategy has proven problematic on many counts. Writing in the mid-1990s, Esping-Andersen highlighted the self-reinforcing negative spiral Bismarckian countries found themselves in, this strategy having resulted in 'prohibitively heavy fixed labour costs which, in turn, discourage[d] employment growth or, alternatively, spur[red] the growth of informal sector jobs or self employment', and which were 'particularly ill-suited to address pressures for greater labour market flexibility and women's demand for economic independence' (Esping-Andersen 1996: 68).

Indeed, women have increasingly sought to enter the labour market, despite policies encouraging them to remain at home. Faced with a lack of care options, either public or private (due to high labour costs), women's increasing participation in the labour market has often been accompanied by a severe drop in fertility rates, and most strikingly so in the most familialistic countries such as Germany, Italy or Spain. Women's aspirations to work have also come into conflict with their capacity or willingness to care for the dependent elderly. These different trends have thus called into question the traditional care arrangements that underpin Bismarckian welfare systems, and this at the same time as the number of elderly people has increased rapidly, thus leading to a 'care crisis'.

Ageing populations are not simply a care issue, but also a financial issue, as fewer workers must bear the cost of a large cohort of pensioners. This has been of particular concern in Bismarckian countries, where the combination of labour-shedding policies and of low female participation rates and low birth rates have exacerbated the dependency burden.

This diagnosis became widely shared in the later part of the 1990s, both at the European Commission level and in the countries under study. At the European Commission level, much emphasis has been placed since the late 1990s on raising employment levels, and especially female employment levels, in order to increase the tax base of the social protection systems. The 1997 European Employment Strategy has set as key objective employment levels of at least 60 per cent for women by 2010, and at least 70 per cent for men. Policies for reconciling work and family life have been presented as crucial measures for simultaneously reaching three aims: raising employment levels, promoting gender equality and raising fertility rates, and member states have been encouraged since the late 1990s to develop appropriate policies (childcare services, parental leave schemes, etc.). However, as we shall see, care policies in Bismarckian countries have mainly pursued the first of these aims (raising employment levels).

The development of elder-care policies has perhaps been less explicitly linked to employment strategies, at least at the European Commission level, but we will see how the shape and content of these policies can nonetheless also be linked to employment strategies specific to Bismarckian welfare systems, based on the development of low-skilled, low-paid personal service jobs.[1]

Trajectories of Reform in Care Policies

This section describes the policy reforms that have taken place in the fields of childcare and elder care in each of the four countries, starting with France and Belgium, as these two countries have long stood out among conservative welfare states for the amount of public childcare services provided.

The French and Belgian specificity with regard to childcare provision is mainly due to the existence of the écoles maternelles, or preschools, which take children from the age of 3. Although compulsory schooling only starts at the age of 6, virtually all children aged 3 to 6 attend preschool (considered part of the national school system). In both countries preschools were developed for educational purposes and to form loyal citizens/republicans, rather than as a care service to help parents reconcile work and family life. Day-care services for children below the age of 3 developed rapidly in the 1970s and early 1980s but expansion then stopped during the 1980s to give way to more private forms of day-care arrangements. France and Belgium have developed a similar mix of seemingly contradictory policies that include both day-care services to facilitate women's employment, and cash benefits that encourage women to stay at home. Finally, both countries share pro-natalist aims and have developed family policies that primarily target and favour large families. With respect to the elderly, care policies have long remained underdeveloped in both France and Belgium. In the mid-1980s, there were still 20 per cent of elderly people living with their children in France – compared to 5 per cent in Sweden (Esping-Andersen 1999: 63). It is only in the early 2000s that both countries (France especially) have developed specific policies to deal with the long-term care needs of the elderly.

Germany and the Netherlands have remained much closer to the traditional male-breadwinner model and, until recently, mothers of small children were not expected to work. The principle of subsidiarity is very strong, and childcare services have traditionally been provided by voluntary welfare organizations. It is only in recent years that these two countries have started to invest more seriously in childcare services. Both countries, however, have a longer history of providing care for the elderly than France and Belgium. The Netherlands developed institutional care for the elderly long ago, while Germany set up a fifth social insurance scheme to deal with dependency as early as 1994.

Despite these initial cultural and policy differences, we argue that these countries have all followed similar patterns of reform and that this can be explained by the shared conservative and corporatist institutional character-istics of these four Bismarckian welfare systems. To strengthen our argument, policy reforms in France are developed at greater length than for other countries to serve as a 'test-case'. We show that despite the prevailing perception of France as different from other Bismarckian welfare states with respect to family policy (Lewis 1992; Anttonen and Sipilä 1996), con-servative and corporatist traits are clearly visible both in the types of policies implemented and in the policy logics that have guided reforms in the past 25 years.

Our analysis shows that from the mid-1980s to the late 1990s, in all four countries, women have been either discouraged from entering the labour market (in Germany and the Netherlands) or, where women had already entered the labour market in the 1970s, as in France and Belgium, measures have been implemented to encourage their withdrawal from the labour market in order to 'free' jobs for men. This is particularly true for low-income women, who have been enticed to make use of long and low-paid parental leave schemes. For higher-income women, on the other hand, various measures facilitating the use of private forms of childcare have been developed. Such measures have typically taken the form of tax deductions and social contri-bution exemptions, thus contributing to a cheapening of the cost of labour in the personal service sector. Such a strategy is highly compatible with the subsidiarist principle of Bismarckian welfare systems as it provides a solution that is entirely based neither on the state nor on the market; instead, the state offers subsidies to help families choose how to service their care needs. Furthermore, such subsidies reinforce one of the characteristic dimensions of Bismarckian welfare systems in that they tend to reproduce and reinforce prevailing patterns of social stratification. Temporary leave schemes and opportunities to reduce working hours have also been on the increase, especially in recent years, and have contributed to a flexibilization of labour, especially of female labour. Finally, despite an expansion of policies to promote the reconciliation of work and family life, these measures have not sought to modify the traditional gender division of labour with respect to care and domestic work, the idea being that it is up to the family to decide 'freely' on how to organize their private life.

France: 'free choice' – for those who can afford it

In the 1970s, as a response to both feminist and labour market demands, France invested quite substantially in the development of day-care services. Despite promises by the Socialist Party for the 1981 elections to further increase the number of day-care places available, the 1980s marked instead a shift towards more private and familial forms of childcare (Jenson and Sineau 2001; Morgan 2002). This shift has been accompanied by a discourse promoting parents' 'free choice' – freedom to choose whether to care for their children themselves or not, and freedom to choose between different types of care options. This 'freedom of choice' rhetoric, also present in the other Bismarckian countries, is perhaps the most defining characteristic of care policies in these welfare systems.

Two types of policies have been pursued in France, both of which have been part of a wider employment strategy: on the one hand, new benefits have been created to promote employment by subsidizing parents who hire childcare workers in the home. On the other hand, parental leave benefits have been expanded to encourage certain parents to leave the labour market to care for their own children (Fagnani 1998; Martin *et al.* 1998; Morgan 2006).

Encouraging low-paid women to withdraw from the labour market. A paid parental leave benefit (APE) was set up in 1985 by the Socialist government, despite strong criticism from some members of the party, who argued that the APE was but a maternal wage in disguise. Indeed, the explicit aim of this new measure was, in a context of falling birth rates and high unemployment, to encourage women simultaneously to have a third child and to withdraw from the labour market (Jenson and Sineau 2001). This benefit, which was only granted as of the third child, gave the parent on leave the right to a non-taxable €225/month allowance for up to two years. The results were somewhat disappointing, however, as only 27,000 mothers took leave in 1986, instead of the 80,000 that had been anticipated (Fagnani 1995). The scheme was therefore modified in 1986 so that one needed simply to have worked two out of the previous ten years (and periods spent on maternity leave or registered as unemployed counted as time worked) to be eligible, and the leave was extended to three years, with the possibility to work part-time during the third year. Pro-natalist aims were thus reinforced, at the same time as the new, more lenient work requirements aimed at getting unemployed women out of the unemployment statistics.

Developing low-skilled, low-paid work by providing subsidies to higher-income women. The year 1986 also witnessed the creation of a special benefit (AGED) for families who hire a private nanny (who does not need to be licensed or qualified) to care for a child in the parents' own home. This benefit covers the employer's social contributions and offers generous tax deductions. Another benefit, the AFEAMA, was set up in 1990 to cover the cost of social contributions when parents employ a registered childminder to care for children in her home. The AFEAMA and the AGED were intended to develop cheaper forms of care than day-care institutions and to increase employment, partly by making it easier to hire someone and partly by bringing women working on the black market into the formal labour market.

Care policies to combat labour market rigidities. In 1994, with unemployment levels over 12 per cent and continually falling birth rates, the Conservative government modified the parental leave scheme so as to make it available as of the second child, and monthly benefits were increased to around €450. The pro-natalist aims remained, but were more clearly overshadowed by employment-related considerations, the explicit aim of this policy being to make the labour force more flexible by encouraging part-time work, and to free up jobs for men by getting some women out of the labour market, as stated by the Conservative minister of social affairs:

the childcare policies that are proposed, in their two components,[2] will contribute significantly to employment. We estimate that these measures should enable the creation of 100.000 new jobs. 50.000 or so of these will correspond to jobs that have been freed. Indeed, the extension of the APE will lead certain parents to diminish or suspend their professional activity, which corresponds to a significant change in behaviour since it would concern about one fifth of APE beneficiaries at the birth of their second child. (Simone Veil, A.N. débats no. 42, 02-06-1994, p. 2483)

This scheme proved successful and considerably modified women's labour market participation: between 1994 and 1997, the number of APE beneficiaries tripled and the percentage of mothers of two children in the labour force dropped from 69 to 53 per cent (Afsa 1998). Indeed, the long duration of the leave and the inadequate job protection associated with this leave have made it difficult for many women to reintegrate into the labour market at the end of the leave period. The amount of the benefit has proven too low to entice men to take the leave and thus 99 per cent of beneficiaries are women.

The 1994 childcare reform also substantially increased the tax deduction that could be claimed by families who hired a private nanny, and increased the benefit for the AFEAMA.

Redomesticating childcare. The AFEAMA and the AGED have met with great success, and spending on these programmes has increased rapidly, while investment in day-care structures has stagnated. Spending on childcare policies by the CNAF (the family social security fund) increased by 169 per cent between 1994 and 2001. The largest increase in financing has gone towards the parental leave benefit (+213 per cent), followed by the financing of the AFEAMA; the third largest increase has been for the AGED (+54 per cent). Meanwhile public day-care services have only benefited from a 39 per cent increase. This means that of the total budget, the proportion spent on day-care services decreased from 16 to 8 per cent between 1994 and 2001, while the proportion spent on families to help them pay for individual forms of care increased from 78 to 84 per cent (Leprince 2003).

While these various schemes are open to all working families, in practice the use of each of these schemes is very much determined by the family's, and especially the woman's, income level. The AGED has been used by high-income families, the AFEAMA by middle-income families, and the parental leave benefit has been too low to attract higher-income earners but has proven very attractive to low-income women (Fagnani 1998; CNAF 2003). Childcare policies have thus served to reinforce prevailing patterns of social stratification.

Finally, though there has been a diversification of childcare over the past 20 years, parental care remains the most common form of childcare for children under 3 (64 per cent), followed by care in the homes of registered childminders (18 per cent). Nurseries only account for 8 per cent of all childcare (DREES 2004).

A new orientation? New reforms have recently been introduced that seem to indicate a progressive change in childcare policies. Since 2002, fathers are entitled to 14 days' paid leave (previously 3) following the birth of a child as part of a move to promote a greater investment of fathers in caring for their children. Also, a new benefit was introduced in 2004, the *Prestation d'Accueil du Jeune Enfant* (PAJE), which brings together and replaces various schemes and child benefits. The aim of this new benefit is 'to better respond to families' needs and expectations by promoting their freedom of choice: freedom to work or to withdraw from the labour market to care for their children, and freedom to decide on the appropriate form of care' (CNAF 2003). It comprises a birth allowance and a means-tested benefit paid out until the child turns 3. Parents also receive a 'free choice supplement', which takes the form either of a paid leave from work until the child turns 3 or of a benefit to help cover the cost of a private nanny or registered childminder. This 'supplement' varies according to parents' income. Though strongly reminiscent of the previous schemes (APE, AFEAMA, AGED), the novelty here is that this new scheme includes special measures to encourage mothers on leave to work part-time and to re-renter the labour force – this is in line with the new (European) agenda of raising female employment rates.

Elder care: encouraging informal care. While France developed childcare policies quite early on, long-term care for the elderly only became a serious issue for policy-makers in the early 1990s. During the discussions on possible solutions to the long-term care issue, policy-makers on both the left and the right were widely agreed on a certain number of points. First, they were all concerned with limiting the cost of a new benefit and were generally agreed that raising social contributions to create a specific insurance scheme was not an option. They were also all generally agreed that it was important to provide incentives to families to keep on caring, both because such a policy would prove less expensive than providing formal care, but also because it has generally been considered that too much state intervention is harmful to society as it undermines the moral fibre of family solidarity (Morel 2006).

A means-tested social assistance benefit for people over 60, the Specific Dependency Benefit (PSD) was set up in 1997. The PSD faced severe criticism for a number of reasons, however, and reform soon appeared necessary.

A new Personalized Autonomy Allowance (APA) was implemented in 2002 to remedy some of the main problems identified with the PSD. Although it remains a social assistance scheme managed at the regional level, it guarantees the same benefit levels everywhere in France. Dependency criteria have been extended, which has considerably increased the number of people eligible for this benefit. The benefit is no longer means-tested but the amount is reduced progressively for beneficiaries whose resources are above a certain ceiling (€949/month in 2002). Finally, the state can no longer reclaim some of the cost on the person's legacy. As with the PSD, the benefit can be used to remunerate an unemployed relative – other than the spouse – who provides care.

This new measure has proven very successful and the number of recipients increased rapidly, leading to higher than expected costs. This prompted the right-wing government to introduce new reforms in 2003 to reduce the cost of the benefit, most dramatically by lowering to €623 the income ceiling below which one is entitled to full benefits.

By providing a cash benefit to the dependent elderly, the idea has been to provide dependent persons with the means to decide on the type of care they want – i.e. to promote free choice – but also to develop low-skilled, low-paid, personal service jobs by transforming the dependent elderly into private employers.

Care as a source of (low-skilled, low-paid) employment. This has proven quite a successful employment strategy: between 1994 and 2004, the number of people employed in personal service jobs (home help, cleaning, childcare) almost doubled, from 639,000 up to 1.26 million. However, these consist mainly of short, part-time jobs, and the great majority of workers have little or no qualifications (CES 2007); wages are consequently quite low.

Thus, whether for young children or for the elderly, care policy reforms in France have increasingly sought to boost employment – albeit low-skilled and low-paid employment – by providing cash benefits to families to become private employers. Such a strategy has been further reinforced by the introduction in 2005 of a universal service cheque to enable people to hire the help they need, and thus to create employment.

Belgium: breaking away from egalitarianism

Just like France, Belgium has gone from policies promoting public day-care services to give all children an equal start in life to policies supporting more private and family forms of care. Also as in France, this shift in policy has been presented as a way to promote 'free choice' for families.

Time to care. In an effort to synthesize both the Socialist demands for more gender equality through the development of childcare services, and the more traditional familialism of the Social Christians who were calling for more support to mothers (especially in poorer families) who chose to remain at home, the Social Christian–Socialist coalition promised, in 1968, to develop public services for the family to promote mothers' labour force participation while simultaneously proposing a childrearing allowance (the ASP – *Allocation socio-pédagogique*) to be paid to mothers who cared for their own children – an allowance which would have effectively discouraged the labour force participation of mothers. The justification for voting these two seemingly contradictory measures was, in the words of a Social Christian senator, to 'respect fully parents' liberty of conscience. They must be able to decide whether they will use a day nursery or they will raise their children themselves' (quoted in Marques-Pereira and Paye 2001: 65).

Although the parliament had passed this reform, the ASP was quickly amended due to budgetary constraints linked to the economic crisis, and was never implemented. The idea was not dropped altogether, however, and was eventually implemented in 1984 as part of a wider leave scheme, the

Voluntary Career Break. This scheme is more than just a parental leave scheme, as workers can request a career break for any reason. It allows workers to take a paid, partial or full-time leave from their job with no risk of being laid off, for a period of six months to a year, renewable for a total of up to five years. The worker on leave must be replaced by another worker receiving full unemployment benefits. The leave benefit is paid at the lowest unemployment insurance rate, that is, the one available to an unemployed worker who is cohabiting (Marques-Pereira and Paye 2001).

Although the break can be taken for any reason, the government and the majority of parliamentarians assumed that the major use would be for childrearing, family reasons, or other personal reasons. The Voluntary Career Break has thus been widely seen as a form of parental leave. Yet this scheme's primary objective was not to help families reconcile work and family life. More fundamentally, it was an attempt to fight the situation of economic crisis and high unemployment that prevailed in Belgium in the early 1980s by redistributing work via part-time employment and flexible working time (*ibid.*).

This measure generated a fair amount of consensus, not least as it was presented under the gender-neutral rhetoric of 'free choice' – the choice to temporarily withdraw from the labour market to care for one's children. A few observers did note that it would probably be mostly women who would ask for the leave, which would constitute an additional labour market disadvantage for them since employers might prefer to hire men in order to avoid such interruptions, but such concerns with gender equality were strongly overshadowed by unemployment concerns. That it would be mostly women who would/could take such a leave was in fact reinforced by the type and low level of benefit paid to the person on leave: being based on the insurance rate paid to an unemployed worker who is cohabiting, it assumes that the person on leave has a (male) breadwinner to rely on.

Developing personal service jobs. The creation of what could effectively be considered as a parental leave benefit was accompanied in the mid-1980s by other measures in the field of childcare that also served to 'redomesticate' childcare. In order to promote more 'free choice', the agency in charge of financing childcare services decided to subsidize home-care services provided by 'day-care mothers', i.e. care provided by childminders in their own homes, alongside the day nurseries. Tax deductions were introduced in 1987, leading to a tenfold increase in the number of day-care childminders in the French Community between 1985 and 1992 (Marques-Pereira and Paye 2001). Since then, the bulk of state subsidies for childcare has gone to this type of childcare and by 1996, there were twice as many places available with day-care mothers as in nurseries in Flanders (Kremer 2002).

Here one can see evident parallels with what was done in France during the same period both to combat 'black' labour and to raise employment levels. Such an approach, although couched in the rhetoric of 'free choice', was again guided by labour-market concerns and, just as in France, marked a notable shift away from the principle of giving all children an equal start in life through the provision of good-quality public childcare. The quality of these private forms of childcare has in fact been a source of debate in Belgium, as unlike workers employed in day nurseries, day-care mothers require no formal training (Marques-Pereira and Paye 2001).

Furthermore, these day-care mothers receive very low wages and pay very little tax or insurance contributions, and they have to rely on a male breadwinner for social rights such as pensions or sickness benefits (Kremer 2002). Day-care mothers therefore constitute a much cheaper and more flexible care workforce for the state than formal day-care institution workers.

Just as in France, this subsidized 'freedom of choice' has allowed higher-income women to combine work and family as they have been able to benefit from tax deductions when hiring a day-care mother, whereas low-income women have had to rely on the Career Break scheme to care for their children themselves. This redomestication of care has thus taken different forms for different women.

Policy developments since the late 1990s have been couched in a more gender-egalitarian language, although the design of these measures does nothing to modify gender roles. Thus, since 1998, each parent is entitled to three months of paid leave as an individual entitlement, but the benefit is flat-rate and paid at a very low level, thus effectively discouraging male take-up. The increase in 2001 from three to ten days of paternity leave is in line with policy developments across Europe.

In 2001, a more flexible time credit scheme replaced the previous system of career breaks. It includes the right to a specific leave (e.g. parental leave or leave to care for an ill family member). The underlying idea of this new time credit is that men and women must be given the opportunity to reconcile a professional career with family responsibilities, thanks to flexible entry and exit options.

The career break or time credit scheme has thus been designed in such a way that the same measure can be used to care for children or/and to care for dependent elderly relatives. The Flemish Community also developed a more specific (but modest) flat-rate care insurance for the dependent elderly in 2001 (Rottiers 2005).

Germany: towards a modified male-breadwinner model?

Germany has long promoted a strong male-breadwinner model, and strong family obligations. Until recently, mothers of small children were not expected to work and childcare facilities for children below 3 have traditionally been scarce (Lewis 1992; Ostner 1998). Some childcare facilities have developed for pedagogical reasons for children over 3 (kindergartens), but these only take children for half days, which means that mothers have tended to work part-time. More recently, new policies have developed to encourage women's labour market participation and to tackle Germany's low fertility problem.

The 1980s and early 1990s: keeping mothers and children at home. In 1986, the government introduced a childrearing allowance (*Erziehungsgeld*) and a parental leave (*Erziehungsurlaub*) as part of a 'family package', which compensated for some of the cuts in family benefits and tax allowances that had been made between 1982 and 1985. The parental leave enables parents to take a three-year leave from work to care for their children until the age of 3, but the childrearing allowance is only paid out during the first two years. It is a flat-rate benefit worth approximately €300 a month for a duration of two years. After the first six months, the benefit is reduced according to income. The parent on leave can continue to work for up to 19 hours a week, with no reduction in benefit. These schemes were introduced against a backdrop of rapidly increasing unemployment, and one of the central motives for introducing these schemes was to encourage women to return to their caring function and to withdraw from the labour market (Schiersmann 1991). That it was specifically women who were thus encouraged to withdraw from the labour market is evident from the very low level of the benefit.

In the early 1970s, less than 1 per cent of all children below the age of 3 and about 30 per cent of children between the ages of 3 and 6 had access to publicly financed childcare (Seeleib-Kaiser 2004). These figures remained stable for over two decades, and it was only in the early 1990s that childcare provision started to increase.

A timid expansion of childcare facilities in the 1990s. In 1992, the Children and Youth Act established a right to childcare for children aged 3 to 6, which was to come into effect in 1996. However, no federal government funds were made available for implementation, and no specification was made of the types of places (full-time or part-time) that were to be made available. Due to financial difficulties at the local level, implementation was delayed until 1999. Between 1992 and 1999, some 600,000 kindergarten places were nonetheless created (Evers *et al.* 2005).

Childcare coverage also improved a little for children under 3, and by 1996 there were 7.5 per cent of children under 3 attending publicly financed day care (*Krippen*) (Rostgaard and Fridberg 1998). This rise in figures, however, is not only due to greater investment in the West, but mostly to the reunification, since coverage levels were much higher in the East (even if they began to decline after the reunification).

A driving factor behind the new interest in childcare provision was the sharp drop in fertility rates. In 1995, fertility rates had plummeted to a very low 1.25 and this was increasingly perceived as a result of the lack of childcare facilities, since women were forced to choose between working and having children. Another key factor was the development of a discourse on gender equality at the EU level, which had an impact on the political debates in Germany. By 1998, supporting families, both financially and through the development of childcare provision, had become a major issue in the Social Democratic Party's election campaign.

New gender norms, new role for the state? Nowadays, mothers of children over 3 are expected to work, at least part-time. Full-time labour force participation has not yet become the norm, however, and the day-care places that were created during the 1990s are mostly for part-time care. By 1998, only one in four children aged 3 to 6 had access to a full-time place (Evers *et al.* 2005).

The development of childcare facilities slowed down after 1999, but in recent years the government has shown renewed interest in the development of childcare facilities for children under 3, including for full-time care (*ibid.*). For the first time, and due to the limited financial capacity of the *Länder*, the federal government has promised financial support for the development of childcare facilities, thus marking a break from the long-standing principle of subsidiarity.

A revised Federal Childcare Payment and Parental Leave Act came into force in 2001, allowing both parents to take parental leave at the same time, extending the permitted level of part-time work during parental leave from 19 to 30 hours a week, and giving parents the opportunity to take the third year of parental leave at any time until the eighth birthday of a child.

Most spectacularly, Germany introduced in January 2007 a parental leave benefit system in line with the Scandinavian model. The existing means-tested parental leave benefit has been replaced by a wage-dependent benefit for a period of one year, paid at 67 per cent of previous net income (up to €1,800). In order to encourage fathers to take a more active part in caring for their children, families can obtain an extra two months if both parents take some leave.

Developing low-paid, low-skilled carers for the elderly. With respect to elder care, Germany voted a compulsory, universal long-term care insurance (*Soziale Pflegeversicherung*) in 1994 (Götting *et al.* 1994; Morel 2006). Despite much discussion regarding the form and financing of the measure that was to be implemented, all political parties and actors involved had agreed on a few important points from the beginning. The first point was that home care should take precedence over care in nursing homes. Second, the scheme was not to cover the cost of room and board in nursing homes, nor, in fact, the whole cost of care. Third, time spent in formal care work deserved credit within the pension scheme. The idea was to make caring more attractive so that caregivers, especially women of working age, would continue to care rather than enter the labour market. Indeed, the reform was by no means intended to reduce the quantity of care provided informally.

Benefits are neither means-tested nor income-related; the amount depends on the level of dependency and on whether the person receives institutional or domiciliary care. In the case of domiciliary care (70.3 per cent of long-term care insurance beneficiaries), recipients can choose between cash benefits, in-kind benefits or a combination of both. The cash benefit is paid to the dependent person, who can use it to remunerate a family member or other informal carer. When the insurance scheme was introduced, 84 per cent of persons receiving domiciliary support chose cash benefits only but this proportion had decreased to 72.6 per cent in 2001 (BMGS 2003), meaning that there is a progressive move towards services and a combination of cash and in-kind benefits, although surveys still report a greater preference for family-provided care (Lundsgaard 2005).

Domiciliary care services have rapidly expanded since the creation of this insurance scheme, but these services have remained low-skilled and low-paid. According to Ostner (1998), the absence of highly defined professional standards in the field of social care can be read as part of an important strategy against unemployment, as politicians of all persuasions perceive these cheap service jobs to be an important source of employment.

Netherlands: the 'combination scenario' as a part-time male-breadwinner model

It is in the Netherlands that the male-breadwinner ideal has been strongest and most long-lasting. Indeed, until the late 1980s, women's participation in the labour market was particularly low (below 40 per cent). Since the 1990s, however, women have worked in ever-greater numbers, and female participation rates are now much higher in the Netherlands than in our other three countries. This massive entry of women on the labour market has been made possible mostly thanks to policies that favour part-time and flexible employment. Indeed, 75 per cent of women only work part-time (Eurostat 2007).

Developing childcare facilities through the workplace. As in Germany, the principle of subsidiarity has been very strong, and childcare services have remained very underdeveloped. In 1988, only 2 per cent of children used subsidized childcare (Kremer 2002). The idea that the family should be the prime provider of care for children has remained well entrenched in the Netherlands, and even today it is considered best for children to attend part-time care only (Knijn 2001).

Childcare policies only began to develop in the 1990s, following a report by the Scientific Council for Government Policy from 1990. The report underlined the large waste of human capital due to women's inactivity and argued that this contributed to the Dutch welfare state crisis. In order to ensure a sustainable welfare state, the government argued that it was necessary to invest in female labour market participation, and thus in childcare (Kremer 2002).

The state therefore introduced a Stimulative Measure on Childcare in 1990, which aimed to get employers to buy 'company places' for their employees in childcare facilities. These places are co-financed by the state, employers and employees, but the contribution by the state decreased from 53 to 33 per cent of the total cost between 1990 and 1998. Parents' contribution also decreased over this period, from 34 to 19 per cent, while employers' share has substantially increased, from 11 to 45 per cent of the cost (Knijn 2001). Despite this, parental fees remain high and most children attending day care therefore come from higher-income groups (Rostgaard and Fridberg 1998; Knijn 2001). This inequality is reinforced by the fact that employers can decide which category of their employees they buy day-care places for. Childcare provision is thus quite socially segmented, once again testifying to the stratifying dimension of this welfare regime.

Parallel to this development, the number of private childminders has also increased rapidly. While children making use of some form of childcare increased from 5 to 15 per cent between 1987 and 1999, the proportion cared for by a private childminder increased from 9 to 31 per cent during the same period (Knijn 2001).

The part-time miracle. Yet expansion in day-care provision has not been the only change in care arrangements to facilitate the reconciliation of work and family life. More important in this respect have been the various policies to promote part-time work. The promotion of part-time work was seen as a way to share work and therefore to combat unemployment. It was also portrayed as a way to allow parents to combine work and care, the idea being to move towards a model where both parents worked and cared part-time – the so-called 'combination scenario'.

Since 2000, all employees are entitled to ask their employer to switch to part-time work. This has been used by mothers of young children mostly as a means to reconcile work and family life, in the face of still insufficient day-care facilities. Today, the Netherlands has both the highest female labour-market participation rate in continental Europe (67.7 per cent), but also the highest level of female part-time work (75 per cent) (Eurostat 2007). However, unlike other countries, part-time work in the Netherlands enjoys strong protections.

Other measures have also been created to increase work flexibility and to respond to the needs of the family. The Work and Care Act of 2001 includes measures offering workers the possibility to put aside part of their salary in order to finance temporary breaks for family reasons.

In 2004, political discussion focused on the government's plans to introduce a 'lifespan leave' arrangement, giving workers greater scope to save for periods of time off during their careers. Care, education and training, leisure time and early retirement are all included and mutually exchangeable in this proposal. The various types of care leave already in existence, combined in the Work and Care Act, will coexist with this new arrangement. Financially, the proposal is directed at reducing government expenditure by giving employees more responsibility and choice in whether to save for time off for care or for early retirement, or even not to save at all. The scope of this scheme may be somewhat limited, however, as only employees with a longer working history and with higher salaries can afford to save enough to take time off for any substantial leave period. For this reason, this measure is unlikely to be of any use as a source of parental leave because of the time necessary with the same employer to save up enough days (Morgan 2006).

Still a conservative welfare regime. Greater investment in childcare policies has not translated into any substantial transformation of the male-breadwinner model – and has not really sought to, either. Rather than invest more massively in day-care infrastructure, the choice was made to reduce working time for parents so that they can both work and care, i.e. care is still considered as something that should be carried out within the family. This policy was implemented without any real consideration of the likely gendered outcome of such a measure (Knijn 2001), the discourse focusing instead, as in the other three countries, on parents' free choice to decide how to arrange their work and family life.

Towards more informal care for the elderly? Surprisingly enough, although childcare provision has been quite underdeveloped, elder-care services on the other hand have long been much more extensive. In the Netherlands, elder care has mainly taken the form of institutional care, but this has begun to change over recent years with the attempt, as in most countries, to shift towards domiciliary care.

A new policy to support the purchase of private care was introduced, first on an experimental basis in 1991, and on a national level in 1995. This new policy takes the form of a 'personal budget', which entitles dependent people to a care allowance to be used for the purchase of care services, whether informal (from relatives) or professional. The introduction of this benefit is part of a move towards providing care recipients with greater freedom in deciding how best to service their needs. It is also, as in France and Germany, a way to offer some form of remuneration to informal carers – and thus to bring them into the labour market. The above-mentioned Work and Care Act of 2001 is another measure that has aimed at supporting informal care towards the elderly by giving it more recognition.

Conclusion: From Labour-shedding to Labour-cheapening

As we have seen, care policies in these four countries have been strongly shaped by, if not instrumentalized in, the ups and downs of Bismarckian labour market policies. From the mid-1980s to the late 1990s, when unemployment was high, women were either discouraged from entering the labour market (in Germany and the Netherlands) or, where women had already entered the labour market in the 1970s, as in France and Belgium, measures have been implemented to encourage their withdrawal from the labour market in order to 'free' jobs for men. A paradigmatic change can be said to have taken place in the mid- to late 1990s, however, and these countries have since then sought to raise female employment rates. This has prompted an expansion of care policies, and signalled a new role for the state, which is taking on new responsibilities. The principle of subsidiarity has thus become weaker, and has been replaced instead by the idea of promoting 'free choice'.

While the aim of raising female employment rates marks a departure from the traditional male-breadwinner model, the care policies that have been developed have nonetheless retained a conservative flavour. Care policies have not attempted to modify the traditional gendered division of labour in the household, and the family (or at least a family-like) environment is still considered as the best locus of care. Care policies have also tended to reproduce and reinforce the social stratification dimension of Bismarckian welfare systems: while low-income women have been encouraged to make use of long, low-paid parental leave schemes, and thus to withdraw from the labour market, various measures facilitating the use of private forms of childcare have been developed for higher-income women. Such measures have typically taken the form of tax deductions and social contribution exemptions, thus contributing to a cheapening of the cost of labour in the personal service sector. A similar strategy has prevailed in the field of elder care, where the dependent elderly are encouraged to buy private personal services.

Thus it appears that, rather than develop good-quality jobs in the public sector, as in the social democratic welfare states, Bismarckian countries are responding to the service sector needs of post-industrial economies by promoting low-skilled, low-paid jobs. Women's entry into the labour market has also enabled a certain flexibilization of the labour force, most notably through the introduction of temporary leave schemes and opportunities to reduce working hours, both of which have proven successful with women looking for ways to reconcile their professional life with their family duties. One can therefore argue that care policies have provided Bismarckian countries with a means to circumvent certain labour market rigidities specific to these systems.

Acknowledgements

I would like to thank Kimberly Morgan and Mary Daly as well as the participants in the research project 'The Politics of Reforms in Bismarckian Welfare Systems' for comments.

Notes

1. Due to space constraints, elder-care policies are treated more succinctly in this article. The article by Da Roit, Le Bihan and Österle in this issue provides a more detailed account of these policies and their link with employment strategies.
2. She is here referring to the proposed modifications of both the parental leave scheme and of the AGED and AFEAMA, which we will discuss below.

References

Afsa, C. (1998), L'allocation parentale d'éducation: entre politique familiale et politique pour l'emploi, *INSEE Première*, 569.
Anttonen, A. and Sipilä, J. (1996), European social care services: is it possible to identify models? *Journal of European Social Policy*, 6, 2: 87–100.
BMGS (Bundesministerium für Gesundheit und Soziale Sicherung) (2003), 'Zahlen und Fakten zur Pflegeversicherung' and 'Soziale Pflegeversicherung. Leistungsempfänger nach Altersgruppen und Pflegestufen am 31.12.2002'. Available at: http://www.bmgs.bund.de
Bussemaker, J. and van Kersbergen, K. (1999), Contemporary social-capitalist welfare states and gender inequality. In D. Sainsbury (ed.), *Gender and Welfare State Regimes*, Oxford: Oxford University Press, pp. 15–47.
CES (2007), *Le développement des services à la personne*, Paris: Conseil Economique et Social.
CNAF (2003), Etat des lieux des prestations petite enfance avant la mise en place de la prestation d'accueil du jeune enfant, *L'essentiel*, 16.
Daly, M. (1997), Welfare states under pressure: cash benefits in European welfare states over the last ten years, *Journal of European Social Policy*, 7, 2: 129–46.
Daly, M. and Lewis, J. (2000), The concept of social care and the analysis of contemporary welfare states, *British Journal of Sociology*, 51, 2: 281–98.
DREES (2004), L'accueil collectif et en crèches familiales des enfants de moins de 6 ans en 2003, *Etudes et résultats*, 356.

Nathalie Morel

Esping-Andersen, G. (1996), Welfare states without work: the impasse of labour shedding and familialism in Continental European social policy. In G. Esping-Andersen (ed.), *Welfare States in Transition*, London: Sage, pp. 66–87.

Esping-Andersen, G. (1999), *Social Foundations of Post-industrial Economies*, Oxford: Oxford University Press.

Eurostat (2007), Employment (main characteristics and rates) – Annual Averages. Available at: http://epp.eurostat.ec.europa.eu/

Evers, A., Lewis, J. and Riedel, B. (2005), Developing child-care provision in England and Germany: problems of governance, *Journal of European Social Policy*, 15, 3: 195–209.

Fagnani, J. (1995), L'Allocation Parentale d'Education: effets pervers et ambiguïtés d'une prestation, *Droit Social*, 3: 287–95.

Fagnani, J. (1998), Lacunes, contradictions et incohérences des mesures de conciliation travail/famille: bref bilan critique, *Droit Social*, 6: 596–602.

Götting, U., Haug, K. and Hinrichs, K. (1994), The long road to long-term care insurance in Germany, *Journal of Public Policy*, 14, 3: 285–309.

Jenson, J. and Sineau, M. (2001), France: reconciling Republican equality with 'freedom of choice'. In J. Jenson and M. Sineau (eds), *Who Cares? Women's Work, Childcare, and Welfare State Redesign*, Toronto: University of Toronto Press, pp. 88–117.

Knijn, T. (2001), Care work: innovations in the Netherlands. In M. Daly (ed.), *Care Work: The Quest for Security*, Geneva: ILO, pp. 159–74.

Kremer, M. (2002), The illusion of free choice: ideals of care and child care policy in the Flemish and Dutch welfare states. In S. Michel and R. Mahon (eds), *Child Care Policy at the Crossroads*, London: Routledge, pp. 113–42.

Leprince, F. (2003), *L'accueil des jeunes enfants en France*, Rapport pour le Haut Conseil de la population et de la famille.

Lewis, J. (1992), Gender and the development of welfare regimes, *Journal of European Social Policy*, 2, 3: 159–73.

Lundsgaard, J. (2005), *Consumer Direction and Choice in Long-term Care for Older Persons. Including Payments for Informal Care: How Can It Help Improve Care Outcomes, Employment and Fiscal Sustainability?* OECD Health Working Papers, 20, Paris: OECD.

Marques-Pereira, B. and Paye, O. (2001), Belgium: the vices and virtues of pragmatism. In J. Jenson and M. Sineau (eds), *Who Cares? Women's Work, Childcare, and Welfare State Redesign*, Toronto: University of Toronto Press, pp. 109–40.

Martin, C., Math, A. and Renaudat, E. (1998), Caring for the very young children and dependent elderly people in France: towards a commodification of social care? In J. Lewis (ed.), *Gender, Social Care and Welfare State Restructuring in Europe*, Aldershot: Ashgate, pp. 139–74.

Morel, N. (2006), Providing coverage against new social risks in Bismarckian welfare states: the case of long term care. In K. Armingeon and G. Bonoli (eds), *The Politics of Postindustrial Welfare States*, London, Routledge, pp. 227–47.

Morgan, K. (2002), Does anyone have a 'libre choix'? Subversive liberalism and the politics of French child care policy. In S. Michel and R. Mahon (eds), *Child Care Policy at the Crossroads*, London: Routledge, pp. 143–67.

Morgan, K. (2006), Les politiques du temps de l'enfant en Europe occidentale: tendances et implications, *Recherches et Prévisions*, 83: 29–43.

Orloff, A. (2006), From maternalism to 'employment for all': state policies to promote women's employment across the affluent democracies. In J. Levy (ed.), *The State after Statism*, Cambridge, MA: Harvard University Press, pp. 230–68.

Ostner, I. (1998), The politics of care policies in Germany. In J. Lewis (ed.), *Gender, Social Care and Welfare State Restructuring in Europe*, Aldershot: Ashgate, pp. 111–37.

Rostgaard, T. and Fridberg, T. (1998), *Caring for Children and Older People: A Comparison of European Policies and Practices*, Danish National Institute of Social Research 98:20, Copenhagen.

Rottiers, S. (2005), The case of the Belgian care insurance. Paper presented at the Young Researchers workshop 'The Governance of Social Policy in the New Europe', Bath University, 1–2 April.

Sainsbury, D. (1996), *Gender, Equality and Welfare States*, Cambridge: Cambridge University Press.

Schiersmann, C. (1991), Germany: recognizing the value of child rearing. In S. Kamerman and A. Kahn (eds), *Child Care, Parental Leave, and the Under 3s: Policy Innovation in Europe*, New York: Auburn House, pp. 51–79.

Seeleib-Kaiser, M. (2004), Germany: still a conservative welfare state? Paper presented at the 2004 Conference of Europeanists, Chicago, 11–13 March.

6

Activation as a Common Framework for Social Policies towards Lone Parents

Trudie Knijn, Claude Martin and Jane Millar

Lone-parent families have always been considered as a 'social risk'. Before the development of modern welfare states lone parents depended on their families or on charity, bearing the risk of morally based exclusion, arbitrary treatment and rigid social control. During the heyday of the 'protective' welfare state in the second half of the twentieth century, arbitrariness declined but lone parents continued to be regarded as an exceptional family type, deviating from the regular breadwinner–housewife model (Knijn 1994; Millar 1996; Lewis 1997; Skevik 2006). However, normative assumptions regarding family structure are now becoming less important in most European countries. Under the new welfare ideology the key normative assumption is that all adults should be in the labour market, even if that means precarious employment (Lewis and Giullari 2005). The new welfare ideology emphasizes full employment and promotes 'active' social policies to achieve this.

In this article,[1] we compare recent social policy reforms for lone parents in three national contexts: France, the Netherlands and the UK. Each of these countries is promoting employment for lone parents, as part of wider welfare state reforms. The main aim of this comparison is to explore whether there are significant differences in activation policies for lone parents between the two continental welfare regimes and the liberal welfare regime of the UK. We thus describe the main reforms of the past decade or so, and seek to highlight similarities and differences. We start with a brief outline of the three national policy trajectories from the social protection model to the current commitment to employment activation. Then we examine the different instruments of these policies and their impact.

From Social Protection to Employment Activation

Under the male breadwinner–female carer model, support for lone parents usually varies according to their previous marital status, with widows treated differently from other lone parents. In the UK, the Beveridge welfare state of the immediate postwar years introduced national insurance benefits for widows and for widowed mothers which provided lifelong support after the death of a husband, but which could be supplemented by earnings without loss of pension.[2] Other lone parents were reliant upon social assistance benefits which were lower, means-tested and paid until the youngest child reached the age of 16 or 18 if still in full-time education. In the Netherlands, legislation in the late 1950s and early 1970s transformed the previously decentralized and strongly personalized system of poor relief but maintained a clear distinction between the deserving and the undeserving poor (Nelson 1990). Benefits for widows were paid for by compulsory and collectively paid workers' premiums and were much more generous than the social assistance benefits for divorced and never-married lone-mother households that were paid for by taxation. Widows could rely on the Dutch welfare state for a guaranteed income for the rest of their lives, while for other lone parents this guaranteed minimum income lasted until their children reached 18. Thus in both the Netherlands and the UK non-widowed lone parents were not expected or required to seek employment. Indeed, there was very little financial support available to people in employment, for either low-paid workers or part-time workers. For non-widowed lone parents, therefore, the options were either full-time employment or full-time receipt of benefits and, in the context of an ideology which emphasized the importance of maternal care for children, most 'chose' to stay at home rather than go out to work.

In France, the situation was rather different. The key reforms were in the mid-1970s, when family policies were reformed to support the more fragile households, including lone parents (Le Gall and Martin 1987; Martin 1995, 1997a, 1997b; Martin-Papineau 2001). A new allowance, the *allocation de parent isolé* (API, or lone-parent allowance), was created in 1976 to guarantee, for a limited period of time (one year or until the youngest child reaches 3 years of age), a minimum income for all the lone-parent families whose resources were under a predefined threshold. It concerned all lone parents, including fathers. A widow's insurance was introduced in 1980, financed by an employee's contribution and provided on a means-tested basis. The API reform took place in a specific context of creating different minimum incomes[3] and the political debate of the time defended this measure as a means to facilitate a 'free choice' between work and life at home or even to pay a 'maternal salary', so that there would be no social discrimination between women who worked and those who devoted themselves exclusively to domestic and caring tasks. The political wish to support lone mothers to care for their young children was explicit.

By the mid-1980s, however, all three systems were coming under increasing criticism, not least as the number of recipients increased. Issues of dependency and disincentives to work became tied up with the appearance of the theme of 'new poverty'. Concern about 'dependence on welfare' appeared in all three countries, and especially in the UK and in France. In the UK there was much negative rhetoric about lone parents in the 1980s, when they were portrayed as selfish and immoral in placing their own needs above those of their children (Kiernan *et al.* 1998). Lone parents were also central to concerns about a supposed 'underclass' of welfare dependants –

non-working and non-contributing to society. In France, where the number of API beneficiaries rapidly exceeded the 53,000 initially anticipated, some argued that these policies were having 'perverse effects'. For example, these recipients were suspected of hiding the existence of a new partner or even of timing a new birth to continue to receive the benefit. The dependency of these lone parents – mostly lone mothers – on the state was firmly condemned, and proposals to abolish the API were made (Sullerot 1984; Dumont 1986). In spite of rising employment rates for French lone mothers in the 1990s, their rates still lagged behind those of married mothers. The numbers of lone parents on API and the *Revenu Minimum Insertion* (RMI) continued to rise, and there was increased concern about the potential lack of work incentives in these benefits. In the Netherlands there was also concern about rising numbers on benefits and issues of cohabitation fraud. Lone parenthood was increasingly perceived as 'a self-selected life style which no longer requires social protection' (Bussemaker *et al.* 1997: 116).

There was also a more positively phrased discourse that stressed the importance of independence and emancipation through participation in employment, and the application of this to all adults. Lone parents were thus just to be treated, generally speaking, in the same way as other social assistance recipients. This has perhaps been taken up most strongly in the Netherlands, where activation for lone mothers is part of the total restructuring of the Dutch welfare state into what Gilbert (2002) calls an 'enabling state' that promotes 'self-responsibility'. The government has argued that lone mothers should be treated as ordinary citizens, that motherhood is not any longer an argument for not participating in the labour market. In 1996 lone parents with children above the age of 5 years were required to take up paid work and in 2004 this work requirement was extended to all lone parents, as discussed in more detail below.

In the UK, the Labour government elected in 1997 made a strong anti-poverty argument for focusing on paid employment. As the welfare reform Green Paper put it, 'work is at the heart of our welfare reform programme ... paid work is the best route out of poverty' (DSS 1998: 3). Lone parents, alongside long-term unemployed, young people, and sick and disabled people, were the key target groups. In France the goal of maintaining a system of minimum income while also sustaining work incentives was central to welfare reform debates, as stated in two official reports at the end of the 1990s (Joint-Lambert 1998; Belorgey 2000). When the Raffarin right-wing government came to power in 2002, the issue of reforming the minimum incomes was central on the political agenda, including proposals to increase work requirements for lone parents.

To sum up, we can state that, by the mid- to late 1990s, the policy goals of these three countries were converging on the objective of getting lone-parent families back to work. These policies are part of wider welfare restructuring, and lone parents are increasingly seen as similar to, rather than different from, other social assistance recipients. Activation is promoted as being in the best interests of those affected, including lone parents. Thus the role of the state is to facilitate employment but also to strengthen work requirements as necessary.

New Instruments for Activation

In this section, we focus on the specific activation policies and instruments for lone parents that have been introduced during the last decade. For each country in turn we provide a description of the nature of these, how they have been implemented, and what impact they have had upon lone parents.

France

Activation programmes. Promoting activation policies has been the main trend of French welfare reforms during the last decade. This concerns all the fragile categories of the population, including minimum income recipients. Faced with the challenge of rising unemployment, the successive right-wing governments of Raffarin (May 2002 to May 2005) and de Villepin (May 2005 to May 2007) have intensified activation policies, with the objective of reducing both the high level of unemployment and the number of recipients of minimum incomes. To reduce the cost of unemployment, a reform of the insurance scheme was implemented in January 2006, including stricter rules of entitlement to obtain an allowance and reductions in the duration of the compensation. With the latter, according to the left-wing syndicate (CGT), about 100,000 unemployed people will see the duration of their allowance reduced by half (from 23 to 12 months). On the other hand, a strong focus is being put on measures to help them come back on the labour market (access to training and qualifications, *validation des acquis* – validation of experience – etc.).

The global orientation of the reforms corresponds to the 'make work pay' philosophy, generally attributed to the UK's 'Third Way'. It has two dimensions: first to subsidize employers by reducing their social security contributions as an incentive to offer low-qualified jobs, but second, to subsidize at the same time employees to encourage them to accept these jobs, by an increase in social transfers and/or by the possibility to cumulate income support with a salary. However, most of the financial support goes to the employer (80 per cent) rather than to the employee (20 per cent). The total reduction in employers' social security contributions corresponds to about 20 billion euros in 2005, with about 16 billion of this relating to tax exemptions for low-paid jobs.

The specific instruments of these reforms include the employment premium (*prime pour l'emploi*), tax credits, and the welfare to work incentives for minimum income recipients, called *mécanismes d'intéressement*. The *mécanisme d'intéressement*, which allows minimum income recipients to cumulate a salary with the RMI or API, was reformed in 2001, to allow the minimum income to be paid alongside salary for six months (Rastier and Maingueneau 2006). For the following nine months, half of the salary is taken into account. Two further measures have also been introduced, which require (in principle at least) minimum income recipients to take up work. For the *revenu minimum d'activité*, created in 2004, this is in the market sector, for 6 or 12 months, at a minimum of 20 hours per week, paid at the minimum wage. For the *contrat d'avenir*, created in March 2006, this is in the voluntary sector[4] for 24 months for an average of 26 hours per week. These measures are intended to provoke a return to employment for minimum income recipients. By September 2006, there were 44,700 people on the *contrat d'avenir* and 9,200 people on the *revenu minimum d'activité* (RMA). In total, the participants in the various different schemes (*mesures d'intéressement*, RMA and *contrat d'avenir*) amounted to about 158,300 people in September 2006, with an increase over the previous twelve months of about 8.8 per cent.

Individualized and decentralized management. To implement these reforms, some non-financial incentives have been introduced, which correspond to a new individualized management: called *politique d'accompagnement*. All minimum income recipients receive a notification from the social services to take stock of their situation, but with the offer of training, etc. On the one hand, this individualized management acts as a control and in some cases, when a recipient does not reply to these notifications, he/she may be struck off and lose the allowance. On the other hand, it is a support for the beneficiaries in order to help them to leave the scheme by accessing the labour market and a salary. In any case, it emphasizes the individual responsibility of the recipients.

The decentralization of the RMI since December 2003 reinforced this perspective. The explicit objective was to increase the efficiency of the minimum income scheme, to facilitate the individualized follow-up of each beneficiary and to reinforce the work obligation. But it has had different impacts in terms of work obligation depending on the local authorities, creating important local variations (Le Bihan *et al.* 2006). The same orientation has been implemented for API beneficiaries by the administration of the *caisses d'allocations familiales*. Each recipient receives a notification in order to be informed of his/her rights but also to control conditions of access to the allowance (level of income, absence of a partner). Again, the aim is to control but also to help and sometimes (no national data on this point) to a striking-off. In October 2006, a new committee was created: the *Comité national de lutte contre la fraude en matière de protection sociale*, whose role is precisely to reinforce the controls in the social security administrations, with a specific focus on income support recipients, considered as at-risk users (Warin 2006).

The impact. For the minimum income recipient, the impact is still relatively limited. The number of API or RMI recipients, whether they are lone parents or not, who also receive a salary has been more or less stable from 2000 to 2005, at 12 to 13 per cent for RMI (about 143,000 people) and 5 to 6 per cent for API (about 11,500 people) (Nivière *et al.* 2006). For API recipients, it is necessary to distinguish between two main types of situation – what the administration calls the 'long' or 'short' API. Long API refers to women who are pregnant or whose younger child is less than 3 years old; short API to those having older children, receiving the allowance for a maximum of a year, after a separation, a divorce or the death of a partner. The percentage of recipients of the 'short API' who cumulate a salary and this minimum income is 8.5 per cent, almost double that of the 'long API' recipients (4.4 per cent). This reflects, first, the problem of reconciliation between work and childcare for those who have a young child, including the problem of atypical working hours which compromise access to public childcare arrangements (Le Bihan and Martin 2004) and, second, the young age of these mothers, who are more often still training or studying.

The Netherlands

Activation programmes. In general, lone mothers on social assistance rely on the same measures and programmes for activation and reintegration as do other people on social assistance. Important policy measures in this context are activating measures – such as sharpening work obligations, stricter sanctions for not meeting work obligations, a redefinition of what constitutes a 'suitable job', tax reductions for working people, etc. Having care responsibilities for (young) children may be treated as a 'social reason' for individual exemptions, and financial incentives like premiums are offered for finishing a teaching programme considered necessary for reintegration, for accepting a job, or for being engaged in voluntary work in the context of social activation.

Concerning work obligation, there has been some recognition of the need for support to enable lone mothers to combine paid work with care, and various measures have been introduced or extended. First, a tax credit was introduced for low-wage households, which also applied to part-time workers. Second, care leave includes maternity leave (16 weeks around the birth of the child, paid leave) and both parents have the right to unpaid parental leave (at a maximum of half of their working time during a period of 6 months) if they have worked for the same employer for a minimum of one year. Employers are not obliged to pay the parent during this leave, but are stimulated to do so by a tax award if they pay at least 70 per cent of the minimum wage to which their employee is entitled. Third, since 2003 employees have the right to ask their employer to either increase or reduce their working hours. Fourth, the provision of childcare has been privatized since 2005, in order to improve quality and to control costs. Working lone parents' costs for childcare are reimbursed with a tax credit if their income is less than 130 per cent of the minimum wage. Welfare recipients with children who participate in a recognized reintegration trajectory are entitled to childcare. Lone parents returning to paid work afterwards are entitled to a reimbursement of 90 per cent of the costs of childcare, although this will be reduced to 10 per cent in 2008 (SZW 2005).

Individualized and decentralized management. The so-called 'individualization principle' – the adjustment of provision to individual need – has always been a central feature of the Dutch social assistance system. During the last decade, decentralization has been strongly pursued because transforming welfare states into active welfare states is also seen as a process of activating the institutional context of the management, implementation and delivery of these policies. This has meant considerable local variation in provisions and outcomes. Studies evaluating the implementation of the first transformation of the social assistance policy at the end of the 1990s found rather large inter-municipal differences in the compensation of childcare costs, part-time work premiums and work-income disregards (Knijn and Van Wel 1999;

Engelen *et al.* 1999). More generally, municipalities may adopt different strategies in activating lone parents on Social Assistance and have substantial discretion in deciding whether or not lone parents should have work obligations.

The impact. Two studies, by Knijn and Van Wel (1999) and by the Dutch General Audit Office (TK 2003), describe the results of the activation of lone parents on Social Assistance and give some insight into what the policy reforms described above mean in practice. Both studies conclude that the number of (partial) exemptions from work obligations is high as a whole, and even more so for lone parents. Since 1996, the proportion of Social Assistance clients fully released from work obligations has increased to about 50 per cent in some municipalities. Also, the General Audit Office's report found that 62 per cent of lone parents on Social Assistance were made an activation offer between 1999 and September 2002. Lone parents with children under 5 are strongly represented among those to whom no offer has been made. In the case of these lone parents, many municipalities only take action when these parents ask for it: a quite 'narrow' interpretation of the voluntary character of activation for this group. Finally, the report showed that, over a period of 14 months in 2001 and 2002, about 20 per cent of lone parents left Social Assistance but 70 per cent of the lone parents that started work in this period are still partly dependent on Social Assistance. Apparently, these lone parents do not earn sufficient income from work to exceed the Social Assistance level. These figures reflect the fact that many lone parents, when engaged in paid work, work part-time and earn insufficient income to become fully independent from Social Assistance. This raises serious doubts regarding the feasibility of two closely connected objectives: fighting poverty, and raising the outflow from Social Assistance of lone parents to a similar level as the outflow of other Social Assistance recipients.

In view of the high poverty rates among lone-mother families, these are not minor considerations (Knijn and Van Berkel 2003). This is rather embarrassing when one takes into account the booming Dutch economy of the late 1990s and the rising prosperity among other categories of the population. Lone mothers' problems in getting out of poverty result from their reliance on part-time work and from the low educational level of most of them: they can only earn low wages in the highly segregated lowest segments of the labour market. Knijn and Van Wel (1999) showed that lone mothers who have at the most a lower vocational education will have to work at least 32 hours per week to earn an income that will make them independent of Social Assistance, while lone mothers with a higher professional or academic level can do so with 21 hours a week. Less educated lone mothers need to work full-time in order to have any financial advantage, and that is exactly what most of them do not want.

All in all, the report of the General Audit Office is quite critical in its conclusion concerning the activation efforts directed at lone parents on Social Assistance. It states that the national government has paid insufficient attention to steering the activation of lone parents, and has neglected to operationalize the comprehensive approach into concrete targets. Moreover, local policies, first, reflect ideological and political considerations and, second, are the consequence of the fact that local social offices decided autonomously on the work obligations while the budgets for social assistance were paid for nationally. Therefore, a reduction in beneficiaries had no financial implications for local budgets, until the introduction of the Work and Welfare Act (Wet Werk en Bijstand) in 2004. That new Act shifted the budgets for Social Assistance to the municipalities in order to force them to get more people out of welfare. If they are not successful, the municipalities will feel it in their purse.

The UK

Activation programmes. The 'New Deal' programmes were started in 1997 with the New Deal for Lone Parents (other programmes target young people, the long-term unemployed, older workers, sick and disabled people and partners of unemployed claimants). The programme for lone parents is voluntary and offers a mix of job-search support, training and practical help to make the transition to work. Lone parents receiving income support are required to attend 'work-focused' interviews at regular intervals and benefits can be reduced if these are not attended. But there is no requirement to participate in the New Deal or to be available for work. Financial support for employment has been substantial in order to increase financial incentives to work and reduce the risk of in-work poverty. These fiscal measures are central to the government aspiration to end child poverty and include the introduction of a national minimum wage, reductions in tax and national insurance contributions, and – most importantly – the introduction of a new system of income transfers to working people, in the form of tax credits. There were two tax credits introduced in 2003. The Child Tax Credit provides means-tested support to most (about nine in ten) families with children, with more help going to non-working and low-paid families. The Working Tax Credit is targeted on low-wage earners. Those with children are eligible if they work for 16 or more hours per week. Childless people may also be eligible but only if they are aged 25 and over and working at least 30 hours per week. The Working Tax Credit also includes a childcare costs element, which is restricted to single-earner couples and lone parents who are using formal care, and pays 70 per cent of costs up to a fixed maximum amount.

There have also been a series of general measures intended to promote 'work/life balance' – improvements to maternity and parental leave, rights to flexible working for parents of disabled children or those aged under 6 (Williams 2005; Millar 2006a). The national childcare strategy has the aim of increasing the provision of nursery education and other childcare services.

Individualized management and local pilot programmes. The New Deal programmes, including the New Deal for Lone Parents, represent an attempt to introduce more of a system of individual case management into the UK. The New Deal 'personal advisers' are central to this. Each participant in the programme is allocated a personal adviser, who provides individual advice and assistance, including help with job search, with working out the financial implications of working, with claiming in-work tax credits and benefits, with finding childcare, and with financial support to meet the costs of making the transition into work. There is some, but fairly limited, opportunity for education and training, but the main focus is on getting lone parents into employment (Millar 2006b). The personal advisers can offer some support in the first few months in work, to help lone parents to sustain employment.

There are also currently a number of pilot and demonstration projects which are extending the provision of support to help sustain employment. For example, lone parents in the 'New Deal Plus' areas can receive an in-work credit (which pays £40 per week for the first 12 months in work) and access an in-work emergency fund pilot (which provides discretionary financial support for specific needs in the first 60 days in work). The Employment Retention and Advancement Demonstration Project is testing the impact of the provision of financial incentives and job coaching in work on employment retention, and includes sole parents among the target groups (Hoggart et al. 2006; Dorsett et al. 2007).

The impact. The UK government has set a specific target that 70 per cent of lone parents should be employed by 2010. Their employment rates have been rising and are now at about 56 per cent, compared with about 42 per cent in 1994. By February 2007, about 748,000 sole parents had taken part in the New Deal for Lone Parents, and about 498,000 had moved into employment (DWP 2007a). The evaluation of the New Deal shows that it is effective in increasing employment, and also that it is generally popular with those lone parents who have taken part (Evans et al. 2003). Tax credits are being received by about one million employed lone mothers and the amounts involved are substantial. For example, in April 2006 a lone mother with one child under 11 working for 20 hours at the national minimum wage of £5.05 per hour would receive about £63 in Working Tax Credit, and about £44 in Child Tax Credit, as well as about £12 in housing and council tax benefit, and £17 in Child Benefit. Thus more than half of her income in work would come from state transfers. The financial help available from tax credits plays a very important role in helping lone parents to take up, and stay in, employment (Hirsch and Millar 2004). The total number of registered childcare places for children aged below 8 has doubled since 1997, and there are now about 1.2 million places, one for every five children. Further increases are planned over the next five to ten years (HM Treasury 2006).

Gregg et al. (2006) review the evidence on the direct impact of policy on lone-parent employment. They conclude that since 1999 policy changes have increased lone-parent employment by about five percentage points. The rest of the increase is due to changes in the characteristics of lone parents and the generally buoyant labour market conditions in the UK. However, it is unlikely that the government will reach the 70 per cent employment target by 2010. Child poverty rates (defined as below 60 per cent of median income, after housing costs) for lone-parent families have also fallen from 55 per cent in 2001/2 to 48 per cent in 2004/5, but it looks unlikely that the targets for reductions in child poverty will be reached (Harker 2006). There is therefore now discussion about what further policies or provisions are needed. A recent review of the direction and nature of welfare reform (Freud 2007) has proposed that lone parents with a youngest child aged 12 and above should be subject to the same work requirements as an unemployed claimant and work requirements be extended to sole parents with progressively younger children from 2010. This is justified by two main arguments. The first relates to the well-being of sole parents and their children ('having a job makes families materially better off . . . work also improves the quality of life and well-being of parents and their children'; 2007: 46). The second reason is that the government support offered through the tax credit and childcare provisions is now, or soon will be, at sufficient levels to make it reasonable to require sole parents to work. The government has broadly accepted this argument and from October 2008 lone parents with a child aged 12 and over will no longer be entitled to income support. Instead, they will only be entitled to Jobseeker's Allowance and so subject to the same availability for work requirements as unemployed claimants. From 2010, this age will be reduced to 7 (DWP 2007a).

Conclusion

First, lone parents face a changing environment of social protection in these three countries, as this policy review has shown. In each country, there has been a shift away from the model of supporting lone mothers to be full-time mothers at home towards an employment-based model. In France the support for some lone parents to stay at home is increasingly tempered by work incentives and work requirements. In the Netherlands lone parents are in theory now subject to the same work obligations as other income support recipients – with the exception of lone mothers of children under 5 – since 2007. In the UK, the rhetoric, focus and direction of policy is towards encouraging and supporting employment, moving towards more compulsory work-related requirements. Lone parents with children aged 12 and over will now be treated in the same way as unemployed claimants in general.

All three countries have changed their rules around work obligations for people receiving income support or minimum incomes. Increasingly, lone parents are seen not so much as a special category (of mothers with care obligations), but as part of the wider group of 'workless' families or the 'hidden' unemployed. This larger group is the focus of policy attention. Although this strategy in general may contribute to the increase in employment and decrease in poverty among lone parents, many obstacles still remain, such as the incompatibility between low-paid, part-time and atypical jobs and caring responsibilities. In spite of some measures concerning paid leave and childcare, there is no systematic prevention of a one-sided implementation of the strategy: introducing work obligations without creating conditions and facilities to realize these, such as paid leave, good-quality childcare, training and reintegration programmes that fit lone parents, and income protection in between precarious jobs. In particular lone-parent families are at risk since they lack the security of a second wage or a second caretaker in the family with whom they can share the burden. As each of the countries under focus has experienced increases in the numbers of the working poor, this activation strategy is far away from an exclusive solution guaranteeing a 'good investment strategy in childhood' – as the increasing poverty rate of children, in particular those in lone-parent families, shows (Esping-Andersen 2002).

Second, these countries have also all introduced or increased financial support for employment, such as means-tested transfers and taxation. However, there are differences in the specific ways in which this has been done. In France, there are provisions for minimum income to remain in payment during the first 15 months in work. In the Netherlands, social assistance guarantees a minimum income if wages are below the minimum. In addition employed lone parents receive (additional) tax credits and get free childcare if their income is below 130 per cent of the minimum wage. In the UK, the child tax credit is paid to families regardless of work status and the working tax credit is specifically intended as a supplement for low wages. Increased expenditure on supporting working people is a key element in activation policies and social security budgets are being retargeted to support employment.

Third, there has also been increasing policy attention to the need for support of various types of working parents – in respect of maternity leave, parental leave, flexible working, and childcare services and subsidies. France was already much ahead of the other two countries in these respects, and both the Netherlands and the UK started from a very low base, in comparison with other northern European countries. But 'family-friendly' employment and 'work/life balance' are now clearly on the policy agenda, either at the European or at the national level. Again, there is less focus on lone parents *qua* lone parents and more on the general needs of working parents (or, more specifically, working mothers).

Fourth, in each of these countries there is a strong focus on the importance of tailor-made and individualized social interventions in activation. Several evaluation studies of activation have made clear that activation is most successful when the activation offers made to clients meet their needs, wishes and capacities (Van Berkel and Valkenburg 2006). Against this background, the increasing emphasis on obligatory activation seems to have a double aim. It should not only activate the target groups, as it is often interpreted, but also the institutions responsible for its implementation. Reforming these institutions (whether they operate at the local level, as in the Netherlands and France, or at the national level, as in the UK) is thus a key part of ongoing welfare restructuring. This has proceeded with differing degrees of success. In the Netherlands local municipalities sometimes act to exclude lone parents from support. In the UK, the commitment to individual and tailor-made support is limited by low resources in staff time and training. The extent to which these services can be developed to match the circumstances, needs and wishes of policy clients will be crucial in future debates over compulsory versus voluntary activation. When activation offers can be transformed from 'an offer you can't refuse' into 'an offer you won't refuse', the issue of work obligations will lose much of its controversial nature.

However, we should also note that policy is not standing still in these areas. In France, the new Fillon right-wing government (since May 2007) has a project to implement a proposition made by Martin Hirsch, a left-wing high civil servant who has agreed to lead the new *Haut commissariat aux solidarités actives contre la pauvreté*. The objective is to experiment a *revenu de solidarité active* for RMI and API recipients, in order to optimize the system of *intéressement* in three ways: (1) by extending this system to the beneficiaries of the RMA and of the *contrats d'avenir* who were excluded from this incentive, (2) by improving the *intéressement* of the part-time workers (below half-time), and (3) by simplifying the different helps into a single premium. In the Netherlands the coalition of Christian democrats and social democrats has recently again freed lone parents with children below the age of 5 from any work obligation, which illustrates the indecisive policies concerning these parents. Also, a new, more promising law has been accepted (but not yet implemented), that tries to find a solution for part-time working lone parents, guaranteeing them the right to payments for care in addition to a part-time job. In the UK there is ongoing debate about the rights and responsibilities of lone parents, and how far to develop work obligation for this group, and new availability for work requirements are to be introduced for lone mothers with older children (aged 12 and above) initially, and to be extended to those with children aged 7 in the next few years.

The extent to which these policies represent a sharp break with the past varies across the three countries. Until the mid-1990s, France was the archetype of the 'social exclusion' rhetoric, which emphasized the state's responsibility to help more fragile citizens. But in the past five years, policy-makers have increasingly promoted workfare arguments and reforms and abandoned the 'social exclusion' rhetoric. The 'dependence' argument and the development of control procedures and practices can be interpreted as a significant step towards a more 'defensive workfare' (Lødemel and Trickey 2000). The recent compromise to accept a left-wing high civil servant's proposition may be interpreted as a hesitation to reinforce this logic of workfare, but we must still wait for the implementation and the evaluation.

The Netherlands appears to have been the toughest of our three countries by legally obliging lone parents to work without any exception for having young children, without paid parental leave and even without introducing reintegration programmes that fit lone parents. This country developed within ten years a 'shock and awe' policy towards lone parents as if it wished to forget its traditional image as a 'motherhood-protecting' nation overnight. Dutch politicians, however, seem not to be quite sure of their case, hence the agreement of the new government to free lone mothers with young children (aged under 5) from the work obligation. In the UK, arguably, these policies for lone parents are less a break with the past, in that reform has proceeded relatively cautiously, and the employment activation policies have been introduced alongside a commitment to ending child poverty – although that in itself is a significant change from the 1980s, when UK conservative governments denied the existence of poverty. But the UK seems to be at a turning point now, ready to shift more decisively to the 'adult-worker' model.

In this process, the hypothesis of convergence is attractive. Nevertheless, it seems more appropriate to consider that each national case is moving towards a common European or even global objective, but by a process of adaptation of its previous system. The importance of the turning point varies across countries. The idea of an alignment is a more adequate way of conceptualizing these changes. However, the theory of continental specificity seems weak once we take social assistance and activation policies into account. The common traits seem larger than the differences between these three welfare states.

Notes

1. With thanks to Anne Skevik for her comments on a preliminary version of this article.
2. Although remarriage would end entitlement – as is consistent with the male breadwinner model.
3. The French minimum income, the *Revenu Minimum Insertion* (RMI), was introduced in 1988. It gives a minimum income to those with income below a defined threshold but also includes a contract that requires recipients to participate in 'insertion' activities such as training or education.
4. Also in territorial communities.

References

Belorgey, J.-M. (ed.) (2000), *Minima sociaux, revenus d'activité, précarité*, Paris: La Documentation Française.
Bussemaker, J., Drenth, A. van, Knijn, T. and Plantenga, J. (1997), Lone mothers in the Netherlands. In J. Lewis (ed.), *Lone Mothers in European Welfare Regimes: Shifting Policy Logics*, London: Jessica Kingsley, pp. 96–120.
Dorsett, R., Campbell-Barr, V., Hamilton, G., Hoggart, L., Marsh, A., Miller, C., Phillips, J., Ray, K., Riccio, J. A., Rich, S. and Vegeris, S. (2007), *Implementation and First Year Impacts of the UK Employment Retention and Advancement (ERA) Demonstration*, Department for Work and Pensions Research Report no. 412, Leeds: Corporate Document Services.
DSS (1998), *New Ambitions for Our Country: A New Contract for Welfare*, Cm 3805, London: Department of Social Security.
Dumont, G.-F. (1986), *Pour la liberté familiale*, Paris: PUF.
DWP (2006), *Households below Average Income, 2004/5*, London: National Statistics.
DWP (2007a), *In Work, Better Off: Next Steps to Full Employment*, London: DWP.
DWP (2007b), *First Release 2007 DWP Quarterly Statistical Summary*. Available at: http://www.dwp.gov.uk/asd/asd1/stats_summary/Stats_Summary_May_2007.pdf
Engelen, M., Bunt, S. and Samson, L. (1999), *Activeringsinstrumenten in de bijstand*, The Hague: Ministerie van Sociale Zaken en Werkgelegenheid.
Esping-Andersen, G. (2002), A child-centred social investment strategy. In G. Esping-Andersen, D. Gallie, A. Hemerijck and J. Myles (eds), *Why We Need a New Welfare State*, Oxford: Oxford University Press, pp. 26–67.
Evans, M., Harkness, S. and Ortiz, R. (2004), *Lone Parents: Cycling in and out of Work and Benefit*, DWP Research Report no. 217, Leeds: Corporate Document Services.
Evans, M., Eyre, J., Sarre, S. and Millar, J. (2003), *New Deal for Lone Parents: Second Synthesis Report of the National Evaluation*, Department for Work and Pensions Research Report no. 163, Leeds: Corporate Document Services.
Freud, D. (2007), *Reducing Dependency, Increasing Opportunity: Options for the Future of Welfare to Work*, London: Department for Work and Pensions.
Gilbert, N. (2002), *Transformation of the Welfare State*, Oxford: Oxford University Press.
Gregg, P., Harkness, S. and Macmillan, L. (2006), *Welfare to Work Policies and Child Poverty*, York: Joseph Rowntree Foundation.

Harker, L. (2006), *Delivering on Child Poverty: What Would It Take?* London: Stationery Office.

Hirsch, D. and Millar, J. (2004), *Labour's Welfare Reform: Progress to Date*, Foundations, York: Joseph Rowntree Foundation.

HM Treasury (2006), *Budget Statement 2006*, HC 968, London: House of Commons.

Hoggart, L., Campbell-Barr, V., Ray, K. and Vegeris, S. (2006), *Staying in Work and Moving Up: Evidence from the UK Employment Retention and Advancement (ERA) Demonstration*, DWP Research Report no. 381, London: Department for Work and Pensions.

Joint-Lambert, M.-T. (ed.) (1998), *Chômage: Mesures d'urgence et minima sociaux*, Paris: La Documentation Française.

Kiernan, K., Land, H. and Lewis, J. (1998), *Lone Motherhood in 20th Century Britain*, Oxford: Clarendon Press.

Knijn, T. (1994), Fish without bikes: revision of the Dutch welfare state and its consequences for the (in)dependence of single mothers, *Social Politics*, 1, 1: 83–105.

Knijn, T. and Van Berkel, R. (2003), Again revisited: employment and activation policies for lone parents on social assistance in the Netherlands. In J. Millar and M. Evans (eds), *Lone Parents and Employment: International Comparisons of What Works*, Sheffield: DWP Research Management, pp. 87–108.

Knijn, T. and Van Wel, F. (1999), *Zorgen voor de Kost*, Utrecht: SWP Uitgeverij.

Le Bihan, B. and Martin, C. (2004), Atypical working hours: consequences for childcare arrangements, *Social Policy & Administration*, 38, 6: 565–90.

Le Bihan, B., Martin, C. and Rivard, T. (2006), L'organisation du RMI et de son volet insertion dans neuf départements depuis la décentralisation, *Etudes et Résultats*, DREES, 535 (November).

Le Gall, D. and Martin, C. (1987), *Les Familles monoparentales*, Paris: Editions Sociales Françaises.

Lewis, J. (ed.) (1997), *Lone Mothers in European Welfare Regimes*, London: Jessica Kingsley.

Lewis, J. and Giullari, S. (2005), The adult worker model family, gender equality and care: the search for new policy principles and the possibilities and problems of a capabilities approach, *Economy and Society*, 34, 1: 76–104.

Lødemel, I. and Trickey, H. (2000), *'An Offer You Can't Refuse': Workfare in International Perspective*, Bristol: Policy Press.

Martin, C. (1995), Father, mother and the welfare state, *Journal of European Social Policy*, 5, 1: 43–63.

Martin, C. (1997a), L'action publique en direction des ménages monoparentaux: une comparaison France/Royaume-Uni, *Recherches et Prévisions*, 47: 25–50.

Martin, C. (1997b), *L'après-divorce: Lien familial et vulnérabilité*, Rennes: Presses Universitaires de Rennes.

Martin-Papineau, N. (2001), *Les familles monoparentales: Emergence, construction, captations d'un problème dans le champ politique français (1968–1988)*, Paris: L'Harmattan.

Millar, J. (1996), Mothers, workers, wives: policy approaches to supporting lone mothers in comparative perspective. In E. Bortolia Silva (ed.), *Good Enough Mothering*, London: Routledge.

Millar, J. (2006a), Families and work: new family policy for the UK. In G. Rossi (ed.), *Reconciling Family and Work: New Challenges for Social Policies in Europe*, Milan: FrancoAngelli, pp. 183–98.

Millar, J. (2006b), Better-off in work? Work, security and welfare for lone mothers. In C. Glendinning and P. Kemp (eds), *Cash and Care*, Bristol: Policy Press.

Nelson, B. (1990), The origins of the two-channel welfare state: workmen's compensation for mother's aid. In L. Gordon (ed.), *Women, the State and Welfare*, Madison: University of Wisconsin Press, pp. 123–57.

Nivière, D., Dindar, C. and Hennion, M. (2006), Les allocataires de minima sociaux en 2005, *Etudes et Résultats*, 539 (November).

Trudie Knijn, Claude Martin and Jane Millar

Rastier, A. C. and Maingueneau, E. (2006), Les dispositifs d'incitation à l'activité dans le système des prestations légales, *Recherches et Prévisions*, 85: 64–70.

Skevik, A. (2006), Lone motherhood in the Nordic countries: sole providers in dual-breadwinner regimes. In A.-L. Ellingsaeter and A. Leira, *Politicizing Parenthood in Scandinavia*, Bristol: Policy Press, pp. 241–64.

Sullerot, E. (1984), *Pour le meilleur et sans le pire*, Paris: Fayard.

SZW (1996), *Nieuwe Algemene BijstandsWet*, Den Haag: Ministerie van Sociale Zaken en Werkgelegenheid. Available at: http://home.szw.nl

SZW (2004), *Wet Werk en Bijstand*, Den Haag: Ministerie van Sociale Zaken en Werkgelegenheid. Available at: http://home.szw.nl

SZW (2005), *Wet Basisvoorziening Kinderopvang*, Den Haag: Ministerie van Sociale Zaken en Werkgelegenheid. Available at: http://home.szw.nl

TK (2003), *Alleenstaande ouders in de bijstand: Vergaderjaar 2002–2003, 28875*, The Hague: SdU.

Van Berkel, R. and Valkenburg, B. (2006), *Making It Personal: Individualising Activation Services in the EU*, Bristol: Policy Press.

Warin, P. (2006), *L'accès aux droits sociaux*, Grenoble: Presses Universitaires de Grenoble.

Williams, F. (2005), New Labour's family policy. In M. Powell, L. Bauld and K. Clarke (eds), *Social Policy Review 17*, Bristol: Policy Press, pp. 289–302.

7
Long-term Care Policies in Italy, Austria and France: Variations in Cash-for-Care Schemes

Barbara Da Roit, Blanche Le Bihan and August Österle

Introduction

Ageing populations, relative increases in morbidity and chronic illnesses, together with pressures on traditional forms of caregiving within families, have made long-term care an important welfare state concern in recent years. In response to increasing needs and decreasing abilities to provide large amounts of family care, calls for the development of comprehensive long-term care systems have been intensified. Many European countries have recently introduced major reforms in long-term care systems, while others are attempting to adapt existing ones to the changing context. Cash benefit approaches are playing an increasingly important role in these attempts (Ungerson and Yeandle 2007; Glendinning and Kemp 2006). As argued by Ungerson (1997), all 'cash-for-care' schemes support the 'commodification' of care through the provision of resources to users and the introduction of a cash nexus into care provision. However, different schemes may support specific 'ways of organizing "commodified care" ' (*ibid.*) with diverse impacts on informal family care relations and/or employment relations.

This article investigates such developments in three social insurance countries – France, Italy and Austria – where long-term care used to be largely understood as the responsibility of the family. In developing more comprehensive long-term care systems, these three countries have not followed, to date, traditional social insurance principles. Rather, either through the introduction of new policies (France and Austria) or the adaptation of old instruments (Italy), all three countries have developed non-insurance-based care allowances in order to support older dependent people. The aim of the article is to show the extent to which these 'cash-for-care' schemes establish a common trend and the extent to which they differ in terms of the specific forms of care commodification that they induce.

After an introduction to long-term care, as it is perceived as a social problem, and an outline of the historical approach of the three welfare states to the risk of dependency in old age, the article presents the main characteristics of the care system in the three countries. The analysis then focuses on the impact of cash for care on care arrangements in the three different forms and contexts, looking at social service provision, informal care and new types of care work between regular employment and traditional informal care. The identification of similarities and differences introduces the concluding discussion on whether these developments are evolving towards a common long-term care approach in the three social insurance countries.

Long-term Care as a Social Risk

All European countries share major challenges in addressing the social risk of dependency. First, European societies are faced with ageing populations. While in 2004, people aged 60 and over represented 21.7 per cent of the population in the EU25, the share will increase to 28.3 per cent in 2020 and 38.4 per cent in 2040. The increase is even larger among the older elderly population. The over-80s represented just 4.0 per cent of the population in 2004, but it is estimated that this share will increase to 6.3 per cent in 2020 and to 10.9 per cent in 2040. Although rapid ageing is a trend common to all European countries, the process has reached different stages and proceeds at different paces. Italy has the highest proportions of the old and very old age groups both at present and in future predictions (see table 1).

Given an increase in morbidities and chronic illnesses in later age, the ageing of populations will produce larger numbers of people in need of long-term care. This increase occurs even when estimates assume a future compression of morbidity. At the same time, it is highly unlikely that a strongly family-oriented system of care provision will be able to deliver the same large amount of care in the future. Changes in employment participation and/or trends in household composition are putting increasing pressure on traditional forms of family care. These and other concerns have generated broad public debate on long-term care in most European countries, but in diverse circumstances and at very different points in time.

Table 1

Estimated proportion of people aged 60+ and 80+ (2004, 2020, 2040)

	Aged 60+ % of total population			Aged 80+ % of total population		
	2004	2020	2040	2004	2020	2040
EU25	21.7	28.3	38.4	4.0	6.3	10.9
EU15	22.4	28.5	38.6	4.3	6.6	11.0
France	20.7	27.7	34.9	4.4	6.5	11.4
Italy	25.0	30.8	43.5	4.8	7.9	12.2
Austria	21.8	27.7	39.2	4.1	5.8	10.9

Source: Eurostat (2006).

France: a step-by-step reform addressing the risk of dependency

In France, the development of policy regarding the frail elderly has been a very slow process. It came on to the political agenda in the mid-1980s, but until 1994 there was no specific policy on dependency, only political debate plus numerous expert reports (Kessler 1994). Until the mid-1990s, the main social care policy for the frail elderly was one which applied to the disabled: the *allocation compensatrice pour tierce personne* (ACTP; compensatory allowance for a third party), which was freely used by older people as well, with no controls.

The political debate centred on certain key issues. The first was the choice between social insurance or social assistance (Frinault 2003). The second, linked to this, was whether the scheme should be universal or concern only people unable to pay for any services. The third issue was how the policy should be funded and managed, and to what extent the state, local authorities and social security funds should be involved. One of the main obstacles was financial. In fact, in the context of budgetary constraints and a policy of curbing public expenditure, it was difficult to promote any policy whose cost had not been properly estimated, until a national inquiry (HID inquiry of INSEE 1998–1999) identified the number of potential recipients (800,000 people).

These challenges – coupled with the government's difficulty in taking a clear decision – may explain the slow process of establishing policy in this field. However, since the mid-1990s, three steps can be identified in creating a specific long-term care scheme and progressively enlarging the number of recipients (Martin 2000). First, in 1994–5, there was implementation of an experimental pilot scheme developed by some local authorities (the *départements*). This was followed, in 1997, by the creation of a temporary national scheme, the *prestation spécifique dépendance* (PSD), implemented at the level of the *départements*. The many criticisms of this scheme, and particularly the fact that only 15 per cent of frail older people received the benefit (150,000 recipients only) made it necessary to reform the care system further. The aim of the second, 2002, reform was clear: to move away from the PSD scheme (whose aim had been to reduce costs, and to increase the number of recipients. The *allocation personnalisée à l'autonomie* (APA) was therefore created. This was based on a universal principle and, unlike the PSD, had no provision for recovery from inheritance.

The final, third step came in 2004 (after the heatwave of the summer of 2003) with the organization of the 'Plan for frail elderly people' for 2004–7 (a second Plan covers the period 2007–12). This introduced a programme to deal with any further heatwaves (air conditioning in retirement homes and hospitals, requisite recruitment of professionals), improved the epidemiological warning system and (in 2005) created a Fund for the frail elderly (*Caisse nationale de solidarité pour l'autonomie*). Financed by an employers' contribution (0.3 per cent of total wages) in return for the abolition of one day of public holidays, plus 0.1 per cent of the *Contribution Sociale Généralisée* (CSG, a tax on income which finances social security), and the transfer of credits for frail elderly and disabled people from the social security fund, this Fund was a step towards the insurance principle (in 2006 the Fund amounted to 14 billion euros). But there have been no further developments since 2005, even though the issue of long-term care insurance is still being debated in France.

Austria: the 1993 reform addressing the risk of dependency

As in France, so in Austria: until the early 1990s long-term care was largely viewed as being the responsibility of the family. This idea was rooted in popular perception, but it also reflected policy approaches. Policies were highly fragmented, with competences mostly devolved to the provincial administrations. There were three types of public support available for the care of the frail elderly. First, there were cash benefits. These were mostly low, restricted to specific groups and only disbursed in specific circumstances. Second, many municipalities had been providing residential care, either in old people's homes and nursing homes or in facilities which mixed both types of residence. The funding of such places was (and still is) based on social assistance principles. The third approach – social services in the community – was available at a substantial level only in a few regions before the 1990s – and even there it was often limited to nursing care (Hammer and Österle 2003).

The Austrian debate that led to the 1993 reform was greatly influenced by representatives of the handicapped. As a consequence, the future of long-term care policies was not focused on the elderly alone, but more generally on the social risk of dependency. And cash provision was strongly advocated as an approach to further the empowerment and autonomy of the recipients. This idea of cash benefits was also favoured by other groups, for reasons of choice and ideas of market-driven developments in long-term care. A further driving force behind the development of a more comprehensive long-term care system was the introduction in three Austrian provinces of new cash benefit schemes which granted cash for care on a needs- and means-tested basis.

This finally led to an Austria-wide consensus on the need to reform long-term care (Pfeil 1994). The 1993 reform programme consisted of two main parts: an agreement between the federal and provincial authorities on responsibilities for long-term care provision, along with cash benefit legislation (to be detailed below). The agreement clarified the division of responsibilities between federal and provincial levels of government. Accordingly, the development of services in the residential, semi-residential and community-care sectors remained a provincial responsibility, while the federal level was responsible for developing arrangements with regard to social insurance coverage for carers. The cash benefit scheme was the product of one Federal and nine Provincial Long-Term Care Allowance Acts. The federal level was responsible for care recipients receiving pensions or similar benefits based on federal statutory provisions, whereas the provinces granted allowances, based on standardized principles, to all those for whom the federal level was not competent, such as handicapped people or the recipients of social assistance. While the cash allowance was established as a social right (with the possibility of appeal to the Labour and Social Tribunal), this was not the case in respect of access to care services.

After 1993, Austria did not see any fundamental change in the principles thus established. However, further developments were to impact on the use of cash benefits, as well as on care arrangements (see the discussion below). Apart from some changes in benefit levels and in the assessment procedure, cash benefits have not been price-adjusted since 1996 (with the exception of 2005). This has led to a substantial decrease in the purchasing power of benefits. During the summer of 2006, amid debates on the grey market economy of immigrant carers, long-term care once again became a matter of public discussion. Together with the focus on how to deal with grey market care and alternative provisions for affordable 24-hour care outside institutions, it is still a major concern at the time of writing (summer 2007).

Italy: a fragmented policy and debate on reform in the 2000s

In Italy the family has long been assumed to be the 'caring' agency, given the existence of only very weak governmental family policies (Saraceno 1998). The needs of dependent elderly people have traditionally had to be met mostly within the (extended) family, owing to a meagre and fragmented system of social protection against dependency. The unpaid work of spouses, daughters and daughters-in-law has traditionally constituted the most important source of care. Moreover, family members have been subject to extensive legal responsibilities in supporting their relatives (Millar and Warman 1996; Saraceno and Naldini 2001).

The most important and widespread governmental measure is a national cash allowance – the *indennità di accompagnamento* – originally intended for adult disabled people, but extended to older people in the mid-1980s. Notwithstanding the diversity of territorial trajectories and degrees of development, formal care – whether provided in institutions or at home – has remained marginal. In particular, the provision of home services has only been residual and administered at the local level, with a limited availability of resources.

Despite the fact that population ageing is a long-term process, the issue has only recently entered public and social policy debate, between the end of the 1980s and the late 1990s. National legislation made explicit reference to institutional services for older people only in 1987, doing so through a national plan for investment in nursing homes for older people. In 1992 Parliament adopted a 'Project Objective for the protection of older people's health'. The national debate – centred on the idea that a new approach to fragility should build a 'network' of territorial services accessed through multidisciplinary professional teams – greatly influenced regional policy-making in this area. Nevertheless, the issue of long-term care was confined to the professional domain for several years, main concerns being the organization of existing services, the need for integration between social and health care, and the need to provide 'protected paths' – in 'technical' and 'profes-sional' terms – following discharge from hospital: all this within the context of a scant supply of services and without questioning the *system* of social protection.

A commission set up to evaluate the macro-economic compatibility of social spending prior to the adoption of new framework legislation recommended (1997), among other lines of reform, a review of the system of disability support and the introduction of a scheme to protect the dependent elderly. This commission proposed the creation of a national fund which would also include existing resources allocated to the *indennità di accompagnamento*: all to be used to provide monetary allowances and services for dependent people (Commissione Onofri 1997: 19).

However, new framework legislation on the social services, introduced in 2000, did not substantially reform the system of social protection for the dependent elderly. The traditional division between national allowances (giving rise to individual rights) and the discretionary local provision of services was maintained. Moreover, the 2001 constitutional reform which introduced the idea of social rights – to be set by the state and ensured by regions and local authorities – has not yet been deployed to any effect. Nevertheless, despite – and probably in relation to – substantial inertia in the social policy arena, important changes have taken place in long-term care arrangements. At the beginning of the 2000s the issue of long-term care merited exposure to public debate, in relation to the onset of an unforeseen and highly visible phenomenon: the increasing use of immigrant labour to care for the elderly living at home. It was the new carer profile of the *badante* – a migrant woman often working irregularly in the grey market – which finally generated public debate over long-term care needs and future prospects.

Cash-for-Care Schemes in Italy, Austria and France

In the 1990s, cash for care developed into a central pillar of policies adopted by the three welfare states to address the risks of long-term care. These cash-for-care programmes will here be described (see also table 2) before comparative analysis is conducted in the broader context of care in the welfare state.

The French 'allocation personnalisée d'autonomie'

In France, long-term care policy is based on a specific scheme – the APA – which has three main features. First, it is a benefit delivered to old people at home and in institutions[1] according to their level of dependency. The French care system is based on a single assessment grid, the AGGIR (*Autonomie Gérontologique – Groupe Iso Ressources*), which distinguishes between six levels of dependency, the APA being allocated up to the fourth level. Because the French scheme is a national one implemented at local level, and in order to guarantee access to the same services right across the country, care packages are defined according to the level of dependency (i.e. the level of GIR) and give entitlement to a certain amount of money (a maximum of €1,189.80 for GIR1, €1,019.83 for GIR2, €764.87 for GIR3 and €509.91 for GIR4). Second – and this is a main characteristic of the French scheme – the benefit is paid to finance a specific care package, determined by a team of professionals, according to their diagnosis of the needs of the recipient. The use of the benefit is therefore controlled and it can only be used to finance services identified as necessary by the professionals. Finally, France has adopted a

Table 2

Cash benefit schemes in France, Italy and Austria

Benefit scheme	France	Italy	Austria
	Allocation personnalisée d'autonomie	*Indennità di accompagnamento*	*Pflegegeld*
Benefit levels and benefit rates per month	4 levels, 2007: up to €509.91 for a Gir4; up to €764.87 for a Gir3; up to €1,019.83 for a Gir2; up to €1,189.80 for a Gir1	Unique level, 2007: €457.66	7 levels, 2007: €148.30 to €1,562.10
Recipients Entitlement criteria (needs, means, age)	Those in need of care Needs-tested means-tested over 60 years old	Those in need of care Needs-tested (100% disability and need of continuous care); not means-tested; no age limits	Those in need of care Needs-tested (>50 hours of care needs; continuous care) not means-tested; no age limits
Assessment tools	A unique grid: the AGGIR grid (6 levels of dependency)	Broad national criteria; implementation by local commissions	Assessment by doctors covering nursing, personal, home and assistance needs
National–local	National legislation; local implementation; mainly local funding	National legislation; national funding	Based on national and provincial legislation, administration and funding; but following the same principles
Benefit recipients, total (% of total population)	2006: 971,000 (1.6% of total pop.)	2006: 1,490,000 (2.5% of total pop.)	Dec. 2005: 381,000 (4.6% of total pop.)
Usage of benefits	Benefit must pay for a care package precisely defined by social and health professionals	Recipients are free in the way they use the benefit	Recipients are free in the way they use the benefit

twofold system to finance the care packages (Le Bihan and Martin 2006a). On the one hand, an 'assistance principle' is applied: below a fixed income threshold (€669.89) recipients do not contribute at all to the funding of their care packages. Above this threshold, on the other hand, a 'user fee' or co-payment system has been introduced, whereby the recipient contributes to the care package according to his or her level of income.

The Austrian 'Pflegegeld'

The 1993 reform based the Austrian long-term care system on a care allowance scheme. This benefit (*Pflegegeld*) is paid to those in need of long-term care, as defined at seven different levels: ranging from €148.30 for level 1 to €1,562.10 for level 7 (in 2007). Level 1 represents care needs amounting to more than 50 hours per month, whereas qualification for level 7 requires care needs of at least 180 hours per month (combined with a lack of coordinated arm and leg movement or comparable conditions requiring regular care-related measures during the day and at night). Benefit entitlement is based on a medical report on the need for long-term care, including the need for personal services and for assistance. Benefits are paid for all age groups and without means testing. At the end of 2005, there were more than 381,000 recipients (BMSK 2007), representing about 4.6 per cent of the country's total population. About 80 per cent of recipients were aged over 60.

Unlike in France, recipients of the benefit are free to decide how to use it. The benefit can be used to co-fund residential care, in which case care allowances are transferred directly to the residence management. When social services are purchased, care allowances are the main source (and calculation base) of the co-payments to be made by users. However, care allowances can also be used to pay family or other informal carers, even if this usually consists of financial support rather than payment. In many informal care arrangements – particularly in the case of care between partners – the allowance becomes part of the common household budget. Finally – and this has been an increasingly important development in the past decade – care allowances are used to pay immigrant carers (Österle and Hammer 2007).

The Italian 'indennità di accompagnamento'

The most important measure of social policy for the dependent elderly in Italy is a national cash allowance – the *indennità di accompagnamento* (literally 'companionship indemnity') – delivered to all disabled people (regardless of age and economic condition) in constant need of help with everyday activities, whether they are living at home or in an institution. In 2006, the beneficiaries amounted to 1.49 million people of all ages, though two-thirds of them were aged 65 and above, i.e. 1.06 million people or 9 per cent of the elderly population (INPS, online). As of 2005, total expenditure was €9.5 billion, i.e. 43 per cent of the total social assistance budget (INPS 2006: 111).

Because the measure was first introduced to provide adult disabled people with additional resources to meet their care needs, the evaluation criteria reflect those used to assess work incapacity. In order to be entitled to the benefit a person must be evaluated as 100 per cent unable to work and, additionally, in need of constant care in order to carry out everyday activities. Nevertheless, such broad criteria can give rise to different interpretations by the local commissions in charge of the assessment and endowed with considerable discretionary power. Beneficiaries are free to use their benefit as they wish. They do not have to justify their expenses.

Recently, regions and local authorities have introduced supplementary care allowances for heavily dependent elderly people living at home in difficult economic circumstances. These cash benefits are territorially dispersed and subject to diverse eligibility criteria. Nevertheless, they are of only minor importance to the target population. The most prominent of these latter regional schemes (in Emilia Romagna, Veneto) reach barely 1–1.5 per cent of the population aged 65 or above and provide monetary support averaging between 1,200 and 2,200 euros per year (Da Roit 2006).

Although all three countries provide cash for care, there are two evident differences. First, the systems differ in how the cash-for-care schemes have developed. In Italy, the *indennità di accompagnamento* has developed separately from social services and the health care system, resulting in a complex and fragmented combination of care services and financial help. In Austria and France, since their major reforms, the care system has been more closely organized around the cash-for-care principle. The second major difference concerns the way in which cash benefits can be used. In France, the benefit is given to finance a specific care package according to the needs of the recipient, as defined and controlled by public services. In Austria, as in Italy, recipients are free to use the cash benefit as they wish. In what follows, we investigate how such differences can affect care work arrangements in the formal sector, in grey care markets and in informal contexts. As will be seen, the effects are not determined by the characteristics of the respective benefit schemes alone, but also by the broader context of the care and welfare system.

Cash for Care and Care Work Arrangements

Cash for care in relation to formal care

As outlined above, care policies in France contrast with the two other countries in that they establish an explicit connection between the provision of an allowance and the consumption of a specific care package. This control principle introduces tighter regulation of the cash-for-care system than in Italy and Austria, because it is a means to prevent the development of a grey market. Even if the old person can still choose the carer, the latter must be declared. Moreover, the creation of the French scheme was directly linked with employment policies and with the desire of French policy-makers to find a way of creating new jobs in the services sector. Indeed, from the outset, the improvement of care services for frail older people was also intended to promote a potential source of employment – be it relational (family, neighbours, friends) or home-help services (which in France are called 'services to individuals' – *services à la personne*). These concern childcare as well as house-cleaning, care for the frail elderly, or any help that the family may receive in its everyday life. In 1997, the creation of a benefit for frail elderly people – the PSD – was therefore considered an opportunity to support the local non-profit service providers managing personal assistants for the frail elderly.

Yet the effects of the PSD were hardly positive. Instead of encouraging the creation of new jobs, the approach chosen actually destabilized existing qualified jobs and created new scope for unskilled labour. With the PSD scheme, families had three ways in which they could pay someone to help them in their everyday lives: direct recruitment when the elderly person was the employer of the carer (it is therefore possible to pay relatives, except for the spouse); the *mandataires* services, when a non-profit organization matched the care user and the care provider; and the *prestataires* services, when a non-profit organization was the service provider and directly employed the care workers sent to the homes of the beneficiaries. Because the price per hour of this last contract was higher than that of the other two,[2] and because there was no incentive to encourage its use, the PSD scheme at first boosted the use of unqualified labour (Le Bihan and Martin 2007). At the end of the 1990s, in order to increase the number of hours paid, families preferred to pay for unqualified workers, and even employed relatives, rather than use the *prestataire* service, even if it was of better quality. However, statistics (Chol 2007) provide evidence that the situation has changed since that period. First, they show a growth in the number of services covered by a 'quality agreement'. (Indeed, in 2005 the number of organizations delivering services to individuals[3] was estimated at 11,000[4] [there were 7,000 of them in 2002], so that there has been an 18 per cent increase since 2004.) Second, the number of employees working for individuals at home increased from 958,475 in 2003 to 1.1 million in 2005. Finally, the number of employees in *prestataires* services also increased, from 166,733 in 2003 to 211,269 in 2005.

In fact, the link between care and employment issues is also important because of the development of measures in favour of employment. Thus, in the 1990s a tax deduction was introduced to encourage the employment of domestic workers. This measure concerned childcare as well as house-cleaning and care for the frail elderly. French families can deduct half of the cost of employing a declared worker from their income taxes. This measure had a major impact and enabled upper- and middle-class families to resort to such a facility. Also introduced was a voucher, the *cheque emploi service* ('service employment voucher'), which simplified the administrative payment procedure for families. More recently, in 2005, the 'Borloo Plan', which concerns 'social cohesion', has organized the development of employment in this sector of services to individuals. The aim is to extend access to such services, to professionalize the sector, and to simplify the administrative procedures. In February 2006 a specific plan for the development of such services announced the creation of between one and two million jobs by 2010 and created a specific agency to organize this sector (*Agence des services à la personne*).

As in France, the cash-for-care scheme was introduced in Austria as the cornerstone of the country's new long-term care policy. But, differently from

France and similarly to Italy, the cash benefit scheme is not directly linked to employment. One of the objectives of introducing the system was, in fact, to support employment creation in the care sector. But policies did not seek to achieve this goal by requiring recipients to use cash benefits in a specific way. Rather, it was expected that the availability of the cash benefit would – via increased purchasing power – increase the consumption of services. One of the key orientations in developing the policy was to enhance autonomy and empowerment.

Despite the lack of an explicit link between the cash benefit and the actual use of services, employment in the care sector has increased substantially in the past ten years. Employment in the mobile care sector – measured in full-time equivalents – increased by about 50 per cent between the mid-1990s and the end of 2002. While the number of total beds remained relatively stable in the residential care sector, there was an increase in nursing beds for people with more extensive care needs requiring extended professional care in institutions. This trend is also reflected in the number of staff in homes, which increased by about 50 per cent in the same period, above all in regard to nurses (Schaffenberger and Pochobradsky 2004). Not least, these developments are a reaction to the availability of care allowances to care recipients. But it is co-determined by a number of factors. According to the 1993 agreement between the federal level and the provinces, the latter must develop an adequate infrastructure in the residential, semi-residential and mobile sectors, giving priority to the last. Moreover, even if perceptions regarding family responsibilities are still strong, the introduction of the cash-for-care scheme has strengthened expectations of public support in the case of long-term care. Together, these factors have helped increase service delivery, in particular of mobile services. All the same, some developments have been hindered. Substantial increases in co-payments, mostly related to the level of the care allowance, have made social services increasingly expensive for users (Österle and Hammer 2004). In addition, alternative care arrangements have been made necessary by the lack of services provided overnight and at weekends (Schaffenberger and Pochobradsky 2004).

In Italy, the *indennità di accompagnamento* was not explicitly intended to be a long-term care measure, nor to be a means of fostering employment in the care sector. Its actual impact on job creation is estimated to be negligible, mainly because beneficiaries are allowed to use the allowance in a completely discretionary manner. First, for instance, the *indennità di accompagnamento* has been partly used to finance residential services (in conjunction with explicit public funding). Because users must pay high fees for institutional care, those entitled to the national cash allowance use it to cover part of such costs. Indeed, during the 1990s there was a relative growth in the number of beds supplied in residential care facilities in some northern regions, even though the overall supply is still limited.[5] Second, the *indennità di accompagnamento* has not served as a means of promoting growth in the home care sector. The supply of home care, despite a certain territorial variability, is still restricted.[6] Third, a regular private care market has not developed as a result of the *indennità di accompagnamento*. This has been due, on the one hand, to the relatively high costs of private services compared to the needs of recipients and the level of the allowance and, on the other, to the absence of controls on the use of the resources. Overall, employment rates in the social and health sectors are still comparatively very low in Italy, having only increased from 3 per cent in 1993 to 3.4 per cent in 2003 (OECD 2003). A certain amount of growth is observable in the social service sector, where employees increased from 122,000 in 1991 to 280,000 in 2001 (Industry and Service Census 1991–2001, Istat online); but this growth – still of small proportions – is attributable rather to direct public subsidies in aid of services (above all private ones).

Developments in the three countries indicate that using cash for care in establishing formal care arrangements concerns not only employment but also the qualifications and working conditions of employees. In this regard, with its impact on professionalization, the reform of the care system and creation of the APA scheme in France has had a real impact on carers. Three main aspects can be identified: the type of services used, the qualifications of carers, and the number of carers working with the frail elderly. First, under the APA scheme, the majority of hours are now paid through the *prestataire* service, considered to be the one of higher quality. This also means that the employer is no longer the care user, but rather the organization itself. In other words, the cash-for-care system in France has been modified and made specific. This shift corresponds to the policy objective of enhancing the quality and professionalization of care. Second, services for the frail elderly are now covered by a 'quality agreement', and the professionalization of personal assistants is organized. Until March 2002, the CAFAD was the only diploma available to personal assistants – and only a few of them possessed one (only 18 per cent of personal assistants had a qualification in the social and health sector, and 9 per cent possessed a CAFAD). Training has since been improved with the DEAVS (*Diplôme d'Etat d'auxiliaire de vie*). Therefore – and this is the third consequence of the APA scheme – although working conditions are still precarious, because professional carers are paid according to the numbers of hours worked and still do not systematically receive a stable monthly wage, the APA has significantly increased the numbers of qualified workers (see above on the growth of the number of employees working in *prestataires* services).

Nevertheless, despite these measures to improve the situation of care workers, changes have only just begun and their impact is still weak. Consequently, working conditions remain precarious. In practice, work schedules are not well defined, and generally no explicit qualification is required. Care workers do not have a monthly defined wage but are paid according to the numbers of hours worked, so that there may be marked variations in earnings from one month to the next.

Whereas, in France, the issues of qualifications and working conditions have arisen in a system where cash for care is explicitly linked with the consumption of services, in Italy and Austria debates on the qualifications and working conditions of carers have been more concerned with the large grey markets in the care sector and the pressure that these create for social service provision in the formal market.

Development of grey markets in Italy and Austria

It is widely recognized in both Italy and Austria that long-term care needs have fostered the development of a broad private-care sector extraneous to social and labour regulations. According to recent estimates, there are currently between 650,000 and 800,000 immigrant care workers in Italy (Da Roit and Castegnaro 2004; Mesini *et al.* 2006), and between 10,000 and 40,000 care workers in grey markets in Austria (Streissler 2004).

The development of these grey care markets is due to the externalization of tasks from families to paid care workers. This trend is based on the availability of monetary resources and on the availability of relatively cheap and undocumented immigrant labour. In southern European countries, Latin America or the Philippines have for long been major source countries for household help workers, organized in grey markets. During the 1990s, care work became a more prominent part of work packages, and workers were increasingly 'employed' specifically for care tasks. In the same period, central and eastern European countries became the main sources of this kind of care labour. This growth has been co-determined by substantial differences in wage levels, the lack of legal opportunities to work in western European countries – and, not least, geographical proximity. This is particularly the case in Austria, where grey care market arrangements are usually based on fortnightly shifts, that is, with two care workers replacing each other every two weeks in a care arrangement (Österle and Hammer 2007). While such 'care work commuters' are mostly from neighbouring central European countries, care workers from eastern European countries with long-term permanence predominate in Italy.

This development of a grey market is driven by three interconnected factors. First, for families with caring requirements, this solution is seen as a more cost-effective alternative to family care and/or to social service provision. Indeed, immigrants can provide 24-hour care which would not be available from social services or would be too expensive for families. Even so, it should be noted that, in Austria, price levels are still too high for low-income families (Österle and Hammer 2007) and that, in Italy, older people often rely on economic support from their children (Da Roit 2007). Second, the arrangements yield better incomes to those providing care, compared to the income opportunities available in their home countries (Österle and Hammer 2007) – all the more so because the arrangements usually include free board and lodging. Third, the grey market system reduces the pressure of increasing demand on social services. This is particularly the case in Italy, where social acceptance of the phenomenon extends well beyond the care sector and has helped attenuate pressures for improved social services in general. Taking these interests together, cash benefits have not directly 'caused' the rise of a grey market in long-term care, but they have certainly helped its development, especially in relation to the fact that the public authorities do not require justifications for the use to which the cash-for-care benefits are put.

However, if immigrant care is an affordable alternative to traditional care arrangements, it is also outside labour and social security regulations. This incurs numerous risks for those providing care on this basis: for instance, a lack of social insurance coverage, a lack of job security, and a lack of health and safety protection (Österle and Hammer 2007). Moreover, this sector undermines the development of social services in terms of the quality of employment relationships and with regard to measures aimed at developing and supervising quality standards in the social services.

An attempt to regularize grey market arrangements was implemented in Italy by means of a mass regularization of undocumented immigrant care workers in 2002–3. In Austria, care work in grey markets became a huge political issue in the summer of 2006, when cases of 'illegal care' were reported to the authorities. The first reaction to this situation was a general amnesty, which currently expires at the end of 2007. At the same time, a broad public debate on grey care work, and policy responses able to ensure 24-hour care, has started. As a result, in June 2007, a new legal procedure was enacted – although it is still subject to fierce debate. According to the new provision, people in need of 24-hour care (or else their family carers) can apply for a subsidy if they employ a carer either working for an organization or on a self-employed basis. The difference between the labour costs for regularly employing household help and what is currently being paid for grey care work is used as a benchmark value. However – and this is a key issue in the ongoing debate – means-testing regulations (referring to the applicant's income and assets) are quite strict.

Regularization in Italy has helped establish some basic employment rights, even if it has been obvious that the effects of regularization are not long-lasting. Austria attempts to limit the extent of grey care markets by subsidizing regular employment arrangements in support of 24-hour care. However, given the restrictive definitions of the target group, strict means testing and limited financial support, its effectiveness in broadly regularizing 24-hour care remains highly questionable.

Cash for care and informal care

Informal family care has been, and still is, the major source of care work provision in the case of long-term care needs. Yet the reforms introduced in France and Austria, and the developments in Italy, may have had a variety of impacts on the role of informal care.

First of all, in all three countries cash for care may have helped to pay for care provided in the informal sector. The Austrian cash-for-care approach, *Pflegegeld*, is – among other objectives – explicitly intended as a means to support informal arrangements. But it attempts to achieve this goal without explicitly linking the provision of family care to the receipt of cash for care. Earlier studies have shown that the *Pflegegeld* receipt is in general related to some kind of financial arrangement between care recipients and informal caregivers (Badelt *et al.* 1997). It is only in particular individual cases that actual employment relationships are established. In the case of care between spouses, *Pflegegeld* usually becomes part of the common household budget. In other circumstances, the benefit can be used to buy care services and/or is transferred to informal caregivers as financial recognition or as a means to arrange for care. The Austrian *Pflegegeld* system has meant relief for many informal care arrangements and is evaluated quite positively by informal carers (Badelt *et al.* 1997; Pochobradsky *et al.* 2005). Similarly, the Italian cash benefit system was initially intended to help disabled people bear the extra costs arising from their disability. Given the extremely low regulation of the use of the benefit, the *indennità di accompagnamento* has variously been used to supplement family income, to pay informal caregivers – or to buy goods and services related to the disability. These benefits were never intended to formalize informal care relations; rather, they were used to supplement the family income and to pay informal carers throughout the 1980s and until the mid-1990s, until the explosion of the grey care market. In the French system, by contrast, regulation is more important. It is indeed possible to use the APA to pay a relative (except for spouses), but, as for the APA in general, the payment is made for the performance of specific tasks, as defined in the care package by social and health professionals.

Second, cash for care has to some extent helped free family members from the need to provide informal care to older dependent people entirely by themselves – and has provided family members with some financial assistance for buying care in the market. From this point of view, cash provisions represent a crucial resource for reshaping family obligations. The availability of cash – together with the availability of low-cost labour in Austria and Italy and controls on the use of resources in France – has enabled a substantial amount of direct care to be switched from the informal to the market sector, be this the formal market sector or the grey market economy.

Nevertheless, in all three countries, care arrangements are still a combination of formal and informal care – and families continue to shoulder the main responsibility for care. First, if the elderly person's resources are not sufficient to access the market for expensive residential care, family members – whether explicitly obliged to do so or otherwise – still contribute substantially to the costs of long-term care. Second, because not all care needs can be managed by a single worker, family members tend to provide a large number of hours of informal care work even in the presence of a paid worker. Care arrangements are usually a mix of informal and formal care. Finally, family members – and more specifically women – are responsible for taking decisions on care responses and, for instance, for choosing a care worker, supervising care activities, and managing the work contract (Attias-Donfut *et al.* 2002; Le Bihan and Martin 2006b; Österle and Hammer 2007). In fact, the system has strengthened the role of informal carers as 'care managers'. It has even been pointed out that care arrangements in the recipient's private sphere are viable only in the presence of an informal carer who, on the one hand, acts as care manager and, on the other, provides complementary care services during the daily, weekly and yearly leaves of paid care workers (Da Roit 2007).

This raises the further question of the broader support schemes available for informal carers. As we have seen, in Italy and Austria the focus is on the benefit as an allowance. Working conditions and social rights are not directly attached to the allowance, although some provisions have been introduced with regard to the specific type of informal care work. An example is provided by the social insurance coverage for informal care provision in Austria – which, however, requires an application, a minimum level of care work provided, and the payment of a reduced premium. In France, the choice has been to treat the benefit as a wage, so that the elderly person cared for becomes the employer of the relative employed (except for the spouse). This choice corresponds to concrete recognition that informal care constitutes work. Nevertheless, professionalization is limited, and only a few daughters or daughters-in-law decide to become personal assistants after having cared for one parent. Giving time off to families so that they can care for their old parents is another possible way to help carers. In Austria, care leave programmes range from a few weeks to a maximum of six months in the case of terminal care. In the latter case, however, the take-up has to date been far below expectations. The situation is the same in Italy, where workers caring for disabled people (who have to be recognized as 'handicapped' according to the law) are entitled, under given conditions, to three days per month of paid leave (since 1992). In France, recognition of informal carers has recently become a political concern, with the adoption of some measures in July 2006. Care leave has been introduced, so that relatives can take leave to care for their parents for a period of three months, which can be renewed up to one year, although with no remuneration. In reality, as some recent studies have shown, parental leave may not be a real solution for women, since it moves them away from the labour market. Also, their investment in their professional activity appears essential, in terms not merely of economic need but also of social identity, to help them cope with difficult situations of dependency (Le Bihan and Martin 2006b). Finally, alternative care settings (e.g. day-care centres) better suited to the reconciliation of work and family life, have been proposed in all three countries – but have not yet been developed to any great extent.

As a consequence, informal carers, above all women of working age, still face substantial risks: the burden of providing long hours of care work, a lack of adequate social insurance coverage and/or a sheer lack of regular income (Hammer and Österle 2003; Weber *et al.* 2003; Kreimer 2006).

Conclusion: Different Paces or Different Paths?

This analysis has highlighted a common trend towards cash for care as a means of addressing the need for long-term care in old age in three European social insurance countries. Yet the cash-for-care schemes here under review differ quite substantially: the context is not the same, nor is the timing of the reforms, nor – to some extent – is their content. Yet are the policy orientations completely different? Can we conclude that different directions have been followed? In fact, these differences do not reflect deeply different ideas of how care and care work should be supported by welfare policies. The question more closely concerns the different pace of policy changes.

The comparison has shown different degrees of development in the debate and the availability of different options at the moment of policy-making. In France and Austria, a specific benefit has been created to meet the needs of the elderly, whereas in Italy there has been no explicit long-term care policy (which in fact results implicitly from the combination of different fragmented measures: debate on the development of a policy for the frail elderly is now taking place in Italy, in 2007).

With respect to the balance between public and private responsibility, the three countries share similar policy orientations. All three approaches are attempting to provide some relief for family care without undermining the role of families as care providers. It is widely recognized that families will not be able to provide the same huge amount of care work in the future as they have done in the past. At the same time, it is emphasized that long-term care must be a shared responsibility, whereby both private and public resources are utilized. The priority given to home care in the three countries confirms the important role of family carers, who become 'care managers'. In this framework, all three countries have adopted a 'cash-for-care' scheme.

However, the ways in which the cash-for-care schemes have been implemented, and their consequences for the specific commodification of care, differ greatly between France, on the one hand, and Austria and Italy, on the other. Whereas the Austrian and Italian schemes grant more autonomy over how to use the benefit, the use of the French APA is controlled and explicitly geared to the purchase of services. The link with employment policies is the main difference between the schemes: strong and explicit in France, where the political objective is also to develop the sector of services to individuals, but weak in Austria and Italy. The analysis has shown the importance of a strong employment commitment both for preventing the development of a grey market in the sector of services to the frail elderly and for improving work conditions – even though the position of home carers in the labour market is still very precarious. If the employment commitment is not backed up with a system that guarantees sufficient means of finance, the only alternative to a grey care market will be a regular labour market with low wages, minimal social security coverage, and mostly precarious employment prospects for employed carers.

Notes

1. In the case of institutions the benefit can either be allocated to individuals or globally to the institution itself, which uses it according to the dependency needs of the residents. The choice between the two options is made by the institution. In France, institutions for the elderly distinguish among three expenditure components: dependency costs (paid by the resident and the APA), accommodation costs (paid by the resident), and health-care costs (paid by the health insurance).
2. The mean costs of services per hour in 1999–2000 by type of contract were the following: direct recruitment: €8.30/hour; *mandataires* services: €10.00/hour; *prestataire* services: €11.50/hour.
3. These statistics concern a larger sector than the 'personal assistants' who care for the frail elderly. Services to individuals include care of the frail elderly, childcare, domestic tasks, and all support needed by individuals (such as gardening, computer help, odd jobs). Care of the frail elderly represents 60 per cent of all services covered by 'quality agreements' and 33 per cent of domestic tasks.
4. Or 12,000 if private firms are included.

5. The national average institutionalization rate of the elderly has never been more than 2 per cent of the population aged 65 or over (the rate being below 1 per cent in the south and around 3 per cent in northern regions).
6. It covers 3–4 per cent of the older population in the most developed cases.

References

Attias-Donfut, C., Lapierre, N. and Segalen, M. (2002), *Le nouvel esprit de famille*, Paris: Odile Jacob.

Badelt, C., Holzmann-Jenkins, A., Matul, C. and Österle, A. (1997), *Analyse der Auswirkungen des Pflegevorsorgesystems*, Vienna: BMAGS.

BMSK (Federal Ministry of Social Security and Consumer Protection) (2007), *Bericht des Arbeitskreises für Pflegevorsorge 2005*, Vienna: BMSK.

Chol, A. (2007), Les services à la personne en 2005: poussées des enterprises privées, *Première Synthèse*, 20, 1.

Commissione per l'analisi per le compatibilità macroeconomiche della spesa sociale (Commissione Onofri) (1997), *Relazione finale*, Roma.

Da Roit, B. (2006), La riforma dell'indennità di accompagnamento. In C. Gori (ed.), *La riforma dell'assistenza ai non autosufficienti*, Bologna: Milano, pp. 287–315.

Da Roit, B. (2007), Changing intergenerational solidarities within families in a Mediterranean welfare state, *Current Sociology*, 55: 251–69.

Da Roit, B. and Castegnaro, C. (2004), *Chi cura gli anziani non autosufficienti*, Milano: Angeli.

Da Roit, B. and Sabatinelli, S. (2005), Il modello mediterraneo di welfare tra famiglia e mercato: come cambia la cura di anziani e bambini in Italia, *Stato e Mercato*, 2 (August), Bologna: Il Milano.

EUROSTAT (2006), *Eurostat Database 2006*. Available at: http://epp.eurostat.cec.eu.int

Frinault, T. (2003), L'hypothèse du 5e risque. In C. Martin (ed.), *La dépendance des personnes âgées: quelles politiques en Europe?* Rennes: Presses Universitaires de Rennes, pp. 69–92.

Glendinning, C. and Kemp, P. (eds) (2006), *Cash and Care: Policy Challenges in the Welfare State*, Bristol: Policy Press.

Hammer, E. and Österle, A. (2003), Welfare state policy and informal long-term care giving in Austria: old gender divisions and new stratification processes among women, *Journal of Social Policy*, 32, 1: 37–53.

Inps (2006), *Rapporto annuale 2005*, Rome.

Kessler, F. (1994), *La dépendance des personnes âgées, un défi pour le droit de la protection sociale*, Strasbourg: Presses Universitaires de Strasbourg, Actes du colloque du Centre de Recherche de Droit Social de l'Université Robert Schuman.

Kreimer, M. (2006), Developments in Austrian care arrangements: women between free choice and informal care. In C. Glendinning and P. Kemp (eds), *Cash and Care: Policy Challenges in the Welfare State*, Bristol: Policy Press, pp. 141–53.

Le Bihan, B. and Martin, C. (2006a), A comparative case study of care systems towards frail elderly people: Germany, Spain, France, Italy, United Kingdom, Sweden, *Social Policy & Administration*, 40, 1: 26–46.

Le Bihan, B. and Martin, C. (2006b), Travailler et prendre soin d'un parent âgé dépendant, *Travail, Genre et Sociétés*, 16 (November).

Le Bihan, B. and Martin, C. (2007), Cash for care in the French welfare state: a skilful compromise? In C. Ungerson and S. Yeandle (eds), *Cash for Care Systems in Developed Welfare States*, London: Palgrave, pp. 32–59.

Martin, C. (2000), Atouts et limites de l'expérimentation: l'exemple de la prestation dépendance, *Revue Française des Affaires Sociales*, 1: 47–58.

Mesini, D., Pasquinelli, S. and Rusmini, G. (2006), *Il lavoro privato di cura in Lombardia*, Milano. Available at: www.qualificare.info/index.php?id=9

Millar, J. and Warman, A. (1996), *Family Obligations in Europe*, London: Family Policy Studies Centre.

OECD (2003), *Labour Force Statistics: 1980–2002*, Paris.

Österle, A. and Hammer, E. (2004), *Zur zukünftigen Betreuung und Pflege älterer Menschen: Rahmenbedingungen – Politikansätze – Entwicklungsperspektiven*, Vienna: Kardinal König Akademie.

Österle, A. and Hammer, E. (2007), Care allowances and the formalization of care arrangements: the Austrian experience. In C. Ungerson and S. Yeandle (eds), *Cash for Care Systems in Developed Welfare States*, London: Palgrave, pp. 32–59.

Pfeil, W. (1994), *Neuregelung der Pflegevorsorge in Österreich*, Vienna: Verlag des ÖGB.

Pochobradsky, E., Bergmann, F., Brix-Samoylenko, H., Erfkamp, H. and Laub, R. (2005), *Situation pflegender Angehöriger: Endbericht*, Vienna: BMSG.

Saraceno, C. (1998), *Mutamenti familiari e politiche sociali in Italia*, Bologna: Milano.

Saraceno, C. and Naldini, M. (2001), *Sociologia della famiglia*, Bologna: Milano.

Schaffenberger, E. and Pochobradsky, E. (2004), *Ausbau der Dienste und Einrichtungen für pflegebedürftige Menschen in Österreich – Zwischenbilanz: Endbericht*, Vienna: BMSG.

Streissler, A. (2004), Geriatrische Langzeitpflege: Eine Analyse aus österreichischer Sicht, *Wirtschaft und Gesellschaft*, 30, 2: 247–71.

Ungerson, C. (1997), Social politics and the commodification of care, *Social Politics*, 4, 3: 362–81.

Ungerson, C. and Yeandle, S. (2007), *Cash for Care Systems in Developed Welfare States*, London: Palgrave.

Weber, F., Gojard, S. and Gramain, A. (eds) (2003), *Charges de famille: dépendance et parenté dans la France contemporaine*, Paris: La Découverte.

8

Family Policies in Germany and France: The Role of Enterprises and Social Partners

Ute Klammer and Marie-Thérèse Letablier

Introduction

Although France and Germany are both commonly categorized as 'Bismarckian' welfare states sharing similar characteristics – like a strong reliance on social insurance systems, group-specific coverage, a high level of social security contributions – they have for decades shown strong differences in the field of family policies, especially with regard to childcare and reconciliation between work and family life. In France, family policy developed largely outside the Bismarckian framework. It was institutionalized as an autonomous branch of the social security system, making of the family a state issue. Compared to (West) Germany, the male-breadwinner model is weaker in France, since women, and especially mothers, have for long been integrated into the labour market. In addition, in France the state not only has an influence on social regulations but it also diffuses republican and secular ideas and values, especially with regard to the education of children. So, family policies have a more long-standing and consolidated tradition in France than in Germany, in particular in the field of childcare, which has been a major issue for more than three decades. Recent developments in German family policy, however, reveal a remarkable shift: driven by demographic concern, long-discussed reform issues – aiming at a better reconciliation between work and family, such as a parental leave scheme with an earnings replacement benefit and an extension of public childcare – have finally been brought into being.

While comparative research on family policy is often restricted to such structures and trends in state programmes, the role of other actors in the field – such as companies and social partners – tends to be neglected. But in the context of an increasing need for childcare and work–family balance facilities that are not entirely being fulfilled by state provision, the role of enterprises and social partners in the framing of these fields is increasing. This article therefore focuses on family policies *in the enterprise sector* for the comparison of recent developments in family policy in France and Germany. The article raises the question of whether recent developments in these two countries are pointing in the same direction or not. The article also links developments in childcare and reconciliation policies to other reform trends, highlighting the facts that family policy issues – in a broad sense – increasingly influence reforms in other branches of social security and that family policy therefore now constitutes a pivotal area for the development of 'Bismarckian' welfare states.

Structures and Trends in Public Family Policy

Family policy design in France and Germany

The male-breadwinner model has been characterized as 'modified' in France, as compared with 'strong' in Germany, with reference to women's working and caring regimes (Lewis 1992). Women in France have a long tradition of working outside the home and from the 1970s onwards have been receiving state support for reconciling work and caring responsibilities. The 'reconciliation issue' emerged on the policy agenda and in political debates while the number of mothers increased in the labour force. Direct family benefits delivered by the National Family Agency (CNAF) increased from 2.5 per cent of GDP in 1973 to 3.1 per cent in 2003. However, the distribution between different types of benefits has shifted: child benefits now account for only 50 per cent of the total direct family benefits delivered by the CNAF whereas they accounted for 87 per cent 30 years ago. Meanwhile, the share of housing benefits has increased from 1.3 to 28 per cent of total family benefits, and the share of social assistance benefits (minimum income, lone-parent allowance, etc.) – which did not exist in 1973 – now accounts for 22 per cent of the same total. This trend indicates a shift from purely family to broader social objectives. But since the family is an autonomous branch of the social security system, family policy receives 49 per cent of its budget from the state.

There is a long tradition of state support for children in France. The state enjoys a high legitimacy for intervening in what is considered a 'private issue' in most other countries. This tradition is embedded in republican ideas about the early education and socialization of children. Children are viewed as a 'public good', a fitting object for social investment (Jönsson and Letablier 2005). However, in spite of this high level of state support for childcare – that in some ways makes France seem close to the Nordic countries – both the forms of support and the objectives are deeply different. Whereas in France policies refer to the liberty of choice for parents to work or care – and also to a diversity of childcare provisions and supply – state support for childcare in Nordic countries is aimed more straightforwardly at supporting working mothers and hence at improving gender equality. In France liberty prevails over equality. Although there are no major objections towards the 'defamilialization of care', and childcare facilities are widespread, some families still encounter problems as far as access to actual childcare facilities is concerned.

In (West) Germany, social and family policy was for a long time focused on the male-breadwinner model of married couples, based on the expectation that women, in particular married women with children, would withdraw from the labour market permanently, or at least temporarily. This model was and still is massively promoted and subsidized by state family policy. By contrast, the expansion of public childcare infrastructure was conspicuously neglected and progressed only very slowly, compared to the situation in many other European countries (Klammer *et al.* 2000: 336–40; Klammer and Daly 2003).

In East Germany (the former German Democratic Republic), a completely different gender model had developed, with a much higher labour market participation of women, including mothers. This was supported by a very high level of public childcare facilities all over the country. After reunification in 1990, however, the East German gender model had no major impact on the West German model and did not lead to a significant improvement in gender equality throughout Germany. Instead, the West German institutional framework was transferred to East Germany and confronted East German women with the established support for married couples and the breadwinner model.

Recent trends in childcare and reconciliation policies in the two countries

In recent years, the emphasis in family policy priority – in both France and Germany – has been on facilitating the work and family balance, within the context of an increasing number of working mothers. While the support for working mothers remained relatively reluctant in Germany for a long time, it has recently been receiving much more emphasis.

The new focus on family policy in Germany. Concern over demographic trends and in particular the low birth rate[1] has refocused attention on family policy in recent years, and this has now become a key point of debate in Germany. During its first period in office (1998–2002), the family policy endeavours of the 'Red–Green' government were mainly concentrated on increasing *monetary* benefits for families (Schratzenstaller 2002). A reform of the parental leave scheme (2001) improved parents' options to combine parental leave with part-time work and provided incentives for mothers to return faster to the labour market. A big pension reform of 2001 upgraded the pension rights of part-time working mothers. In addition, the general right to part-time employment was improved by law in 2001. A central problem for many (West) German parents remained the missing availability and flexibility of public childcare. The right to a nursery place for children above the age of 3 does not extend to full-day care places. When it comes to children *below* the age of 3, West Germany is even near the bottom end of the EU, with a quota below 5 per cent. In East Germany, however, the coverage of childcare is (still) much more comprehensive. In their second period in office (2002–5), the Red–Green government finally declared the extension of state childcare facilities for small children as a high-priority family policy objective, but the success remained moderate.

After the change of government in 2005, when a grand coalition between Christian Democrats and Social Democrats came into power, the support for families was strengthened once more. Although the Christian Democrats always supported the privileges for married couples and the male-breadwinner model, the new Christian Democrat family minister now pushes forward the extension of public childcare and in addition introduced a new parental leave benefit (*Elterngeld*) imitating the Swedish scheme. Since January 2007, parents who interrupt their employment to care for a newborn baby get a parental leave benefit replacing 67 per cent of their net income from work – up to €1,800 per month – for up to 14 months (two months of which are reserved to the father). This new tax-financed scheme can be interpreted as a significant reorientation in German family policy. It will not only lead to a considerable overall increase in spending for families (estimated costs: €3.87 billion per year – BmFSFJ 2006f), but it will shift resources from needy parents to working parents. The cash benefits during parental leave are therefore no longer (primarily) oriented to help poor parents, but to compensate working parents for a temporary loss of income. One motive was to give well-educated women incentives to have children, since a growing number of them remain childless in Germany.[2] While the new benefit, oriented towards wage replacement, seems to be in line with the Bismarckian insurance system, the new benefit is not financed through social security contributions, but through general taxes. It therefore marks a completely new structure in the German welfare state.

Priorities on work and family life balance in France. In France, the work–life balance has been a major issue in family policy over recent decades, focusing on public support for childcare facilities, on fathers' share of family responsibilities and on parental leave. A paternity leave was introduced in 2002 and the childcare package reorganized in 2003. Among the topics tackled by the 'family conferences', held annually since 1996, have been the issues of solidarity and redistribution between families, support for families with numerous children, parenthood and the sharing of parental responsibilities, intergenerational solidarity within families – and childcare. As in Germany, the demographic issue has been constantly on the agenda, although the birth rate remains relatively high in France. Instead of implementing direct support for families to encourage fertility, the focus of family policy has moved to support for childcare facilities, based on the hypothesis that the good ranking of France with regard to fertility may be a result of generous state support for working mothers.

Over the last 10 years, irrespective of the government (socialist until 2002, then conservative), family policy has focused on the development of childcare facilities as well as on the quality of childcare. The main difference between the two policy streams lay in the forms of state support: whereas left parties are in favour of collective childcare structures with an emphasis on quality of childcare, right parties show preferences for support in cash, giving a choice to parents between working and mothering. Policy objectives highlight the 'liberty of choice' for parents, as well as the diversity of childcare supply and forms of state support.

The restructuring of the public childcare support system has been the major development in family policies. In 2003/4 the *prestation d'accueil du jeune enfant* (PAJE) replaced five benefits that had been developed in the 1980s and 1990s. The objective was to simplify the childcare benefit system while confirming its underlying principles. A further objective was also to reduce the costs of private childcare services by childminders, especially for medium- and low-income families, in order to support this form of childcare – and maintain the principle of liberty of choice. Since 2004, parents of a first child are eligible for a six-month parental leave allowance following maternity leave, while parents of two or more children are eligible until the youngest child is 3 years old. In fact, the reform has extended eligibility for the parental leave allowance, giving prominence to home care over other forms of childcare.[3] The childcare allowance is paid to parents who employ a childminder or a person at home caring for children under 6 years. The objective of the PAJE is to increase families' solvency so that they have a real chance to choose between working or caring, and also the precise form of childcare. However, the new childcare package does encourage low-income mothers to care for their children themselves – and hence to leave the labour market, with the risk of being trapped in unemployment and poverty (Méda and Périvier 2007). It also favours individual rather than collective forms of childcare – and therefore just may reduce the quality of care.

The long tradition of public support for childcare in France has led to a very different picture by comparison with Germany. In 2005, almost all children from 3 to 6 years attended preschool (*école maternelle*), which is viewed as a preparation for primary school. Catering and care services may be offered by local authorities to facilitate the reconciliation between children's hours of care and parents' hours of work. Parents may receive support for meeting the costs of additional care. CAF expenses dedicated to childcare are now higher than those dedicated to child benefits. Between 1995 and 2005, the number of families hiring a childminder has increased from 200,000 to 605,000, while the number of places in collective structures rose from 250,000 in 1992 to 320,000 in 2005. However, the needs are not yet entirely covered.

From benefit provision to regulation, motivation and moderation: new roles for the state in Germany's Alliance for the Family

In addition to the considerable changes in the traditional fields of family policy – cash benefits, legal rights and childcare infrastructure – an additional trend has become visible in Germany (more than in France): since the second period of the Red–Green government (2002–5), much emphasis has been put on the involvement of other actors in the development of a family-friendly society. This hints at a new welfare mix in this field of the Bismarckian welfare state.

The launching of the new initiative 'Alliance for the Family' by the Red–Green government in 2003 is an example of the new policy orientation, bringing together a broad range of measures and activities intended to improve the work–life balance in Germany.[4] The basic idea was to create a new conscience among the different societal actors about the importance of the family for the whole society – and to stimulate awareness about the need to support families. The project – initiated by the German Family Ministry in cooperation with the Bertelsmann Foundation – aimed at uniting the activities of different actors, such as employers' associations and trade unions, local governments, companies, etc. The main goal, as laid down in a consensus paper, is the development of a 'sustainable family policy' based on three (normative) assumptions that (a) German society needed a higher fertility rate, that (b) the economy needed qualified workers and a higher labour market participation of women, and that (c) children needed (better) education and guidance in their early years.

Activities include the regular exchange of experiences between actors at different levels. Representatives of the institutions and associations involved built a 'competence group for balance' to work towards a consensus between the interest groups. A competence network of scientists supports the process; scientific studies have been commissioned. Press conferences, publications and detailed information about the Alliance for the Family on the Family Ministry's website (www.bmfsfj.de) provide the transfer into the public sphere.

One project under the remit of the Alliance for the Family, by which the new approach can be illustrated, is the initiative 'Local Alliances for Family'. Following the assumption that the local context is essential for families' living conditions and well-being, the initiative Local Alliances for Family was launched by the Family Ministry in 2003. The aim was to initiate the assemblage of local round tables – alliances of the relevant local actors capable of helping to improve the context for family life in the municipalities. Such networks can include the local administration, the town council, companies, representatives of employers' associations and trade unions, churches, third sector initiatives, families and other actors. By November 2004, only 11 months after the start of the initiative, the family minister was able to announce the founding of the 100th Local Alliance for Family.[5] The number increased to 364 in January 2007.[6]

The Ministry has installed a service office to support towns and municipalities running a Local Alliance for Family. By January 2007 a total of 629 towns and municipalities expressing interest in this field had received assistance.[7] A broad range of services and help is offered, with a focus on counselling and workshops on the spot. In these workshops individual approaches designed to fit in with the workings of the respective municipality are developed. The services offered follow the principle of subsidiarity, the idea being to assist engaged partners to find their own, locally feasible strategies. Another aim of the service office is to bring different local alliances together for an exchange of ideas and experiences. PR workshops offered by the service help local actors to develop instruments (e.g. websites, newsletters) for going public and informing citizens about their activities. The whole project is scientifically accompanied and evaluated by a research institute, the German Institute for Youth (DJI).

Evaluation suggests that local alliances are focusing on different aspects of family life and work–life balance, according to the needs and resources identified in their local contexts. The topics treated range from the organization of public childcare and elder care, to flexible working time arrangements, family-friendly opening hours for the administration, modified timetables for public transport and many more issues. In order to spread examples of good practice, each month one local alliance is declared 'local alliance for family of the month'.

Although some municipalities and actors claim that activities they had started long before the invention of the Alliance for the Family have only been reorganized under a new name, there is widespread approval and support for this initiative. When the government changed in 2005 and the Family Ministry was taken over by a conservative minister, there was no doubt about the continuation of the ministry's engagement in this initiative – and a scientific evaluation has meanwhile confirmed the positive economic effects of these Local Alliances for Family (BmFSFJ 2006a).

In both countries it has become obvious during recent years that *state* family policy has not sufficed to enable families to achieve a satisfactory work–life balance, due to changes in living and working environments, to demographic changes and tight public budgets. In the following sections we shall examine the involvement of other actors, especially enterprises, in family policy issues.

Family Friendliness in Collective Agreements and at the Company Level: Are the Social Partners and Enterprises Taking Over?

Concerning the particular role of the social partners and enterprises for work–life balance, three factors have to be considered: the place of reconciliation issues in collective agreements, the family-friendly strategies of employers, and the policies and support brought to employees by work councils.

Work–life balance in legal regulations and collective agreements

Family-friendly regulations in German collective agreements. Apart from the new 'motivating' approach of the Family Ministry and the growing interest in a qualified female workforce in times of demographic change, there is another factor which may lead to the social partners becoming more active with regard to work–life balance and reconciliation issues in Germany. In 2001, the government failed with their plan to implement an encompassing equality law for the private sector, which would have obliged all companies to take measures to improve their gender equality arrangements and their family-friendliness. Employers and their associations succeeded in preventing the law by declaring their willingness to improve the situation on a voluntary basis. So have the social partners and enterprises now taken over, as far as family-friendliness and reconciliation policies are concerned?

As is clear from an analysis of collective agreements by the WSI archive for collective agreements, family-friendliness is still not a high profile issue in German collective agreements (CAs) (Klenner 2005). Nevertheless, a considerable number of CAs contain some relevant items geared to supporting reconciliation between work and family life. Most of these regulations had already been agreed in the collective bargaining rounds of the 1990s. New regulations from 2000 feature a (soft) right to return from part-time to

---

Box 1

Regulations concerning the reconciliation between work and family in
German collective agreements

- Transition from full-time work to part-time work and vice versa.
- Prevention of problematic working times in the evening and at the weekend when childcare cannot be arranged.
- Adjustment of working times to the opening times of childcare institutions.
- Equal treatment of part-time and full-time employees.
- (Extra) options to take time off when children or elderly relatives are ill or in need of care.
- Organization of parental leave, qualification measures during parental leave.
- Organization of telework.

Source: WSI-collective agreement archive (Klenner 2005: 62).

---

full-time work in some collective agreements in the retail trade, a right to claim qualification during parental leave (metal industry of Baden-Württemberg) and some comprehensive agreements on family-friendly measures and gender equality in selected collective agreements at the enterprise level, e.g. in the agreements of the German Telekom, the privatized telecommunications company. As Klenner (2005: 61) sums it up, relevant regulations can in particular be found in branches with a high percentage of female employees, as well as in branches that depend on women with high qualifications (e.g. the chemical industry, banking sector, IT sector). Company-level collective agreements in formerly public companies also have a higher probability of containing family-friendly regulations. In these cases, issues from public sector equality law have often been adapted to the new collective agreement, once a company was privatized.

Some collective agreements, in branches with long or flexible working hours which raise special reconciliation problems for the (female) workforce (such as the retail and metal industries), regulate the (better) matching of working time with school times and the opening hours of childcare institutions, or again specify the scope for taking time off if a child is ill (beyond the legal right). Many collective agreements now contain regulations concerning part-time work and the organization of parental leave, e.g. measures for staying in contact with the company during parental leave. Some collective agreements contain an extended job guarantee beyond the legal right to three years of parental leave, this policy being in contradiction to the latest trend in family policy – which has been to increase incentives for a *quick return* to the labour market after giving birth. Box 1 sums up the main issues concerning reconciliation between work and family life, as so far taken up by German collective agreements.

As far as the relationship between legal regulations and collective agreements is concerned, there are different patterns to be found. In some cases, collective agreements were progressive and similar legal regulations followed later, e.g. introducing the right to combine parental leave with part-time work, or the general right to work part-time. In some cases, collective agreements built on existing legal regulations and specified and extended them. In other cases collective agreements took up proposals of the draft equality law for the private sector which the Red–Green government failed to implement in 2001 after fierce protest by the employers and their associations.

Work–life balance with regard to legal regulations and collective agreements in France. In France, work–life balance issues with regard to working time and flexible working arrangements have been included in legal regulations and notably in the 35-hour laws at the turn of the century. Collective agreements that have been negotiated in companies have more or less explicitly undertaken engagements on this topic, secondarily with regard to employment issues.

The 2005 law on 'equal pay' attempts to reduce the prevailing gender wage gap by stimulating collective bargaining on issues of gender equality. It includes several points on the reconciliation of work and family life. It stipulates that indicators of family-friendliness should be integrated into reports on the situation of men and women which companies have to produce every year for the government (art. 5). Support is to be given to companies for replacing employees on maternity leave, so as to eradicate obstacles limiting the hiring of women by companies, due to the anticipation of maternity leave (art. 7). The training allowance was raised for employees facing costs of childcare during training (art. 8) and access to training after parental leave was encouraged (art. 9). Employees on maternity leave are eligible for paid leave, the same as if they had been working (art. 12). In short, by eradicating obstacles to the hiring or to the career of mothers, these measures support women's labour market participation, completing a set of measures promoting gender equality in the workplace that have been implemented over the last five years, especially the *label égalité* and the 'interprofessional agreement' signed in 2004 by all the social partners. This latter agreement frames collective bargaining at the branch and enterprise level, concerning hiring, training, equal pay and parents' work–life balance. Two stipulations of this agreement have been included in the legal programme on social cohesion in 2005: the neutralization of the parental leave period in the calculation of eligibility for training rights and the opportunity for employees to discuss professional projects (before or after maternity or parental leave) with their employers, so as to maintain links with the enterprise.

Work–life balance and family-friendliness at the company level

An agglomeration of literature has proved that family-friendliness at the company level constitutes not merely a cost factor, but can also, used well, point to ways ahead, to the economic benefit of the company (Yasbeck 2004; Juncke 2005). Benefits can include a reduction in staff turnover, increased returns on training investment, reduced absenteeism, reduced use of sick leave, stress reduction, greater staff loyalty and commitment, increased return from parental leave, etc.

Family-friendly regulations in German enterprises. In a German study commissioned by the Family Ministry, the research institute Prognos came to the conclusion that the introduction of family-friendly measures at company level resulted in a positive return on investment of +25 per cent (Prognos AG 2003). According to this study, family-friendly policies in the company saved over 50 per cent of the costs incurred as a result of the lack of reconcilability between work and family, in particular bridging, fluctuation and reintegration costs. Although it was a small study and although the extent of the positive effects depended heavily on the labour market segment in question, this study has stirred a lot of interest among German employers.

Company agreements on reconciliation or work–life issues typically take up one or several of the four fields differentiated by the OECD (OECD 2001; Maschke and Zurholt 2005):

- options for shorter or longer interruptions of work (e.g. for parental leave or elder care, sabbaticals, illness of a child or relative);
- adaptation of the work organization (including part-time work and particular working hours, teleworking);
- organization of or support for childcare;
- information and qualification.

While in 2002 only 4 per cent of German companies offered childcare facilities[8] and 12 per cent provided special offers for parents in parental leave, flexible working time as a measure to combine work and family life was much more widespread (Klenner 2004a). The survey shows that, in the overwhelming majority of German companies (i.e. in 9 out of 10 companies), employees already had options for adapting their working hours. The option of taking free time to compensate for overtime previously worked existed in 3 out of 4 companies – and was the most frequently cited means of adapting working time to family needs. Other options were flexitime, part-time work or informal arrangements with superiors and other team members. The data did not clarify, however, how conflicts were solved and who (the employer or the employee?) really decided on the use of time. A survey by Bauer *et al.* (2004) has revealed that the coverage and possible use of working time accounts differ according to levels of qualification as well as to gender. Highly qualified white-collar employees have a working time account more often than blue-collar workers and they also have more power to decide on the use of their own time credits.

In 2001, the goal of reconciling work with family life was included in the amended Works Constitution Act (BetrVG), governing the rights and obligations of the employee representatives in German companies. The law now states that work councils are responsible for promoting reconciliation between work and family life (section 80I,2b BetrVG). Since the introduction of the law this topic has been the subject of debates in many companies (WSI work council survey; see Klenner 2003, 2004a). In companies where the topic was put on the agenda, the initiative has often come from the work councils (80 per cent, multiple answers) – often in combination with interested colleagues (44 per cent, multiple answers). Until 2003, only 8 per cent of companies with more than 20 employees had a company agreement on the reconciliation between work and family, compared to 20 per cent of companies with more than 1,000 employees. Initiatives in the company or company agreements on family-friendliness and equality are much more widespread in companies with a work council than in others.

According to the latest wave of the representative survey 'Enterprise Monitor on Family-friendliness' (BmFSFJ 2006e), the awareness of German companies concerning family-friendliness and the need for reconciliation policy has steadily grown over recent years. By 2006, 72 per cent of the interviewed employers regarded the topic of family-friendliness as important for their company, compared to 47 per cent as of 2003. Family-friendly measures have, in short, become more widespread. Almost every fourth enterprise in 2003 practised between 7 and 9 measures characterized as 'family-friendly'. In particular, flexible working time models and the active organization of the parental leave period – issues that were mentioned by employees to be particularly important for them (Klenner 2004b) – are more widespread today than three years ago. Questioned about the motives behind the introduction or extension of family-friendly measures, 83 per cent of employers mention the aim to keep qualified employees in the company, 81 per cent want to increase the work satisfaction of their staff and 78 per cent mention economic motives (BmFSFJ 2006e).

Although this survey was carried out by the research institute affiliated to the Employers' Association (IW) that has an interest in demonstrating that the voluntary declaration of the employers to improve family-friendliness is working and that legal regulation is thus unnecessary, it cannot be denied that typical issues of family policy are increasingly being taken up by German companies. The Family Ministry has commissioned and published several guidebooks to help employers and work councils developing company-specific agreements on work–family reconciliation and equality (BmFSFJ 2005, 2006b, 2006c, 2006d).

Nonetheless, the 'working culture' of a company could be more important than any particular company-level provision. More knowledge about new processes of inclusion and exclusion will be necessary to redefine the options and obligations of different actors to improve family-friendliness and work–life balance.

France: from working time arrangements to childcare incentives. In France, companies contribute to the reconciliation of work and family life mainly through three types of measures: working time arrangements, parental/care leave arrangements and the supply of services aimed at facilitating employees' caring arrangements. Whereas working time was the main focus in the 1990s onwards, due to the implementation of the 35-hour law, services and other family-friendly facilities have now moved forward on the agenda. However, family-friendly regulations are still more often to be achieved by laws than by collective agreements (Lanquetin and Letablier 2005).

Working time arrangements include flexible hours for parents with young children and the possibility of shifting from full-time to part-time work, plus a range of leaves for parents. The significance of these measures varies across sectors of activity and company size. Cash benefits may be offered by work councils – such as bonuses for childbirth, financial supports for childcare, for education expenses or for holidays. Only about 5 per cent of all companies (having at least 20 employees) offer a day-care service for children at the workplace, or in collective childcare structures elsewhere.

Although this reconciliation between work and family life was only a secondary aim of the laws framing working time reductions in the late 1990s, the impact on family life has been highlighted by several publications (Méda and Orain 2002; Fagnani and Letablier 2004, 2006; Letablier 2006). According to the surveys, about two out of three parents (fathers or mothers with school-age children) reported that the reduction of working time has facilitated their work and family life combination.

Part-time work for women is more common in Germany (44 per cent) than in France (31 per cent), though it has increased rapidly during the last 20 years in both countries. Both France and Germany provide examples of policies designed to stimulate part-time job creation, especially for low-wage workers. However, average weekly working hours in the main part-time job are longer for female part-timers in France (23.3 hours) than in Germany (17.8 hours), and the share of involuntary part-time work is again larger in France, stressing the differences in attitude towards part-time work in the two countries.

The company survey on working time and work–life balance for the European Foundation provides information on companies' practices and perceptions about working time and other work–life balance arrangements in 21 EU countries (see Riedmann et al. 2006). A glimpse at companies' practices, in respect of part-time and parental leave in France and Germany, shows interesting similarities and differences (Anxo et al. 2007a, 2007b). Until the introduction of the new parental leave scheme in Germany in 2007, the two countries shared similar parental leave patterns: concerning the length of parental leave, the earnings replacement ratio, opportunities for part-time leave and flexible arrangements. Take-up rates were lower in France than in Germany, where childcare facilities were underdeveloped. The length of leave taken up also depended on the overall work–family reconciliation package parents had access to. In Germany, the return rate to work was rather low (50 per cent), and many mothers returning to work switched to part-time. Whereas enhancements of parental leave exist in collective agreements for various economic sectors in Germany, this is rare in France. Public sector establishments are more likely – as against those in the private sector – to have some experience of parental leave, in particular in Germany (Anxo et al. 2007a).

Until recently, only a limited number of French companies offered childcare facilities. In general, public opinion is reluctant with regard to the role of companies in this field, arguing that childcare is mainly a state responsibility (Letablier et al. 2003). However, some companies offer such facilities because of their unsocial working schedules (hospitals, transportation) or to be attractive for their employees. Companies are more and more encouraged to invest in childcare in order to contribute to national challenges with regard to raising the birth rate or the employment rate of mothers.

Since 2004, enterprises investing in services for their employees are eligible for tax deductions (*crédit d'impôt famille*). Companies may also sign 'childhood contracts'[9] with local family agencies and local authorities, contributing to the funding of childcare structures at local level. Companies' investment in childcare services can take various forms: they can open a crèche, be a partner in a *contrat enfance* or subsidize part of the childcare expenses of their employees. Their investment is framed by local family policy agencies and local social services. But two years after the introduction of the measure, results turn out to have been limited, and so far only few companies have made such investments (Daune-Richard *et al.* 2006).

In addition to their task of representing employees, work councils also have the role of supporting employees' needs, in relation to family costs and responsibilities, and especially with regard to leisure, culture, holidays and various provisions for children. In French companies with at least 50 employees, work councils receive subsidies to fulfil this role. Some large companies own holiday residences, but more of them offer financial support to their employees for leisure activities (e.g. holiday vouchers). Such family-friendly benefits have been reactivated over recent years, especially in connection with policies aimed at stimulating the development of care services for families. The law launching the social cohesion programme (2005) includes a programme on care services, and receives various forms of support related to job creation. Families buying care services are eligible for reductions to their social contributions and taxes, reducing the costs of such services, mainly in childcare and elder care, but also on housekeeping. The service voucher (*chèque emploi-service*) that is the pillar of this programme is being renewed as a main tool of home care services development. The service voucher is now universal, companies and work councils having been encouraged to fund the voucher, totally or partly. All of the competent organizations are eligible for tax deductions in respect of their investment in all kinds of care services. This prefunded service voucher is coming to be viewed as a modern and efficient tool in aid of corporatist (company) social policy. Employees can pay a child-minder or another care service with this voucher. Large companies – such as the post office – can offer comparable vouchers, though the outcomes are yet to be evaluated.

Family-friendliness or equality? The German career and family audit versus the French 'label égalité'

One group of instruments in the new toolbox of voluntary company engagements consists of audits. Their coverage and focus differ between Germany and France, however.

The German 'career and family audit'. The German 'career and family audit' was introduced in order to give private sector companies – as well as public establishments – incentives and ideas for the development of family-friendly strategies in accordance with the particular situation and goals of each company. Run by the Hertie Foundation, the programme is supported and promoted by the Family Ministry under the roof of Alliance for the Family.[10]

Companies applying for this audit get support to develop firm-specific strategies. Within the auditing process, already existing family-friendly measures are scrutinized and the firm-specific potential to develop additional family-friendly activities is analysed. Since there is no legal obligation for companies to activate family-friendly policies, the audit is based on their voluntary engagement.

More than 140 single family-friendly measures are found in the portfolio checked within the auditing process (Schmidt and Mohn 2004: 183 ff.). One main focus turns out to be on working time arrangements that can help to improve the balance between work and family. Other measures encompass monetary benefits on the company level, company childcare facilities, measures concerning the location of work or the work organization. Up to November 2006, some 372 German enterprises had successfully undergone this auditing process and received their certificates.[11] The government ostensibly underlines its support for this audit by hosting the annual certification ceremony.

The French 'label égalité'. In France, family-friendly recommendations have been included under the gender equality issue at the workplace. The work–life balance issue was incorporated in collective bargaining about working time reduction and flexible arrangements in the context of the 35-hour laws implementation. Since then, focus in the negotiations between the social partners has been on gender equality rather than on family-friendly measures. Since the law (May 2001, reinforcing the 1983 law) obliges employers to negotiate gender equality at the workplace and to report on the comparative situation of men and women in companies, a survey indicates that 72 per cent of enterprises have not yet negotiated this issue, for all its being compulsory.[12] Moreover, even companies that have negotiated have not as yet given priority to issues of work–family balance (Laufer and Silvera 2005).

The inter-professional agreement between employers and trade unions in March 2004 has stimulated negotiation on gender equality at firm level, including in respect of family-friendly issues. The *label égalité* gives new incentives for companies to develop family-friendly strategies in line with the gender equality issue. It was launched in 2004 by both social partners and the minister of women's rights as a tool aimed at stimulating companies to invest in gender equality and family-friendly strategies. The idea is supported by the minister of women's rights, implemented by audit agencies and attested by a certification agency. However, the certification procedure is unusual since social partners participate in the process. Certification is delivered for a period of three years. Companies applying for the audit can get support for developing specific programmes aimed at improving gender equality along three dimensions, one of them referring to 'how companies take into account the parental responsibilities of their employees'. Among the criteria related to work–life balance are the possibilities of flexible working time arrangements, working conditions, and maternity and parental leave arrangements.

The audit is based on the voluntary engagement of companies; the precondition to participate is to engage in a programme aimed at improving gender equality and family-friendliness at the workplace. Until 2006, about 15 enterprises had got the label. In some ways this procedure is comparable to the German 'career and family audit'. Firms' participation in the programme, however, is so far much lower than in Germany and the focus is more on gender equality, as against family and balance in Germany.

Different Starting Points – But Similar Trends?

Despite different starting points with regard to the role of the state and the development of family and childcare policies, France and Germany are experiencing similar trends, especially in stressing work and life balance issues and in pushing enterprises to become active in this field. Yet clear differences are nonetheless visible between the two cases.

The logics underlying social policy funding in France have not undergone a remarkable change, in family policy or in other related fields. Reforms of the family benefit system have been rather an adaptation to changing contexts than radical reforms in themselves. The system of family tax-splitting remains untouched. And non-working women continue to depend on their husbands/partners for their social rights, remaining a person à *charge*. Labour market reforms may have increased the pressure on welfare mothers to seek work, but reforms of the childcare benefits system have not deeply changed the conceptualization of care. Liberty of choice remains the principle behind family policy in France and the restructuring of the childcare benefit system has not really changed this: conditions of eligibility have been revised but childcare by parents (mothers) is still encouraged. Parental leave allowance has been extended to parents with one child and the duration has remained unchanged for parents with two or more children. It has been argued that the focus on 'choice' in combination with the extension of eligibility for family benefits – and in particular the new support for part-time work and private care solutions – might point towards a refamilialization of France (Veil 2007). Unlike the German reform, the parental leave allowance in France remains a flat-rate allowance not to be considered as a wage replacement so much as a care allowance, encouraging mainly mothers on low incomes to trade off a job for a caring allowance, thus deepening the social class gap between the two categories of earners: medium- and high-income families on the one hand and one-earner low-income families on the other.

In addition to the principle of liberty of choice guiding family policy decisions in France, the decision to maintain diversity in childcare provision encourages the prevalence of a domestic/individualistic conception of childcare; i.e. the focus on childminders is one way of pushing a 'family conceptualization' of childcare to the detriment of the pedagogical conception prevailing in collective structures. In this context, the opening of the childcare sector to companies indicates a preference for diversity to the detriment of the idea of a public service regulated by the state. It also generates wide inequalities between sectors of activity and therefore between families. Finally, these reforms sustain a dual system of childcare – individual and collective – and have not deeply attempted to reduce social and gender inequalities. State support still combines allowances, tax deductions and social contribution deductions for families.

To sum up, French family policy has – in spite of the extended system of public childcare – not said 'farewell to maternalism' (Orloff 2006): few policy measures have attempted to promote gender equality in the private sphere. The whole system remains focused on women assuming care responsibilities either at home or in the public sphere. Reforms have not changed the family foundations of the social system. The influence of the family movement explains why the family cause is still well defended in France, more than that of women or children (Chauvière 2006). Thus the restructuring of French family and social policy over recent years has not called into question the Bismarckian foundations of the welfare state model, but has rather contributed to its so-slow adaptation to a new European economic and social context.

The analysis of *recent trends in Germany* comes to somewhat different conclusions. On the one hand, some fundamental structures and regulations of German family policy still remain unchanged. Most privileges for the married bread-winner family, as the system of matrimonial tax-splitting, remain untouched, and small part-time jobs are still promoted as an option for married women. On the other hand, considerable changes in recent family policy (and social policy in general) are taking place in Germany.

- The first important finding is that some reforms of the benefit system, in particular the new parental leave benefit (*Elterngeld*) clearly supporting the idea of the working mother, are much more than reluctant adaptations of the existing system. The *Elterngeld*, introduced in 2007 and copying the Swedish approach, definitely marks a considerable shift in the logics of German family policy. It is strongly geared towards the idea of the working mother who only interrupts work for a short period after childbirth. This reform would at least have to be classified as a 'second-order change', if not as a 'third-order change' (Hall 1993).[13] The same holds – even more – for other reforms, in particular the pension reform of 2001, the four 'Hartz laws' from 2003–5 that thoroughly changed unemployment protection and active labour market policy, and probably also the health reform from 2007 (see also Hinrichs 2004, for the pension reform; Bothfeld 2006 and Klammer and Schulz-Nieswandt 2006, for the Hartz reforms; Leiber 2006, for the health reform).
- A second important finding is that family issues have surpassed the restricted field of family policy and have increasingly entered into other fields of social policy reform, such as pensions, labour market and/or health care reforms. Concerns about demographic developments have led to a situation where welfare state reforms in Germany are being more and more influenced by family issues, and welfare state change in Germany can only be understood when this debate is taken into account.
- Finally, a third important finding is that the developments hint at a broader concept of social policy for the future German welfare state. As has been shown in this article, the Family Ministry is increasingly assuming new roles: from benefit provider to regulator, motivator and

moderator, integrating other social actors, in particular companies, in fields such as childcare and reconciliation policy. This hints at a broadening of the future welfare mix in Germany beyond Bismarckian social insurance.

If the foregoing analysis is right – i.e. that the speed of change is faster and the quality of change is more significant in Germany at the moment – what could be the reasons for this? First, one could point to the fact that Germany has been for some time (and still is) lagging behind France, in respect of the coverage of public childcare, mothers' labour market participation, etc. Therefore, the pressure for change (also with respect to the Lisbon goals of the European employment strategy) is quite high. In addition, the demographic pressure – with birth rates much below the French situation and a quickly ageing workforce – has pushed the public discussion and political action, as well as companies' increasing awareness of the needs of their (qualified) female workforces. Finally the need to motivate new actors and companies' willingness to develop more family-friendliness have to be seen in the context of the employers' promise to take action on the basis of a voluntary agreement when they succeeded in blocking the equality law for the private sector that the Red–Green government intended to implement in 2001. This is different from France, where such an equality law already exists, and where the state still lays claim to a strong leadership role in family policy – a leadership *taken over* after conflicts from strong, paternalistic companies (and the Catholic church) in the Third Republic (1871–1940) (Veil 2007).

Empirical data for Germany so far only partly reflect the ongoing changes. The family type based on the male-breadwinner model is still predominant, mainly in Western Germany, although it is no longer anything like the norm for the majority of households today. Attitudes among both men and women are increasingly in favour of the greater participation of women as well as – to a lesser extent – the mothers of small children in the labour market. The labour market participation rate of women in Germany has increased to a middle place (11th) in a ranking of the 25 EU member states (Bothfeld *et al.* 2005: 116, 123, based on Eurostat; France: rank 14), and it is in particular the labour market participation of mothers that has gone up in recent years. However, if one compares activity rates for mothers with children below the age of 12 throughout the EU, Germany is still in the bottom half (rank 15 – France: rank 10; Bothfeld *et al.* 2005: 173, based on Eurostat). In addition, due to the high part-time rate of Western German working mothers, many women in (Western) Germany only contribute a small share to household incomes and still depend economically on their male partners. This reflects the ongoing support for the male-breadwinner model. These contradictory signals have repeatedly been identified as one of the main reasons why, compared to other European countries, women have still made so little headway in (Western) Germany in their efforts to attain some kind of equality with men in the area of employment and incomes (e.g. Dingeldey 2002).

As has been shown, family policy issues in both France and Germany – in spite of different patterns and speed of change – more and more overlap with other actors and other fields of social policy. Companies are obliged by law (France) or motivated by incentives and assistance (Germany, to a lesser degree also France) to become active in the fields of gender equality and family-friendly working conditions. In both countries, family policy is increasingly linked to labour market, pension, health and anti-poverty policy, as well as to issues of gender equality. In times of labour market and demographic change, the 'family issue' is being shifted into the centre of political interest and increasingly shapes the reform trends of these Bismarckian welfare states.

Notes

1. The German birth rate currently ranks 181st worldwide out of 191 surveyed countries.
2. Among German women born in 1960, more than one in four is childless, whereas in France, Spain or Norway this applies only to one in ten of the respective birth cohort (Schmidt and Mohn 2004: 189; Eurostat data).
3. The PAJE includes four allowances: a flat-rate birth premium (€840) paid to parents at childbirth; a monthly allowance (€168) paid to parents with children under 3 years of age; a parental leave allowance called *allocation de libre choix d'activité* paid to the parent who stops or reduces their activity to care for a child, and a childcare allowance called *allocation de libre choix du mode de garde* aimed at reducing the costs of childcare for working parents. The first two benefits are means-tested, but 90 per cent of parents receive these allowances aimed at reducing childrearing costs for parents. The two other allowances concern childcare.
4. The following description of the Alliance for the Family is primarily based on Schmidt and Mohn (2004) and on the information provided on the website of the Family Ministry (www.bmfsfj.de).
5. Website www.bmfsfj.de, press information from 22 November 2004.
6. Website www.lokale-buendnisse-fuer-familie.de, accessed 12 January 2007.
7. Website www.lokale-buendnisse-fuer-familie.de, accessed 11 January 2007.
8. However, companies have developed a variety of measures to support childcare. While company kindergartens are rare, more companies pay for external childcare and support parents' initiatives as well as local childcare agencies, or they offer emergency care options (BmFSFJ 2005: 34).
9. 'Childhood contracts' were launched in 1988 in order to promote childcare policies for children under 6 years. The contract aims at increasing childcare equipment and services. Contracts are concluded between the local family agencies (CAF), local authorities, and other possible partners such as enterprises. They allow local family agencies to have institutional partners while playing a major role in the management of local childcare policies. Some 50 to 70 per cent of childcare expenses are covered. At the end of 2000, 3,200 'childhood contracts' had been achieved, covering 2.8 million children under 6, and 1,820 'leisure contracts' covering 2 million children.
10. Two other certifications that have been developed to promote family-friendliness on the company level are *Erfolgsfaktor Familie* (success factor family, www.erfolgsfaktor-familie.de) and *Total E-Quality* (www.total-e-quality.de).
11. Website www.beruf-und-familie.de, accessed 10 January 2007.
12. *Délégation aux droits des Femmes, rapport d'information*, no. 103 (2003–4).
13. In a 'first-order change', goals and instruments of a system remain unchanged; only slight adaptations (such as an increase of social security contributions) are implemented. Reforms can be classified as a 'second-order change' when a change of instruments is implemented while the overall goals remain the same.

A 'third-order change' requires a significant change in the goals or 'philosophy' of a system as well as in the instruments (Hall 1993).

References

Anxo, D., Fagan, C., Letablier, M.-T., Perraudin, C. and Smith, M. (2007a), *Parental Leave in European Companies*, European Foundation for the Improvement of Living and Working Conditions, Luxembourg: Office for Official Publications of the European Communities.

Anxo, D., Fagan, C., Letablier, M.-T., Perraudin, C. and Smith, M. (2007b), *Part-time Work in European Companies*, European Foundation for the Improvement of Living and Working Conditions, Luxembourg: Office for Official Publications of the European Communities.

Bauer, F., Groß, H., Lehmann, K. and Munz, E. (2004), *Arbeitszeit 2003. Arbeitszeitgestaltung, Arbeitsorganisation und Tätigkeitsprofile*, Köln: Berichte des ISO.

BmFSFJ (2005), *Familienfreundlichkeit im Betrieb: Handlungshilfe für die betriebliche Interessenvertretung*, Berlin: BmFSFJ.

BmFSFJ (2006a), *Die Initiative 'Lokale Bündnisse für Familie' aus ökonomischer Sicht, prognos*, Berlin: BmFSFJ.

BmFSFJ (2006b), *Informationen für Personalverantwortliche: Familienfreundliche Maßnahmen im Unternehmen*, Berlin: BmFSFJ.

BmFSFJ (2006c), *Familienorientierte Personalpolitik: Checkheft für kleine und mittlere Unternehmen*, Berlin: BmFSFJ.

BmFSFJ (2006d), *Familienbewusste Personalpolitik: Informationen für Arbeitnehmervertretungen, Unternehmens- und Personalleistungen*, Berlin: BmFSFJ.

BmFSFJ (2006e), *Unternehmensmonitor Familienfreundlichkeit 2006*, Berlin: BmFSFJ.

BmFSFJ (2006f), *Bundesministerin Ursula von der Leyen: Heute ist ein guter Tag für Familien in Deutschland*, Pressemeldung, Berlin: BmFSFJ.

Bothfeld, S. (2006), Ein Ende, kein Anfang: Wie die Hartz-Reformen das Konzept der deutschen Sozialbürgerschäft verändern. In C. Schäfer and H. Seifert (eds), *Kein bisschen leise: 60 Jahre WSI*, Hamburg: VSA, pp. 91–104.

Bothfeld, S., Klammer, U., Klenner, C., Leiber, S., Thiel, A. and Ziegler, A. (2005), *WSI-FrauenDatenReport 2005*, Berlin: Sigma.

Chauvière, M. (2006), Enjeux de la néo-familialisation de l'Etat social. Colloque CNRS/Matisse/Université Paris 1 on 'Etat et régulation sociale', Paris, 11–13 September.

Daune-Richard, A. M., Odena, S. and Petrella, F. (2006), *Innovation et diversification des modes d'accueil de la petite enfance: quelle participation des entreprises pour quelle gouvernance?* Rapport LEST pour la Caisse nationale des allocations familiales.

Deutscher Bundestag (2006), *Siebter Familienbericht: Familie zwischen Flexibilität und Verlässlichkeit – Perspektiven für eine lebenslaufbezogene Familienpolitik*, BT-Drucksache 16/1360, Berlin.

Dingeldey, I. (2002), Das deutsche System der Ehegattenbesteuerung im europäischen Vergleich, *WSI-Mitteilungen*, 3: 154–60.

Fagnani, J. and Letablier, M.-T. (2004), Working time and family life: the impact of the 35 hours law on the work and family life balance in France, *Work, Employment and Society*, 18, 3: 551–72.

Fagnani, J. and Letablier, M.-T. (2006), The French 35-hour working law and the work–life balance of parents: friend or foe? In D. Perrons, C. Fagan, L. McDowell, K. Ray and K. Ward (eds), *Gender Divisions and Working Time in the New Economy: Changing Patterns of Work, Care and Public Policy in Europe and North America*, Cheltenham: Edward Elgar, pp. 79–90.

Hall, P. (1993), Policy paradigm, social learning and the state: the case of economic policy in Britain, *Comparative Politics*, 25, 3: 275–96.

Hinrichs, K. (2004), Alterssicherungspolitik in Deutschland: Zwischen Kontinuität und Paradigmenwechsel. In P. Stykow and J. Beyer (eds), *Gesellschaft mit beschränkter Hoffnung, Reformfähigkeit und die Möglichkeit rationaler Politik*, Wiesbaden: VS-Verlag für Sozialwissenschaften, pp. 266–86.

Jönsson, I. and Letablier, M.-T. (2005), Caring for children: the logics of public action. In U. Gerhard, T. Knijn and A. Weckwert (eds), *Working Mothers in Europe: A Comparison of Policies and Practices*, Cheltenham: Edward Elgar, pp. 41–57.

Juncke, D. (2005), *Betriebswirtschaftliche Effekte familienbewusster Personalpolitik: Forschungsstand*, Working paper 1, Forschungszentrum Familienbewusste Personalpolitik, Münster.

Klammer, U. and Daly, M. (2003), Die Beteiligung von Frauen an europäischen Arbeitsmärkten. In U. Gerhard, T. Knijn and A. Weckwert (eds), *Erwerbstätige Mütter: Ein europäischer Vergleich*, München: Beck, pp. 193–217.

Klammer, U. and Schulz-Nieswandt, F. (2006), Logik des Sozialstaats und, Arbeit am Menschbild, Die Auswirkungen von Hartz IV auf verschiedene sozialpolitische Felder, *Sozialer Fortschritt*, 7: 157–9.

Klammer, U., Klenner, C., Ochs, C., Radke, P. and Ziegler, A. (2000), *WSI-FrauenDatenReport*, Berlin: Sigma.

Klenner, C. (2003), WSI-Betriebsrätebefragung 2003 zur Vereinbarkeit von Familie und Beruf, zur Chancengleichheit und zur Beschäftigungssicherung, Erste Ergebnisse. Available at: http://www.boeckler.de/pdf/WSI_BR_Befragung_2003_Erste_Thesen.pdf.

Klenner, C. (2004a), Gender: Ein Fremdwort für Betriebsräte? *WSI-Mitteilungen*, 5.

Klenner, C. (2004b), *Erwartungen an einen familienfreundlichen Betrieb*, Berlin: BmFSFJ.

Klenner, C. (2005), Gleichstellung von Frauen und Männern und Vereinbarkeit von Familie und Beruf, Eine Analyse von tariflichen Regelungen in ausgewählten Tarifbereichen. In R. Bispinck and WSI-Tarifarchiv, *WSI-Tarifhandbuch 2005*, Frankfurt a. M.: Bund-Verlag, pp. 39–65.

Lanquetin, M.-T. and Letablier, M.-T. (2005), *Concilier travail et famille en France: approches socio-juridiques*, Rapport de recherche 22, Paris: Centre d'études de l'emploi.

Laufer, J. and Silvera, R. (2006), Les accords d'entreprise sur l'égalité professionnelle. In *Regards sur l'actualité 317*, Paris: Ministère de la Parité et de l'Egalité Professionnelle.

Leiber, S. (2006), Wohin steuert die 'Bismarck'sche' Sozialversicherung? Aktuelle Gesundheitsreformen im Vergleich. In C. Schäfer and H. Seifert (eds), *Kein bisschen leise: 60 Jahre WSI*, Hamburg: VSA, pp. 57–74.

Letablier, M.-T. (2006), Childcare in a changing world: policy responses to working time flexibility in France. In J. Lewis (ed.), *Children, Changing Families and Welfare States*, Cheltenham: Edward Elgar, pp. 201–19.

Letablier, M.-T., Pennec, S. and Buttner, O. (2003), *Opinions, attitudes et aspirations des familles vis à vis de la politique familiale en France*, Rapport de recherche CEE 09 (January).

Lewis, J. (1992), Gender and the development of welfare regimes, *Journal of European Social Policy*, 3: 159–73.

Maschke, M. and Zurholt, G. (2005), *Chancengleich und Familienfreundlich. Betriebs- und Dienstvereinbarungen. Schriftenreihe der Hans-Böckler-Stiftung*, Frankfurt a. M.: Bund-Verlag.

Méda, D. and Orain, R. (2002), Transformations du travail et du hors travail: le jugement des salariés, *Travail et Emploi*, 90: 23–38.

Méda, D. and Périvier, H. (2007), *Le deuxième âge de l'émancipation: La société, les femmes, l'emploi*, Paris: Seuil (La république des idées).

OECD (2001), *Employment Outlook 2001*, Paris: OECD.

Orloff, A. S. (2006), L'adieu au maternalisme? Politiques de l'état et emploi des mères en Suède et aux Etats-Unis, *Recherches et Prévisions*, 83: 9–28.

Prognos AG (2003), *Betriebswirtschaftliche Effekte familienfreundlicher Maßnahmen: Kosten-Nutzen-Analyse*, Köln: BmFSFJ.

Riedmann, A., Bielenski, H., Szczurowska, T. and Wagner, A. (2006), *Working Time and Work–Life Balance in European Companies, Establishment Survey on Working Time 2004–2005*, European Foundation for the Improvement of Living and Working Conditions, Luxembourg: Office for Official Publications of the European Communities.

Schmidt, R. and Mohn, L. (eds) (2004), *Familie bringt Gewinn: Innovation durch Balance von Familie und Arbeitswelt*, Gütersloh: Bertelsmann.

Schratzenstaller, M. (2002), Familienpolitik – wozu und für wen? Die aktuelle familienpolitische Reformdebatte, *WSI-Mitteilungen*, 3: 127–32.

Veil, M. (2007), Geteilte Verantwortung: Neue familienpolitische Entwicklungen in Frankreich, *Dokumente*, 1/2007.

Yasbeck, P. (2004), *The Business Case for Firm-level Work-Life Balance Policies: A Review of the Literature*, Wellington. Available at: www.dol.govt.nz/PDFs/FirmLevelWLB.pdf

Websites

www.bmfsfj.de
www.erfolgsfaktor-familie.de
www.lokale-buendnisse-fuer-familie.de
www.total-e-quality.de

Index

Index

defamilialization of 9
  informal 84, 98; Netherlands 96, 97
  see also childcare; elder-care; long-term
  care allowances
    Austria 120, 124, 127
    Italy 125
    long-term care 117
    Netherlands 98
care crisis 85
care insurance: Germany 95
care leave programmes 132
care managers: informal carers as 131, 133
care packages: France 122–4, 125
care policies
  and employment 16, 83, 90–1, 99
  gendered division of labour in 17
  long-term 6, 15, 117–35
  social stratification in 17, 89, 96, 98
  trajectories of reform 86–98
care service vouchers: France 148
care workers
  immigrant; Austria 121, 124, 129–30;
    Italy 122, 129–30; working
    conditions 129–30
  working conditions 128, 133
  see also childcare workers
career and family audit: Germany 148–9
career breaks, voluntary
  Belgium 91–2, 93
  see also care leave; lifespan leave; maternity
    leave; parental leave; paternity leave
carers, women as 84, 131
  in Bismarckian system 2–3
  France 151
cash-for-care systems: for long-term care
    6, 117–35
change, conversion type of 59
changes: Bismarckian welfare systems 3–8
  sequential process of 8–16
childcare 6
  France 86, 136, 146, 147–8; free
    choice 87–90, 137, 139–40, 150–1
  Germany 86, 93–6, 136, 138–9, 145
  lone parents 111
  Netherlands 86, 96–7, 107
  policy reforms 82–101
  private: for high-income women 17, 87, 93,
    98
  UK 109, 110
childcare workers
  Belgium 92–3
  France 88, 89–90
  Netherlands 96
childrearing allowances
  Belgium 91
  Germany 93–4
choice, freedom of
  Belgium 91, 92
  in care policies 6, 84, 98
  France 87–90, 137, 139–40, 150–1
class *see* stratification, social; underclass
clusters, welfare state 82–3

cohabitation fraud: Netherlands 104
collective agreements (CAs)
  France 144
  Germany 142–4
collective protection 2
combination scenario 97
commodification of care 117
companies: family-friendly policies 136,
    142–50, 152–3
competition
  in health care systems 8, 55–6, 58, 59
  in hospitals 54
compulsion: in second-pillar pension
    provision 32
confidence: pensions 35–6
conservative regime: criticism of 82–3
consolidation reforms: Germany 12–13
contracts, childhood: France 148
contributions, social
  in Bismarckian system 3
  Germany 70
  increase in 11, 12, 25
  linked to benefits 13–14
  and unemployment benefits 67
convergence 7
conversion type of change 59
cost containment
  health care systems 46, 47–52, 57
  unemployment insurance systems 5, 64, 66,
    69, 75, 76
crisis, welfare state: causes of 10
crisis narratives: and unemployment
    reform 68
CSG (France) 15, 16
culture, working 146
CWI (Netherlands) 74
Czech Republic: Bismarckian welfare system 3

day-care services 132
  Belgium 86
  France 86, 87, 89
  Germany 94–5
decentralization: Netherlands 107–8
demographic imbalances
  Germany 151, 152
  and pension reform 24
  see also ageing populations; birth rates; fertility
Denmark
  national health system 41–2, 44, 45, 46
  unemployment reform 77
dependency 103–4, 113
  Austria 120
  of elderly 15
  France 119
deregulation: labour market 85
development: cumulative but
    transformative 8–9
diagnosis-related group method 54, 55
Dini pension reform (Italy) 28–9
disability policy 85
  Austria 120
  Italy 121, 122, 124–5, 131, 132

Index

Index

Index

women in 8, 82–3; in Bismarckian
    system 3; discouragement of 85, 87,
    91, 98; France 136, 137, 144;
    Germany 141; (re-)entry 6, 7, 90, 96,
    99
see also employment
labour shedding strategy 4, 9, 12, 67, 69, 85
    Belgium 71
    shift from 5, 83
layering: in unemployment reform 62–3, 77
leave see care; lifespan; maternity; parental;
    paternity
life insurance
    France 32
    for pensions 36–7
lifespan leave: Netherlands 97
Local Alliances for the Family (Germany)
    141–2
lone mothers
    activation 9
    employment levels 83
    Netherlands 104, 107, 108
    social policies for 6
lone parents
    poverty 83
    social policies for 6, 102–16
long-term care 6, 15, 117–35
Luxembourg
    Bismarckian welfare system 3
    health insurance system 42

'make work pay' philosophy 105
management: activation policies
    France 106
    Netherlands 107–8
    UK 109–10
managerialization: of hospitals 54–5
maternalism, farewell to 83, 151
maternity leave 99
    France 140, 144
    see also parental leave
men workers
    job and income security for 2
    see also breadwinners; parental leave; paternity
    leave
morbidities: increase in 118
mothers
    labour market participation: Germany 138,
    152
    working: Germany 151
    see also lone mothers

NABW (Netherlands) 73
nannies see childcare workers
national health systems 41–2
    access 42–3
    benefits 43–4
    organization and regulation 44–5
    problems 45–7
Netherlands
    Bismarckian welfare system 3
    care reforms 82, 83

childcare 6, 86, 96–7, 107
elder-care 6, 86, 97–8
health insurance reform 5, 40–1; cost
    containment policies 47, 48, 50, 52;
    structural changes 52, 54, 55–6, 58, 59
health insurance system 42, 43, 44–5, 45–6
lone parents 6, 102, 103, 104, 107–9,
    111–12, 113–14
pensions 36
unemployment reforms 62, 68–70, 71, 73,
    74, 78
welfare state reform 15
New Deal programmes: UK 109–10
Norway: national health system 41–2, 44, 45,
    46
NWW (Netherlands) 71

OECD 7, 64, 66
older people, pensions: Germany 30
organization: health care systems 44–5
outsiders, labour market 5, 6, 9, 16
    unemployment reform 65, 70, 78

pacts, social 69
PAJE (France) 90, 139–40
PARE (France) 72, 73
parental leave 132
    Belgium 92, 93
    France 88–9, 90, 140, 146, 147, 150
    Germany 93–4, 95, 136, 138, 139, 143–4,
    145, 146, 151
    increase in 87
    lone parents 111, 112
    low-income women 17, 87, 98
    Netherlands 97, 107
    see also maternity leave; paternity leave
parents see lone mothers; lone parents; mothers
part-time work see employment, part-time
parties, political: negotiation of
    retrenchment 13
partners, social
    family policies 136, 142–50
    involvement in social security 15
    negotiation of retrenchment 9, 13–14
paternity leave
    Belgium 93
    France 90, 139
    see also parental leave
pay-as-you-go (PAYG) pension systems 21, 22,
    23–4, 24–5
pension consensus: Germany 26
pension reform 4–5, 9, 15, 21–39
    delaying impact of 24
    first wave 4–5, 25–8
    Germany 151
    Italy 13
    second wave 5, 28–31
    Spain 13
    stages 22–3, 25–32, 35–7, 37–8
pension systems
    funded 22, 23, 24–5, 29, 31–2
    Germany 29, 31–2, 138

Index

multi-pillar 8, 21, 22, 23, 25
second-pillar 32
PERCO (France) 31
PERP (France) 31, 32
personal advisers: New Deal 109–10
PES (Belgium) 73
pharmaceutical industries: taxation of 53
pharmaceuticals 48
Germany 56
phasing-in periods, long: pension reform 22, 32–5, 37
Italy 29
Plan Juppé 50, 52, 58
plans, unemployment 65
Plegegeld (Austria) 124, 130–1
political actors: in health care systems 58–9
politics
and pensions 35–6, 37
and unemployment reform 68
poor: deserving and undeserving 103
Portugal: national health system 41–2
poverty: lone parents 83, 111–12
Netherlands 108
UK 104, 109, 110, 113
preschools
Belgium 86
France 86, 140
prescriptions 43, 44, 48, 49
primary health centres 44
privatization 9
procrastination
in pension reform 24
see also phasing-in periods, long
professionalization: care workers 128, 132
PSD (France) 90, 119, 126

qualifications: care workers 128

recalibration of benefit rights
reactionary 5, 70
unemployment reform 64–5, 65–6, 69–72, 75, 76
reform cascade 77
regularization: immigrant care workers 130
regulation: health care systems 5, 44–5
France 49
reorientation interviews: Netherlands 73
retirement
delaying: France 30
early 12, 85; cutting back on 5;
Germany 27; Italy 26;
Netherlands 97
retirement age
Germany 30
Italy 26
and pension reform 24
retrenchment 4
negotiation with social partners 9, 13–14
opposition to 11–12, 67
pensions 23, 37
policies of 7–8
1990s 12–14

reunification, German
and childcare 94
gender equality 138
and health care system 50
and pensions 27
Riester Rente (Germany) 29, 31–2
rigidity: of Bismarckian welfare systems 3–4
RMA (France) 106, 113
RMI (France) 16, 70, 72, 104, 106, 113

Scandinavian countries
childcare 84, 137
see also specific countries
sectorial reforms: France 13
security: for men workers 2
Seehofer Reform 50–1, 56
seniority pensions: Italy 26
sequential changes *see* incremental changes
service sector employment 63
sickness funds 48, 49
France 45
Germany 53, 54, 56
role of 55–7
skills training 65
social policies, new
adoption of 15–16
traits of 7–8
social services: and grey markets 129–30
solidarity fund, old-age (France) 27–8
Spain
Bismarckian welfare system 3
fertility rates 85
national health system 41–2
pension reform 4–5, 13
specialists, medical 48
spending, social
increase in 12
see also retrenchment
springboard jobs 65
stasis, shared: and unemployment reforms 67–8, 68, 74
state
care policies 84
and health insurance systems 59;
France 9, 57–8; Germany 57
stratification, social: in care policies 17, 98
France 89
Netherlands 96
structural reforms 9–10, 14–15
Bismarckian welfare systems 4
health insurance systems 52–9
2000s 15–16
subsidiarity, principle of 98
care policies 84, 87
family policies 141
Germany 86, 95, 141
Netherlands 86
support schemes: for informal carers 131–2
Sweden
elder-care policies 86
national health system 41–2, 44, 45, 46
Switzerland

Printed and bound by CPI Group (UK) Ltd, Croydon, CR0 4YY

09/06/2025